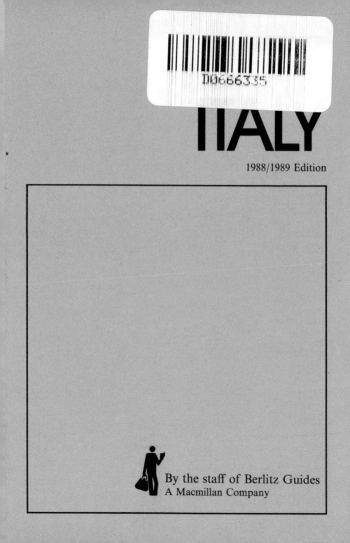

ITALY

1988/1989 Edition

By the staff of Berlitz Guides
A Macmillan Company

How best to use this guide

These 256 pages cover the **highlights of Italy,** grouped into five regions. Although not exhaustive, our selection of sights will enable you to make the best of your trip.

The **sights** to see are contained between pages 47 and 193. Those most highly recommended are pinpointed by the Berlitz traveller symbol.

The **Where to Go** section on page 42 will help you plan your visit according to the time available.

For **general background** see the sections Italy and the Italians (p. 8), Facts and Figures (p. 16), History (p. 17) and Historical Landmarks (p. 40).

Entertainment and **activities** (including eating out) are described between pages 194 and 217.

The **practical information,** hints and tips that you will need before and during your trip begin on page 218. This section is arranged alphabetically for easy reference.

The **map section** at the back of the book (pp. 244–251) will help you find your way around and locate the principal sights.

Finally, if there is anything you cannot find, look in the complete **index** (pp. 252–256).

CONTENTS

CONTENTS

Cover photo: Botticelli's *Birth of Venus* in Florence's Uffizi.

Text:	Jack Altman
Staff Editor:	Christina Jackson
Layout:	Doris Haldemann
Photography:	Daniel Vittet
	p. 36 SCALA, Florence;
	pp. 53, 63, 209 Walter Imber;
	pp. 75, 171 PRISMA/Schuster GmbH;
	pp. 79, 85, 89, 93, 97, 103 Jean Mohr;
	pp. 134, 139, 201 Claude Huber;
	pp. 188, 193 Kurt Ammann;
	p. 213 Jean-Claude Vieillefond.
Cartography:	Falk-Verlag, Hamburg
	pp. 6–7, 47, 57, 77, 113, 144, 166, 178
	Max Thommen

Acknowledgments

We would especially like to thank Adrienne Farrell for her help in the preparation of this guide. We are also grateful to Francesca Rahimi, Don Larrimore and Lyon Benzimra for their assistance.

Found an error or an omission in this Berlitz Guide? Or a change or new feature we should know about? Our editor would be happy to hear from you, and a postcard would do. Be sure to include your name and address, since in appreciation for a useful suggestion, we'd like to send you a free travel guide.

Although we make every effort to ensure the accuracy of all the information in this book, changes occur incessantly. We cannot therefore take responsibility for facts, prices, addresses and circumstances in general that are constantly subject to alteration.

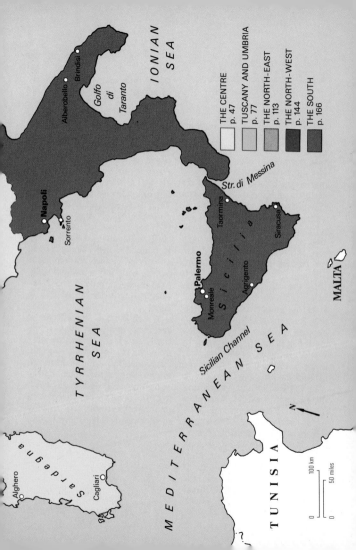

ITALY AND
THE ITALIANS

From the Alps right down to the southern tip of Sicily, Italy provides the most tangible proof that the world indeed is a stage. Architects and sculptors treat the myriad parks and gardens as set designs, and nature itself turns the landscapes, with their characteristic statuesque cypresses, tortuous olive and fig trees or chorus rows of vineyards, into just so many artful backdrops for the daily histrionics of Italian life.

In the cities, the cathedrals, palaces or town halls are planned as harmonious elements in stage-sets for the streets and the all-important piazzas, just as much monuments in their own right. In Venice, dazzling as the Basilica, Doges' Palace and Marciana Library may be, the focus of life is in the Piazza San Marco and the Piazzetta beyond. The same is true of Rome's piazzas—Navona, del Popolo or di Spagna; Siena's Campo; Turin's Piazza San Carlo. Conceived as a theatre emphasizing the decorative space more than the buildings around it, the piazza satisfies the need of Mediterranean peoples to conduct their lives in the open air.

For we mustn't forget the players. In each town, at that magic moment at the end of the afternoon, they stroll across the piazza, find themselves a well-placed seat at their favourite café or stand in groups to argue business, politics or football—more often football than politics—and never merely discuss when it's possible to argue. Their celebrated gift for gesticulation has not deserted them nor that keen look that reassures them of the appreciation of their audience. No people more joyfully lives up to its legendary image than the Italians. As Orson Welles put it, all 50-odd million of them are actors, with only a few bad ones, and those, he added most unfairly, are on the stage and in films.

Watch them at the wheel of a car: every time they stop, reluctantly, at a traffic light, the men, even more than the women, check their looks in the rear-view mirror and comb their hair—ever ready to go on stage. Driving, of course, has become a major opportunity to display their dramatic talents. An Italian

The gondolier rests
his vocal chords before serenading
the afternoon's passengers.

8

designer observed that a nation's cars are like its people: Scandinavian and German models are solid, strong and reliable, built to resist an accident; Italian cars tend to be more fragile, but slick and spirited, built to *avoid* an accident.

Built, above all, to indulge the national sense of style. The imaginative flair of Neapolitans zigzagging out of a traffic jam forces the admiration of the most nerve-shattered onlooker. In the purely visual sphere, style has been a national preoccupation from the Golden Age of Michelangelo or Leonardo da Vinci in the Renaissance to the grandiose cinematographic fantasies of Fellini or Visconti in the modern era. It is there not only in the splendour of the frescoes and monumental fountains but also in the dazzling design of a scarlet Ferrari, a coffee pot or a fountain pen. The smart international man-about-town insists that good "English" tailoring is now only to be found in the meticulous workshops of Milan or Rome. And Italianized by such

The Dukes of Milan built Pavia's Charterhouse as a flamboyant family mausoleum.

10

Italian lovers are perfectly comfortable even on a bicycle not made for two.

national quirks as the overcoat almost invariably draped over the shoulders like a cloak or, in the summer, the sleek leather moccasins imperatively worn *without* socks.

In 1401, a cool French scholar told his Milan colleagues: "Art without science is nothing". The Italians replied: "Science without art is nothing", and today, pasta manufacturers employ architects to design new forms for noodles.

In the simplest *trattoria* or most elegant of restaurants, your choice of a meal begins before you sit down. Not with the menu, but with yet another theatre décor, sprawling across a long table as you enter: plates of pink scampi and purple squid, stuffed eggplant and zucchini, red, yellow and green peppers, cascades of grapes and figs.

And if you take a plane or train the length of the peninsula, Italy offers itself as another long table of delights spilling out into the Mediterranean. In the north, the snowcapped Alps and jagged pink rocks of the Dolomites; the gleaming lakes of Como, Garda and Maggiore; the fertile and industrious plain of the Po stretching from Turin and Milan across to ancient Verona, the hills of Vicenza and lagoons of Venice.

On the west coast, the Italian Riviera curves from San Remo to Viareggio on either side of the venerable port city of Genoa. Behind the sandy beaches, from the marble quarries of Carrara, the mountain chain of the Apennines climbs into Tuscany—where lie the ageless beauties of Pisa, Lucca, Florence and Siena and the magical hill towns of Montepulciano, Volterra and San Gimignano.

Umbria's rich green countryside surrounds a golden triangle of historic cities, the Assisi of St. Francis, the noble university town of Perugia and medieval Gubbio. To the east, the grand Byzantine citadel of Ravenna dominates the seaside resorts of the Adriatic.

And, half-way down the west coast, the unique golden universe of Rome, witnessing countless declines, falls and rebirths, resists all the assaults of brutal modernity.

In another world unto itself, the exhilarating chaos of Naples commands a magnificent bay, the isles of Ischia and Capri and the ruins of Pompeii in the shadow of the Vesuvius volcano. To the south, the fishing villages of Sorrento and Positano spill down the craggy cliffs of the Amalfi coast. Meanwhile, on the other side of the peninsula, well off the beaten tourist track, are the strange prehistoric landscapes of Puglia and the medieval fortresses of the German emperors.

Italy's western approaches are guarded by the islands of Sardinia and Sicily, rugged, mysterious, at once bright and sombre.

The Italian people, with Latins and Etruscans mixing over the centuries with Greeks, Lombards, Normans and Spaniards, are as diverse as this panoply of landscapes. Each region sustains a solid and pugnacious local pride from historic division into the city-states, duchies, kingdoms and republics of Florence, Naples and Venice, Lombardy, Piedmont and Sicily. Nurtured within the geographical separations of the Alps, the Po valley and the coasts on either side of the Apennines, it was this very diversity that created the richness of Italian art with its competing regional schools of painting and architecture. Significantly, the move towards national unity in the 19th century coincided with a dramatic artistic decline from which the country is only now recovering.

Given its short history as a unified nation, Italy's patriotic sense is invested almost exclusively in the national football team. After the devastating experience of Mussolini's fascism, national government is rarely regarded as an obvious solution to the people's daily problems. If some form of government proves necessary, they prefer the local town hall to the parliament in Rome.

Most Italians are naturally cheerful and friendly towards foreigners, with an almost total absence of "racist" terms. They reserve their scorn for each other—Venetians and Romans or Milanese and Neapolitans.

Over and above the regional identifications, the country remains divided culturally, economically, psychologically between the prosperous, industrial North and relatively backward South, the *Mezzogiorno* ("noon"). This division was perpetuated by centuries of feudal rule in Naples and Sicily while the North developed more progressive forms of economy and government, almost to the point of regarding the South as Italy's own Third World, offer-

It's the children who lend colour to a greystone village in the Abruzzi mountains.

ing a supply of cheap migrant labour.

But at the personal level, the warm-hearted, high-spirited Neapolitans, for instance, in no way feel themselves inferior to the cool, pragmatic "manager" types of the big northern cities. Italy's two halves come face to face in Turin, where Fiat's automobile factories have attracted thousands of workers from the *Mezzogiorno*. Sociologists have noted that the transplanted southerners tend to support the populist Juventus football team, owned by Fiat's Agnelli family, while the other, more bourgeois local team, Torino, is favoured by the longer-established Turin citizenry.

Foreign visitors are not obliged to take sides. We can fall in love with the whole country.

FACTS AND FIGURES

Geography:	The Italian landmass covers 301,245 square kilometres (116,228 sq. mi.). The familiar boot-like silhouette stretches 1,200 km. (750 mi.) from the north-west Alpine frontier with France to the south-east "heel" of Puglia. Below the three great lakes, Maggiore, Como and Garda, the fertile plain of the Po river separates the Alps from the rugged chain of the Apennines running like a wall down the middle of the peninsula to the arid and poorer south. Other major rivers are the Tiber at Rome, Arno in Tuscany and Adige in the Tyrolean Dolomites. Across the Adriatic to the east lies the rocky coastline of Yugoslavia. Off the Tyrrhenian (west) coast are the mountainous islands of Sardinia (south of France's Corsica) and Sicily (off the boot's "toe"), largest of the Mediterranean islands. Three major volcanoes in the south, Vesuvius, Stromboli and Sicily's Etna, are still active. Highest point: on Mont Blanc (Monte Bianco) 4,760 metres (15,616 ft.).
Population:	57 million
Capital:	Rome (pop. 2,830,000)
Major cities:	Milan (1,500,000), Naples (1,200,000), Turin (1,000,000), Genoa (700,000), Palermo (700,000), Bologna (400,000), Florence (400,000), Catania (380,000), Bari (370,000), Venice (340,000).
Government:	By its constitution of 1948, Italy is a republic of provinces grouped into 20 regions. A President with honorary rather than political powers is chosen by an Electoral Assembly of parliamentary and regional representatives. Government is in the hands of a Prime Minister and his cabinet selected from among the parliament's Senate of 322 members and more powerful 630-strong Chamber of Deputies. A parliamentary mandate is 5 years.
Religion:	99% Catholic, 1% Protestant, Greek Orthodox and Jewish.

HISTORY

Italy as a nation has existed only since 1871. Before then, despite the peninsula's obvious geographical unity bounded by the Alps and the Mediterranean, its story is a fragmented tale of independent-minded cities, provinces and islands.

We have abundant evidence of the ancient Etruscan, Greek and Roman communities in Italy, but know very little of the country's earlier, prehistoric settlers. Vestiges of dwellings survive—cabins on stilts in the frequently flooded Po valley, larger clay houses on the western marshlands of Tuscany, and Sardinia's still visible domed dry-stone *nuraghi*. But the inhabitants? Perhaps North Africans and eastern Europeans peopled the Ligurian coast, while the Adriatic and south may have been settled from the Balkans and Asia Minor.

Nobody knows where the Etruscans came from. During the millennium before the Christian era, their civilization reached beyond Tuscany north to the Po valley and south towards Naples. At a time when Roman and other Latin tribes were still primitive, Etruscan society was aristocratic and highly sophisticated. Gold and other metal ornaments showed Greek influence, but the Etruscans' vaulted architecture was indigenous, as were their roads, canals and sewers.

Arriving in the 8th century B.C., the Greeks set up city-states in eastern and southern Sicily, dominated by Syracuse, and others on the Italian mainland, at Naples, Paestum and Taranto. Pythagoras squared his hypotenuse in Calabria, and it was at Agrigento that Empedocles concluded the world was divided into four elements—fire, air, earth and water.

After defeats by Greeks in the south, Latins in the centre and Gallic invaders in the north, the Etruscan empire ended in the 4th century B.C. As Greek colonial power weakened through Athens-Sparta rivalry back home and pressure from Phoenicians in Sicily, the vacuum was filled by an uppity confederation of Latin and Sabine tribes living on seven hills known collectively as Rome.

The Romans

Legend says Rome was founded by Romulus, sired with twin brother Remus by Mars of a Vestal Virgin and abandoned on the Palatine Hill to be suckled by a she-wolf. Historians agree that the site and traditional founding date of 753 B.C. are just about right.

Under Etruscan domination, Rome had been a monarchy until a revolt in 510 B.C. established a patrician republic which lasted

On their sarcophagi, Etruscans recline in dignified repose.

five centuries. In contrast to other Italian cities weakened by internal rivalries and unstable government, Rome drew strength from a solid aristocracy of consuls and senate ruling over plebeians proud of their Roman citizenship and only rarely rebellious.

Recovering quickly from the Gallic invasion of 387 B.C., the Romans took effective control of the peninsula by a military conquest reinforced by a network of roads with names that exist to this day: Via Appia, Flaminia, Aurelia. From chariots to Ferraris, Italians have always liked careering across the country on wheels.

Roman power extended around the Mediterranean with

victory in the Punic Wars against Carthage and conquests in Macedonia, Asia Minor, Spain and southern France. The rest of Italy participated only by tax contributions to the war effort and minor involvement in commerce and colonization. Resentment surfaced when former Etruscan or Greek cities such as Capua, Syracuse and Taranto supported Hannibal's invasion in 218 B.C. Rome followed up defeat of the Carthaginians with large-scale massacres and enslavement of their Italian supporters. National solidarity was still a long way off.

Under Julius Caesar, provincial towns won the privileges of Roman citizenship. His reformist dictatorship, bypassing the senate to combat unemployment and ease the tax burden, made dangerous enemies. His assassination on the Ides of March, 44 B.C., led to civil war and the despotic rule of his adopted son Augustus, who consolidated the empire.

Conquest of the Greeks accelerated rather than halted the influence of their culture in Italy. Romans infused Greek refinement with their own energy to create that unique mixture of elegance and realism, delicacy and strength that have remained the essence of Italian life and art.

In architecture, the Romans made a great leap forward from the Greek structures of columns and beams by developing the arch, vault and dome, well suited to the needs of empire—basilicas for public administration, the new engineering of aqueducts and bridges, and triumphal arches for victorious armies. If they adopted the Greeks' gods, turning Zeus into Jupiter, Aphrodite into Venus, the cult placing the emperor at its apex served the interests of the Roman state.

19

In the centuries of imperial expansion, decline and fall, Italy took a back seat as power moved with the armies away from Rome east to Byzantium and north to Gaul or Germany.

Despite persecution under Nero in the 1st century A.D., Christianity spread from Rome through southern Italy, later to the north. With Constantine (306–337) in Byzantium, Milan and then Ravenna became the capital of Italy. Christianity was made the state religion. At the end of the 4th century, Emperor Theodosius organized the Church into dioceses and declared paganism and heresy a crime. He himself was excommunicated by St. Ambrose, Bishop of Milan, for massacring 7,000 rebels in Thessalonica. The position of Bishop of Rome as primate of the Western Church was asserted by Pope Leo I (440–461), tracing the succession back to St. Peter.

The invasion of Attila's Huns and the sacking of Rome by Goths and Vandals brought an end to the Western Empire.

After the Empire

Wars between the Goths and Byzantines and new waves of invasions made Italian unity impossible.

The dual influence of Greek and Latin culture persisted. In the 6th century, Justinian reannexed Italy to his Byzantine Empire and codified Roman law as the state's legal system. Under Heraclius (610–641), Greek was extended to Italy as its official language.

Hellenistic and oriental influences were most evident in religion. Byzantine ritual coloured the Roman liturgy. The Roman basilica's long colonnaded nave leading to an apse gave way to the Greek cross with a central space surrounded by arches and topped by a dome. Sculptural reliefs flattened out to symbolic decorative, non-human forms, and painting and mosaics were high in colour, but more rigid and formal. Spiritual preoccupations turned away from the world's few joys and many woes in the present to mystic contemplation of the ineffable hereafter.

Much too ineffable for Italian tastes. The monastic movement founded by St. Benedict in the 6th century reasserted involvement in the realities of social life. The Benedictine order emphasized moderation in the austerity of its food, clothing and sleep, not unlike the habits of any peasant of the times. Flagellation and similar rigours introduced into other Italian

Modern Verona contemplates its Roman arena across a sundae.

20

monasteries by the Irish monk Columbanus were soon modified by the gentler Benedictine rule.

Monasteries in Italy remained modest affairs as bishops moved faster than abbots to take over lands laid waste by barbarian invasions. The Church ordered monasteries to forget secular matters and devote themselves to liturgy.

By the 8th century, the Byzantines held the balance of power with the Lombards (a Germanic tribe), who had invaded Italy in 568 and set up their capital at Pavia four years later. The Lombards controlled the interior in a loose confederation of fiercely independent duchies. Lombard territory split Byzantine Italy up into segments ruled from the coasts—Veneto (Venice and its hinterland), Emilia (between Ravenna and Modena) and Pentapolo (between Rimini and Perugia), plus Rome and Naples (with Sicily and Calabria).

In Rome, the highly political popes played the Lombard duchies off against those of the Byzantine Empire. They cited a forged document, the *Donation of Constantine,* supposedly bequeathing them political authority over all Italy. Seeking the powerful support of the Franks, Pope Leo III crowned their king, Charlemagne, ruler of the Holy Roman (in fact, mostly German)

Empire, in 800. But the pope had in turn to kneel in allegiance, and this exchange of spiritual blessing for military protection laid the seeds of future conflict between the papacy and the German emperors.

Venice, founded on its lagoons in the 6th century by refugees from Lombard raiders, prospered from a privileged relationship with Byzantium and uninhibited readiness to trade with Muslims and other infidels further east. The merchants of Venice were only too happy to bring a little oriental spice and colour into the dour lives of Lombards in the Po valley and beyond the Alps to northern Europe.

Naples held on to its autonomy by prudently combining links with Rome and Constantinople. When Arabs conquered Sicily in the 9th century and turned to the mainland, Naples at first sought an alliance. But as the invaders advanced towards Rome, Naples linked up with neighbouring Amalfi. Despite military expeditions by the Franks and Byzantines, the Arabs remained on the Italian scene for two centuries.

The Middle Ages

In the 11th century, the adventurous Normans put an end to Arab control of Sicily and southern Italy. Exploiting a natural genius for assimilating the useful elements of the local culture rather than indiscriminately imposing their own, they adopted Arab-style tax-collectors and customs officials and Byzantine fleet-admirals for their navy. In Palermo, churches and mosques stood side by side, feudal castles next to oriental palaces.

The Crusades against the Islamic threat to Christendom brought great prosperity to Italy's port cities. Pisa sided with the Normans in Sicily and profits from its new commercial empire in the western Mediterranean paid for its Cathedral, Baptistery and Leaning Tower. Genoa's merchant empire spread from Algeria to Syria.

Supreme master of the art of playing all sides, Venice stayed out of the first Crusade to expand its trade with the East while ferrying pilgrims to Palestine. Later, when Byzantium threatened its eastern trading privileges, Venice persuaded crusading armies to attack Constantinople in 1204, thereby strengthening its position even more.

The Po valley's economic expansion through land clearance and new irrigation works brought a rapid decline of feudalism. Dukes, administrators and clergy lived in towns rather than isolated castles, absorbing the hinterland into communes, forerunners of the city-states.

The communes were strong enough to confine German Emperor Frederick Barbarossa's Italian ambitions to the south, where he secured Sicily for his Hohenstaufen heirs by marrying his son into the Norman royal family. Ruling from Palermo, Barbarossa's cultured but brutal grandson Frederick II (1194-1250) was a prototype for the future Renaissance prince.

His power struggle with the papacy divided the country into two highly volatile camps—Guelfs supporting the pope and Ghibellines supporting the emperor. The backbone of the Guelfs was in communes such as Florence and Genoa. In 1266, they financed the mercenary army of Charles d'Anjou to defeat the imperial forces—and take the Sicilian throne. But Palermo rose up against the French in the murderous Sicilian Vespers of 1282, when the locals massacred everyone who spoke Italian with a French accent and forced Charles to move his capital to Naples. The Sicilians offered their crown to the Spanish house of Aragon.

The Guelf-Ghibelline conflict became a pretext for settling family feuds (such as the one in Shakespeare's *Romeo and Juliet*) or communal rivalries from which Genoa and Florence

*In St. Francis' Assisi,
the gentle monastic life
continues.*

emerged stronger than ever. In Rome, the dissolute popes repeatedly switched factions for temporary advantage and lost all political and moral authority in the process.

After two centuries of religious heresy, the Church needed a spiritual renewal, finding the perfect ally in Francis of Assisi (1182–1226), pious without being troublesomely militant (see p. 110). His sermons had immense popular appeal. He chose not to attack Church corruption but to preach instead the values of a Christly life. By involving religion in a love of nature, preaching even to sparrows, he appealed to an old pagan Italian tradition. The Franciscan order

The City-States

By the end of the 13th century, with the independent-minded communes growing into fully fledged city-states, Italy was clearly not to be subjugated to the will of one ruler.

The Middle Ages in Italy were far from being the murky era that many humanist scholars liked to contrast with the brilliance of the Renaissance. Bologna had founded Europe's first university, famous above all for its law studies, in the early 11th century, followed by Padua, Naples, Modena, Siena, Salerno and Palermo. Unlike in other Church-dominated European universities, sciences, medicine and law prevailed over theology.

In the absence of political unification, it was the universities that awakened the national consciousness. Scholars travelling from town to town across the country needed a common tongue beyond the elitist Latin to break through the barriers of regional dialects. It had been a foreigner, German Emperor Frederick II, who launched the movement for a national language at his court in Palermo, but Dante Alighieri (1265–1321) provided the ardour, moral leadership, and unmatched literary example to bring it to fruition.

Genoa rose to challenge Venice's supremacy. It dislodged

provided a much needed *manageable* revival. The architecture of the church built in his name at Assisi contradicted Francis's humble testament denouncing "temples of great dimension and rich ornament". But Assisi's frescoes of the saint's life, painted by Cimabue and disciples of Giotto, proved an immensely effective act of artistic propaganda against the prevalent libertinism and heresy.

Pisa in the western Mediterranean, whittled away at Venice's hold on eastern ports, and set up colonies on the Black Sea for trade with Russia and the Far East. But Genoa's 1381 participation in the ruinous Chioggia war on the Venetian lagoon exhausted its resources. Its newly formed Bank of St. George had to sell off overseas colonies and ran the town like a private company for the benefit of a small local oligarchy seeking future prosperity as international financiers for the kings of Spain or France.

Venice rebounded to turn to the mainland, extending its Veneto territory from Padua across the Po valley as far as Bergamo. After relying exclusively on overseas trade, Venice created a new land-owning aristocracy through this expansion.

In its fertile Po valley, Milan prospered from trade with Germany, principally in textiles and armour. Escaping unscathed from the Great Plague of 1348 and subsequent epidemics, it built up a sound economic base and maintained a strong army with its plentiful manpower.

From this Gothic palace, the Doges presided over the great Venetian empire.

Florence was the first Italian town to mint its own gold coin (*fiorino* or florin), a prestigious instrument for trade in European markets, and organized textile manufacture on a large-scale industrial basis. Although outside troops were called in to crush an uprising of the Ciompi (woolworkers), the people of Florence were well-fed and highly literate compared with the rest of the country. The Medici emerged as the dominant merchant family with Cosimo becoming the city's ruler in 1434. A building boom underlined the prosperity: Giotto's Campanile was at last completed, as were Ghiberti's great Baptistery doors, Brunelleschi's dome on the Cathedral, and palaces by Alberti and Michelozzo.

Divided in the 14th century between the Spanish in Sicily and the French in Naples, southern Italy remained solidly feudal. Its almost exclusively agricultural economy suffered much more than the north from plague and famine. Landlords resorted to banditry to replenish their treasury. If Palermo was in decline, Naples flourished as a brilliant cosmopolitan capital. In 1442, it was reunited in one kingdom with Sicily, under Alfonso of Aragon.

With the papacy in comfortable exile in Avignon since 1309, the brutal rule of the Orsini and Colonna families reduced Rome to a half-urban, half-rural backwater. Self-educated visionary Cola di Rienzo governed briefly in 1347 until the nobles drove him out. Thirty years later, the papacy returned.

The Renaissance

A new national fraternity of scholars with multiple expertise in the arts, sciences and law, emerged as itinerant consultants to rulers eager to make their city-states centres of cultural prestige and political propaganda.

Men like Leon Battista Alberti, architect-mathematician-poet, brought a new spirit of inquiry and scepticism. From their detailed study and translation of the Greek philosophers, they developed principles of objective scientific research, independent of the political, religious or emotional bias characterizing medieval scholarship. The emphasis switched from heaven to earth. Leonardo da Vinci eagerly applied the new method to architecture, civil and military engineering, urban planning, geography and map-making. It was Giorgio Vasari, facile artist but first-rate chronicler of this cultural explosion, who dubbed it a *rinascita* or rebirth of the glories of Italy's Greco-Roman past. But even more, it proved, with the humanism of Leonardo and Michelangelo and the political realism of Machiavelli, to be the birth of our modern age. Including the blood and thunder.

For the creative ferment by no means precluded new horrors of war, assassination, persecution, plunder and rape. It was the heyday of the brilliant but lethal Spanish-Italian Borgias: lecherous Rodrigo, who became Pope Alexander VI, and treacherous son Cesare, who stopped at nothing to control and expand the papal lands. (His sister Lucrezia, forever smeared by anti-Spanish propaganda of the day as mistress of both her father and brother, was in fact, as Duchess of Ferrara, a generous patroness of the arts and benefactress of the poor.)

In Florence, where his family had to fight tooth and nail to hold on to their supremacy, Lorenzo de' Medici also found time to encourage the art of Perugino, Ghirlandaio, Botticelli, the young Leonardo and tempestuous Michelangelo. But decadence set in and Dominican preacher Girolamo Savonarola denounced the corruption of a Church and society more devoted to pagan classics than the Christian gospel. At the Carnival of 1494, he shamed the Florentines into throwing their "vanities"—clothes, jewellery and cosmetics, but also books and paintings, with Botticelli

contributing some of his own— onto a giant fire on the Piazza della Signoria. Four years later, when Savonarola declined to test the validity of his apocalyptic prophesies with an ordeal by fire, he was arrested, hanged and burned anyway, on the Piazza della Signoria.

On the international scene, the Turkish conquest of Constantinople in 1453 closed Genoa's Black Sea markets, but Venice worked out a new deal in Cyprus and even a *modus vivendi* in Constantinople itself. But the Venetians' empire declined as they lost their taste for the adventure of commerce in favour of the safety of their landholdings. From 1494 to 1530, the Spanish Habsburgs and the French turned Italy into a battleground for the Kingdom of Naples and the Duchy of Milan. Genoa threw in with the Spanish to give Emperor Charles V access, via Milan, to his German territories and later became a lucrative clearing-house for Spain's American silver. Rome was plundered by imperial armies in 1527; the Medici were driven out of Florence and returned to power under tutelage of the Spanish, who won effective control of the whole country.

But the dust of war settled and it was the dazzling cultural achievements that left their mark on the age. True father of Rome's High Renaissance, Pope Julius II (1503–13) began the new St. Peter's, commissioned Michelangelo to paint the ceiling of the Vatican's Sistine Chapel and Raphael to decorate the Stanze. Architect Donato Bramante was nicknamed *maestro ruinante* because of all the ancient monuments he dismantled to make way for the pope's megalomaniac building plans. With the treasures uncovered in the process, Julius founded the Vatican's magnificent collection of ancient sculpture.

The Sistine Chapel's new brilliance startles those familiar with the prerestoration grime.

Counter-Reformation

Badly shaken by the Protestant Reformation, the Church convoked the Council of Trent (north of Lake Garda) in 1545. Non-Italian bishops urged the Church to carry out its own reform, hoping to democratize relations with the pope. But the threat of Lutherans, Calvinists and other heretics shifted the emphasis to repression, culminat-

ing in the Counter-Reformation formally proclaimed in 1563. The Church reinforced the Holy Office's Inquisition and the Index to censor the arts. The Jesuits, founded in 1534, quickly became an army of militant theologians to combat heresy. Italian Protestants fled and Jews in Rome were shut up in a ghetto (50 years later than in Venice) and expelled from Genoa and Lucca.

Cardinal Carlo Borromeo, nephew of Pope Pius IV and Archbishop of Milan (1565–84), was the exemplary spiritual leader of Italy's Counter-Reformation. In alliance with the Jesuits, he weeded out corrupt clerics and the, for him, too soft Umiliati order of Catholic laymen. As a symbol of his crusading spirit, he consecrated the new Flamboyant Gothic cathedral, which took centuries to complete.

Art proved a major instrument of Counter-Reformation propaganda, but it had to undergo some important changes. The vigour and intellectual integrity of the High Renaissance had softened into Mannerism's stylized sophistication. Condemning the preoccupation with pagan gods and worldly decadence, the Church urged artists to deliver a strong, clear message to bring the troubled flock back to the fold. The

31

Madonna and saints of Annibale Carracci attracted the faithful with a sensuous image of ideal beauty, while Caravaggio made a more brutal, but no less effective appeal with a proletarian Mary and barefoot Apostles. As the Church regained ground, it promoted a more triumphant image, epitomized by Bernini's grandiose Baroque altar in St. Peter's.

But the self-confidence rang hollow when, in 1633, the Vatican ordered Galileo to deny the evidence of his own eyes, through the new telescope he had designed, and stop teaching that God's earth was only one of many planets in orbit around the sun.

After a 16th century in which Naples had become the largest town in Europe—and one of the liveliest—the south was increasingly oppressed and impoverished. The army had to crush revolts in Sicily and Naples against heavy taxes and conscription for Spain's wars in northern Europe.

Towards Nationhood

Lacking the solidarity to unite and too weak to resist by themselves, Italian kingdoms and duchies were reduced to convenient pawns in Europe's 18th-century dynastic power plays. At the end of the Wars of Spanish, Austrian and Polish Succession, the Austrians had taken over north Italy from the Spanish.

The Age of Enlightenment engendered a new cultural ferment. The theatre of La Scala opened in Milan and the Fenice in Venice. Stimulated by the ideas of Voltaire, Rousseau and Diderot, intellectuals were more keenly aware of being Europeans, but also *Italians,* a national consciousness they promoted in the Milan magazine, *Il Caffè.*

The hopes of progressives were raised by Austrian reforms in Lombardy and Tuscany (where the Medici dynasty ended in 1737): fairer taxes, less Church influence in schools, more public education, removal of the Inquisition, Jesuits, death penalty and instruments of torture. Outside the Austrian sphere of influence, Italy remained stolidly conservative. Venice stagnated under the rule of a small entrenched élite, drawing nostalgic comfort from the city's petrified beauty as painted in the *vedute* of Guardi and Canaletto. The papacy in Rome had lost prestige with the dissolution of the Jesuits and the crippling loss of revenue from the Habsburg Church reforms. The south's aristocracy resisted all significant social reforms proposed by the Spanish. Don Carlos, descendant of Louis XIV who saw himself as a southern Sun King—with Caserta Palace as his Versailles—is best remembered for launching the excavations of Pompeii in 1748.

On the north-eastern Alpine frontier, a new state had appeared on the scene, destined to lead the movement to a united Italy. With Savoy split in the 16th century between France and Switzerland, its foothill region south-east of the Alps, Piedmont, had come into the Italian orbit. Sidestepping the stagnant economic burden of Spanish domination, the sparsely populated duchy expanded fast. Turin was little more than a fortified village of 40,000 inhabitants in 1600, but it rose to 93,000 a century later. The pragmatic dukes of Piedmont liked French-style absolutist monarchy but tempered it with a parliament to bypass local fiefdoms. They copied Louis XIV's centralized administration and tax-collection and, by the 18th century, Turin was a sparkling royal capital built, quite unlike any other Italian city, in classical French manner.

Napoleon Bonaparte was welcomed with his seductive ideas of Italian "independence" after driving out the Austrians and Spanish in 1797. But the French soon proved just as great a burden on Italian treasuries to support their war effort and the Bonaparte family. If Napoleon did not exactly "liberate" Italy, he did shake up the old conservatism from Lombardy to Naples by creating new universities and high schools, streamlining the bureaucracy, creating a new legal system with his Napoleonic Code and generally awakening the forces of Italian nationalism. Clandestine political clubs like the *Carbonari* sprang up around the country.

Caution was the watchword among Italian rulers restored to their lands after Napoleon's defeat. Austria seized the occasion to add the Veneto to its Lombardy territories. The 1823 conclave of *zelanti* (zealot) cardinals elected arch-conservative Leo XII to help the papacy recover from its Napoleonic shock. On the lookout for any contagiously progressive movement, the Austrians helped Bourbon King Ferdinand of Naples crush an 1821 revolt for constitutional monarchy and foiled a similar uprising in Piedmont. The danger became clear in 1831 when insurrection spread through Bologna, Modena and Parma to the Papal States of central Italy. But the Austrians defeated a rebel government of "united Italian provinces", weakened by regional rivalries and conflicting personal ambitions.

The Risorgimento, the "resurrection" of national identity, took two conflicting paths. Genoese-born Giuseppe Mazzini's *Giovine Italia* (Young

Italy) movement sought national unity by popular-based insurrection. He opposed Piedmontese patricians and intellectuals of the Moderates party seeking reform through a privilege-conscious confederation of Italian princes blessed by the papacy, with Piedmont providing the military muscle. They feared a new proletarian militancy among factory workers. Landowners bringing in cheap migrant day-labour faced mounting peasant resentment. Food riots broke out in Lombardy, revolts in Tuscany, and southern peasants demanded a share-out of common land.

Composer Giuseppe Verdi was the Risorgimento's towering artist. His operas' romantic humanism inspired fellow patriots, who saw in the *Nabucco* Freedom Chorus a positive call to action.

Outright rebellion erupted in Milan on March 18, 1848, year of revolution all over Europe. Emissaries flew by balloon to nearby cities for reinforcements that freed Milan from the 14,000-strong Austrian garrison. The Venetians restored their republic, a Piedmontese army joined up with troops from Tuscany, the Papal States and Naples, and a new democratic Roman Republic was proclaimed. But the hesitant Carlo Alberto of Piedmont gave the Austrians time to recover and Italian gains toppled like dominoes. National unity was again sabotaged by provincial rivalries.

Conceding the need for more reform, the new king of Piedmont, Vittorio Emanuele II, became a constitutional monarch with a moderate-dominated parliament. Prime Minister Count Camillo Benso di Cavour, a hard-nosed political realist, won over moderate left-wing support for a programme of free-trade capitalism and large-scale public works construction. Among the political exiles flocking to Piedmont was a veteran of the earlier revolts, Giuseppe Garibaldi.

With their French allies, Piedmont defeated Austria at Magenta and Solferino to secure Lombardy in 1859. A year later, Cavour negotiated the handover of Emilia and Tuscany. But it was the adventure of Garibaldi's Red Shirts that imposed the unification of the peninsula in 1860. With two steamers, antiquated artillery and 94,000 lire in funds, Garibaldi set sail from Genoa with his "Expedition of the Thousand". The heroic Red Shirts seized Bourbon Sicily and crossed to the mainland. At Teano, outside Naples, they met up with Vittorio Emanuele, who was proclaimed King of Italy. National unity was completed with the annexation of Veneto in 1866 and Rome, the new capital, in 1871.

Garibaldi, bravest of Italy's freedom fighters, is known simply as "The Hero" (l'Eroe).

The Modern Era

Despite its extraordinary fragmented history, unified Italy took its place among modern nations as an unexceptional centralized state, careful to protect the interests of its industrial and financial establishment and granting reforms to the working classes only under the pressure of their united action.

From migrant labour in France and Germany, where they were known as Europe's Chinamen, factory and farm workers brought back expert knowledge of union organization and strikes. But in keeping with the Italians' traditional local attach-

35

ments, their first unions were *camere del lavoro,* regionally based chambers of labour linking workers to their town or commune rather than their individual trade.

Both left and right wanted Italy to join the European race for colonies—their eyes fixed on Ethiopia and Libya. Conservatives supported expansion for reasons of national prestige. Socialists talked of Italy's "civilizing mission" in the Mediterranean, seeking to divert the flow of emigrants (heading increasingly to the Americas) to experimental collective land management in new African colonies in Tripoli and Cyrenaica.

At home, in addition to traditional textiles, industry was expanding fast in metallurgy, chemicals and machinery. The national love affair with cars had begun—from seven produced in 1900 and 70 in 1907, there were 9,200 rolling out of the factories by 1914, most of them from Fiat, founded in 1899.

With wily Prime Minister Giovanni Giolitti manoeuvring the forces of capital and labour, Italy began its 20th century in a blithe state of calm and prosperity known as *Italietta:* holidays by the sea or in the mountains, soothing operas like Puccini's *La Bohème* and *Madame Butterfly,* the first silent-movie extravaganzas of *The Last Days of*

Pompeii and *Quo Vadis*, relaxed conversations in city squares at the hour of the *passeggiata,* the evening walk. Avant-garde artists enraged by the smug bourgeoisie seemed harmless enough, futurists declaring war on spaghetti and preferring the beauty of Maseratis and Alfa Romeos to that of Greek statues.

They were less amusing when hailing World War I as the "world's hygiene". Previously committed to a Triple Alliance with Austria and Germany, Italy remained neutral in 1914. The following year, acting with what Prime Minister Antonio Salandra acknowledged to be *"sacro egoismo",* Italy signed a secret treaty to enter the war on the side of Britain, France and Russia in exchange for the post-war annexation of Austrian-held Trento, South Tyrol (now Alto Adige) and Trieste.

The people were at first cool to the war, despite the jingoism of flashy aristocratic aesthete Gabriele d'Annunzio and his friend, an ex-socialist newspaperman named Benito Mussolini. The Italian Army was the least well prepared of the combatants, lacking artillery, machine guns, trucks and properly trained officers, but the infantry showed remarkable courage in the trenches. After disaster at Caporetto, the Austro-German 1917 advance across the Veneto plain was held until the Italian counterattack of October–November 1918 permitted a triumphant entry into Trento and Trieste.

For the peasant, worker and petit bourgeois, war in uniform was their first real experience of Italian nationality. Enthusiastic war-supporters like d'Annunzio, who captured the popular imagination by flying over Vienna to drop propaganda leaflets, were acclaimed as patriots, while democrats and pacifist republicans were dismissed as defeatists. Parliament, which was denied knowledge of the secret war treaty till the Peace Conference of 1919, was exposed as impotent.

The left was in disarray. The Socialists won the elections but split over support for the Russian Revolution, leading to the formation in 1921 of the Italian Communist Party. In an atmosphere of economic crisis—stagnant productivity, bank closures and rising unemployment—conservatives wanted somebody tougher, more dynamic than eternally compromising old-style politicians. With black-shirted *Fasci Italiani di Combattimento* (Italian combat groups) beating up Slavs in Trieste and union-workers in Bologna, Mussolini filled the bill. Threatened by the Fascists' March on Rome in 1922, King Vittorio Emanuele III invited Mussolini, *il Duce,* to form a government.

The now all-too familiar process of totalitarianism set in: opposition leaders assassinated, their parties, free unions and free press all abolished. The Vatican did not complain, though it was upset when the fascist youth movement dissolved the Catholic Boy Scouts. After the Lateran Treaty of 1929 had created a separate Vatican state and perpetuated Catholicism as Italy's national religion with guaranteed religious education in the schools, Pope Pius XI described Mussolini as a man sent by Providence.

Italian fascism remained a style rather than a coherent ideology, typified by the raised-arm salute replacing the "weakling" handshake, bombastic architecture and Mussolini's arrogant harangues from the Palazzo Venezia's "heroic balcony" in Rome. The Duce's motto of "Better to live one day as a lion than 100 years as a sheep" contrasted with the one he gave the country: "Believe, obey, fight." Neither lions nor sheep, most Italians survived with lip-service and good humour, while communists re-allied with socialists in the anti-fascist underground whose partisans linked up with the Allies during World War II.

In 1936, Mussolini diverted attention from the worsening

economic climate at home with an invasion of Ethiopia and proclamation of the Italian Empire. With the Vatican's enthusiastic support, Italian war planes joined Hitler's Luftwaffe on General Franco's side in the Spanish Civil War (5,000 Italian communists and socialists fought on the Republican side). In 1938, German-style racist legislation was introduced against the country's 57,000 Jews. The next year, Italy invaded Albania and, after France's collapse in June 1940, plunged with Germany into World War II. Its poorly equipped armies were defeated by the British in the African desert and by the mountain snows in the Balkans. The Allies landed in Sicily in June, 1943, and liberated Rome one year later. Mussolini, toppled soon after the Allied landings and reinstated briefly as a German puppet in the north, was caught fleeing in German uniform to the Swiss border and executed in April, 1945.

The sordid hardships of postwar Italy—unemployment, the black market and prostitution—have been made graphically familiar through the brilliant neo-realist cinema of Rossellini, de Sica and Fellini. Today, the remarkable economic recovery has silenced the old condescension about Italy's technological and managerial talents. In the European Common Market, it has more than held its own in heavy industry, agribusiness and the new electronics. A specifically Italian ingredient came from the highly productive clandestine—and so untaxable—manufacturing and other activity parallel to the open market.

Italians didn't take easily to national government. They had gone most of their history without it and Mussolini had spoiled their appetite. Now, fatigued by his excesses, they rejected the militant left for a little *dolce vita* with the less adventurous but less disturbing Christian Democrats. Their perpetually changing coalitions hardly constituted real national government, but the people seemed to function quite well anyway. In the 1980s, a pragmatic socialist coalition government with the Christian Democrats brought a few years of unusual stability. Corruption, *combinazione* and tax-evasion continued, but police clamped down on the political terrorism of the Red Brigades and neo-fascists and the age-old criminality of the Mafia.

In Tuscany, the cypresses recover from their blight. As Fellini puts it, *E la nave va,* "And the ship sails on."

Most charming "flags" of Italy are the ubiquitous laundry.

HISTORICAL LANDMARKS

Early Settlements	9th c.B.C.	Etruscans settle in Italy.
	8th c.	Greeks in Sicily and south.
Roman Era	753	Rome founded.
	510	Establishment of Roman Republic.
	202	Rome defeats Carthage.
	44	Julius Caesar assassinated.
	27	Augustus instals empire.
	64 A.D.	Christian persecutions in Rome.
	79	Vesuvius volcano buries Pompeii.
	312	Constantine becomes Christian.
	410	Visigoths sack Rome.
Invasions	6th c.	Lombards invade Milan; Venice founded on lagoon.
	800	Pope crowns Charlemagne.
	827	Arabs invade Sicily.
	1000–1100	Normans conquer south.
Middle Ages	1182–1226	St. Francis of Assisi.
	1198–1250	Frederick II's court in Palermo.
	1271–95	Marco Polo in Orient.
	1305	Giotto paints Padua Chapel.
	1309–77	Popes exiled to Avignon.
	1312	Dante writes *Inferno*.
	1347	Cola di Rienzo rules Rome.
	1378–1381	Venice and Genoa fight for supremacy.
Renaissance	1434	Cosimo begins Medici rule in Florence.
	1442	Spanish rule Naples and Sicily.
	1494–1559	Spanish and French fight over Naples and Milan.
	1497	Leonardo da Vinci's *Last Supper*.
	1498	Savonarola burned in Florence.

	1508–12	Michelangelo paints Sistine Chapel ceiling.
	1527	Sack of Rome by imperial troops.
Counter-Reformation and Enlightenment	1545–63	Council of Trent.
	1633	Trial of Galileo.
	1748	Excavations of Pompeii begin.
	1778	La Scala theatre opens in Milan.
	1796	Napoleon invades north.
Risorgimento	1821	Austrians crush insurrection.
	1831	Mazzini founds *La Giovine Italia*.
	1848–49	Abortive countrywide revolts.
	1859	Franco-Piedmontese alliance takes Lombardy from Austria.
	1860	Garibaldi's Expedition of 1,000.
	1861	Kingdom of Italy proclaimed; capital Turin.
	1871	Rome capital of unified Italy.
Modern Era	1915	Italy joins British, French and Russians in World War I.
	1919	Trento, South Tyrol (Alto Adige) and Trieste acquired from Austria.
	1921	Italian Communist Party founded.
	1922	Mussolini begins Fascist regime with March on Rome.
	1929	Lateran Treaty establishes separate Vatican state.
	1936	Italy invades Abyssinia, bombs Republican Spain.
	1940	Italy joins Germany in World War II.
	1943–44	Allies liberate Sicily, then Rome.
	1945	Mussolini caught and executed.
	1978	Red Brigades assassinate Christian Democrat leader Aldo Moro.

WHERE TO GO

Not an easy decision. "Doing" Italy is a lifetime job and many devotees are so in love with the place that they don't even think of any other holiday destination. After a first romance with, say, Rome, Venice or Florence, they spend the rest of their lives systematically working their way through the country, region by region, year after year. But if this is your first trip, without being too ambitious, you might like to get at least a first over-all impression. If the seduction works, and it usually does, you'll want to come back for more, to fill in the gaps. If that's not possible, what we propose here will still give you a feel for Italy and things Italian.

The book includes all the most important towns and regions to help you make your choice. We've divided the country up into five areas, each with a principal city as a focus or starting point: *Rome* for central Italy, plus Sardinia; *Florence* for Tuscany, Umbria and the Adriatic seaside resorts; *Venice* for

Loafers, workers and pigeons meet on Milan's Piazza del Duomo.

42

Veneto, the Dolomites and Emilia's historic towns from Parma to Ravenna; *Milan* for Lombardy, Piedmont and the Italian Riviera; and *Naples* for the south and Sicily.

As always, we try to be representative rather than encyclopaedic in our coverage of the country. Given the sheer richness of Italy, our selection of places within those five areas is not in any way exhaustive (nor, by the same token, exhausting). Those who know something of Italy already will inevitably feel that a few of their favourite spots have been neglected (though they may also be grateful we've kept their secret), while they'll find others they never dreamed of. Newcomers will have more than enough to choose from.*

Depending on how much time you have for that all-important first taste, we suggest you try to visit at least two, even three of the regions. Those with a passion for the big city can combine Rome or Milan with the artistic delights of Florence and Tuscany or the romance of Venice. But for many, the key to Italy's Mediterranean soul is to be found in Naples and the south. After the intense emotion, you can always

cool off at the seaside resorts on the Riviera or the Adriatic.

The trick is in the mix. Not just geographically, in exploring the variety and contrasts of north and south, but in combining the attractions of town and country and the different facets of Italy's daily life. Nowhere is it easier to overdose on museums and monuments than in Italy. A dear old lady returned from her first visit with the observation: "Italy's very nice, very nice indeed, but for my taste, too much history." While it would be a crime to ignore the churches, palaces and museums chronicling the glories of Italy's history, the best way to enjoy them is also to spend plenty of time lazing around in cafés or on the beach or just sleeping under an olive tree out in the country. The siesta is one of the greatest of all Latin institutions, and the most important Italian expression you may ever learn is *dolce far niente* (how sweet to do nothing).

Many people cannot manage to go to Italy outside the major holiday periods—Easter, July and August. But if your options are more flexible, the most enjoyable months are May, June, September and October, especially for Rome, Venice and Tuscany. Certainly, July and August can be almost unbearably hot and humid in the big cities, but some find a perverse ghostly

---

*For more detailed information on specific destinations in Italy, look for the Berlitz Travel Guides to *Rome, Venice, Florence, Italian Riviera, Italian Adriatic* and *Sicily*.

pleasure in being in Rome on Ferragosto (on and around August 15) when the city is abandoned to the cats and the crazy. And remember, Italians make no bones about public holidays (see p. 237), they just close the country down.

Getting Around

Even the most free-spirited traveller can use a little help occasionally. With the tourist industry such a vital factor in the economy, Italy has an elaborate network of information offices. Bureaucrats being bureaucrats, efficiency and amiability vary from place to place, but they all provide useful maps and brochures.

For general information, the state tourist office ENIT *(Ente Nazionale Italiano per il Turismo)* has offices in major foreign cities as well as regional capitals. APT *(Azienda di Promozione Turistica)* gives more detailed regional sightseeing information and can also help with hotel and camping accommodation. CIT *(Compagnia Italiana Turismo)* is a national travel agency for transportation, excursions and hotel bookings.

The Berlitz-Info section at the back of the book (pp. 218–243) gives detailed practical guidance on the technicalities of travel through Italy, but here are some general thoughts to help you plan your trip.

Not Too Much

Museum-going in Italy is not always simple. Even the local tourist office cannot always keep up with the changes in opening hours. Some museums are closed temporarily, for days, months or even years, for restauro (restoration). This is a blanket term covering budgetary problems for museum staff and modern security systems or genuine, long overdue programmes of renovation of the buildings and restoration of the paintings. Many ancient Roman monuments may also go into prolonged hiding under protective scaffolding.

When you do go to one of the really big museums like the Uffizi in Florence, the Vatican in Rome or Milan's Brera, treat it like Italy itself: unless you're a museum-fiend, don't try to do it all. Before you go in, look at the guide, study the museum plan in the lobby and head for the things you really want to see. Or, if you prefer the serendipity of coming across beautiful surprises, just wander around, but not for much more than an hour. Otherwise, you may get a sharp attack of visual overload and won't be able to tell the difference between a Fra Angelico and the sign for the fire extinguisher.

Except for a major journey from one part of the country to another, say, from Milan to Rome or down to Naples, touring by train, given the uncertainties of schedules and frequency of strike action, is best reserved for train-buffs with plenty of time, timetables and patience. If you are making a long rail journey, don't rely on the generally dreary dining car service. Make up your own picnic hamper of cold meats, salad, cheese, fruit and Chianti from the local market before you get aboard. Very often, you end up sharing it with Italian passengers who offer their own local delicacies.

But the great breathtaking Italian adventure remains the road. The *autostrada* (toll motorway or expressway) runs the length and breadth of the peninsula, a challenge to the imagination and survival instincts of Western civilization. Only to the uninitiated do Italian drivers seem dangerous. Most of them are highly skilful—they have to be—and proud of their reflexes. Two attitudes to avoid: recklessness and excessive caution. Don't try to match their improvisations, you will only raise their competitive spirit into the realm of high risk. They may be similarly provoked by indecisive slowcoaches.

Keep your car for use on the open road. In the overcrowded cities, just drop your bags off at the hotel, park your car and walk, take a bus or rent a bike. Most big towns have solved the problem for you by closing off their old centre *(centro storico)* to private cars.

Try to vary the kind of places you stay in. Little old hostelries and country inns are charming, but, depending of course on your budget, it's worth splashing out at least one night on the special comforts and pampering of the great hotels. Look out, too, for converted monasteries: the frugality has long gone, the heating is modern and the medieval well has been replaced by a swimming pool, but the setting is still conducive to meditation.

One last tip: even if you're a linguistic dud, do speak a couple of Italian words. The pronunciation is remarkably easy. Italians are usually delighted by anyone making the effort. A cheerful *buon giorno* (good day) or *buona sera* (good evening) can work wonders when coming into a shop. In a land where politeness is much more important than you might imagine, *per favore* (please), *grazie* (thank you), *prego* (don't mention it) and, when pushing through a bus, *permesso* (excuse me) will be greatly appreciated. You'll find some further simple phrases at the back of the book, p. 243. Now enjoy it, *buon viaggio!*

CENTRAL ITALY

The centre of Italy is the cradle of Latin civilization, administrative headquarters of that ancient conglomerate known as the Roman Empire. Immediately surrounding Rome, Lazio is the old province of Latium. On the eastern flank of the Apennines, the Abruzzi region, of which the province of Molise is a recently created offshoot, came under Roman domination in the 3rd century B.C. While first-time visitors will want to spend most of their time around Rome, the wilderness of the Abruzzi National Park makes a pleasant excursion within fairly easy reach of Rome.

The rugged island of Sardinia deserves at least a week to do it any kind of justice, but you may want to spend just a long weekend at one of its attractive little seaside resorts.

ROME

Within and beyond its seven hills and along the winding banks of the River Tiber, Rome has four or five different personalities: ancient Rome of the imperial ruins; Catholic Rome of the Vatican and churches; the Renaissance city of Michelangelo and Raphael or the Baroque of Bernini and Borromini; and a modern metropolis of interminable traffic jams, fashionable boutiques and cafés, but also factories and high-rises in the industrial suburbs.

You may choose one, two or all of them, but none is easily separable from the others. Churches are built on the ruins of Roman baths or pagan temples. The flights of fancy of the T-shirted, designer-jeaned café crowd on Piazza Navona draw natural inspiration from Bernini's grandiose 17th-century fountain. The secret of the Eternal City is that it has lived all its ages simultaneously. The road-building Caesars *knew* their descendants would be obsessed with cars.

Park yours, get into some comfortable walking shoes and ease yourself into the city gently. Before you face the daunting challenge of the ancient city around the Colosseum or the Vatican's formidable complex, we suggest you get to know the modern Romans' town.

The Centre

Make an early start with breakfast on **Piazza del Popolo** at a veritable Roman institution, meeting-place of the city's brighter spirits, the **Caffè Rosati** (and come back for an evening apéritif). Its terrace is a perfect vantage point for admiring the gracefully curving piazza as an exemplary piece of open-air urban theatre, designed in 1816 by Giuseppe Valadier, architect to Napoleon.

On the north side, the austere **Santa Maria del Popolo** is important for Raphael's Chigi Chapel, exquisite frescoes by Pinturicchio and, above all, two profoundly disturbing early 17th-century paintings by Caravaggio, the *Conversion of St. Paul* and *Crucifixion of St. Peter,* in the Cerasi Chapel left of the choir.

Next to the church, an arched gateway marks what was the entrance to ancient Rome along the Via Flaminia, leading from Rimini on the Adriatic coast.

The **obelisk** in the centre, dating from the Egypt of Rameses II (13th century B.C.), was brought here from the Circus Maximus and re-erected by Pope Sixtus V in 1589. Rounding off the south side are the twin Baroque churches, **Santa Maria dei Miracoli** and **Santa Maria in Montesanto,** completed by the 17th-century masters, Gianlorenzo Bernini and Carlo Fontana.

Above the piazza to the east, the **Pincio** gardens offer a magical view of the city, especially at sunset. (For the great art museum in the Villa Borghese behind the Pincio, see p. 66.) The Pincio promenade lined with pine trees and open-air restaurants takes you past the **Villa Medici,** home of French artists visiting on national scholarships, to the 16th-century French church, **Trinità dei Monti.**

Its twin belfries loom over the **Spanish Steps** *(Scalinata della Trinità dei Monti)*, eternal hangout of guitar-playing youths, lovers and pedlars of trinkets and flowers. The pleasant daze induced on the three-tiered travertine staircase, festooned in spring with pink azaleas, was celebrated by John Keats as a "blissful cloud of summer indolence" before he died here in 1821. His house at the bottom of the steps has been preserved as a museum.

Named after a palace used as the Spanish Embassy, the steps and the **Piazza di Spagna** are the heart of the city's most

They must have already thrown their coins in the fountain.

fashionable shopping area, leading over to the Via del Corso. The piazza's 17th-century boat-shaped marble fountain, **Fontana della Barcaccia,** is by the great Bernini's father. The venerable **Babington's Tea Rooms** are a relic of the days when Romans called the piazza the "English ghetto". More quintessentially Roman, on nearby Via Condotti, is the city's oldest coffee house, the 18th-century **Caffè Greco,** popular, as you'll see from pictures, busts and autographs, with Goethe, Byron, Baudelaire, Liszt, Gogol and Fellini.

The **Trevi Fountain** *(Fontana di Trevi)* benefited from Fellini's keen sense of Baroque aesthetics when he dipped the sumptuous Anita Ekberg in its legendarily purifying waters for his film *La Dolce Vita.* Most people are content just to toss in a coin over their shoulder—causing daily fights between street urchins and the municipality for the considerable revenues in high season. Nicola Salvi's astounding 18th-century fountain is in fact a triumphal arch and palace façade (to the old Palazzo Poli) framing mythic creatures in a riot of rocks and pools, with a rearing horse symbolizing the ocean's turmoil and a calmer steed its tranquillity. Tucked away behind narrow alleys, this extravaganza is out of all propor-

tion to its tiny piazza and no amount of signposts leading to it can prepare you for the marvellous shock of discovery. Romantics go at the dead of night, to be alone with its illumination.

That other symbol of the *dolce vita,* the **Via Veneto,** has been deserted by its starlets and *paparazzi* and only the expensive cafés, shops and hotels remain.

On one of the seven hills of ancient Rome, the fortress-like **Palazzo del Quirinale,** once residence to popes fleeing the malarial swamps of the Vatican down by the Tiber, housed the king of Italy after 1870, and is now the presidential palace. The only embellishment on its formidable façade is Bernini's graceful porch, but its piazza is worth the climb for the view over the city and the Vatican.

You couldn't miss **Piazza Venezia** if you tried—and many do try, because of its endless traffic jams and the grotesque **Vittorio Emanuele Monument,** celebrating the first king of unified Italy with inimitable 19th-century pomposity. North-west of the monument, the 15th-century **Palazzo Venezia** is a fine example of severe but elegant early Renaissance architecture, now containing a museum of medieval and Renaissance arms, furniture and sculpture. Mussolini had his office there and harangued his followers from the balcony.

Behind the Piazza Venezia, one staircase leads steeply up to the austere 13th-century **Santa Maria in Aracoeli**, while another, more graceful and gradual, takes you up between statues of Castor and Pollux to Michelangelo's beautifully cambered square of the **Campidoglio** (Capitoline Hill). This haven of quiet, away from the traffic, forges a superb link between the Renaissance

---

Dental Surgery

Few edifices have known such universal hostility as the Vittorio Emanuele Monument or "Vittoriano". Popularly known as the "wedding cake" or "Rome's false teeth", the bombastic colonnade with its pedestrian equestrian bronzes and almost unclimbable steps are a true monument of urban catastrophe. Begun in 1885, the 40-year construction entailed the demolition of a piece of the ancient Capitoline Hill. Parts of the Palazzo Venezia were dismantled for a clearer view. The gigantic proportions completely dwarf the surrounding splendours of ancient Rome and the dazzling white Brescia marble clashes with the city's preference for gentle amber, ochre or pink travertine. In 1944, art historians pleaded with the Allies to suspend Rome's status as an open city—protecting it against bombardment—just long enough to destroy the Vittoriano.

---

and ancient Rome's most sacred site, where sacrifices were made to Jupiter and Juno. The grand central bronze equestrian **statue of Marcus Aurelius** (undergoing prolonged restoration) is to be sheltered in a museum and replaced by a copy. At the rear of the square is the handsome 16th-century façade of the **Palazzo Senatorio** (now the City Hall), flanked by the **Palazzo Nuovo** and **Palazzo dei Conservatori.** These last two house the Capitoline Museums (see p. 66), whose Greek and Roman collections provide an excellent introduction to the Forum.

The church of **the Gesù,** severe and relatively discreet on its own square west of the Piazza Venezia, was a major element in the Jesuits' Counter-Reformation campaign. Begun as their Roman "headquarters" in 1568, its open ground plan was the model for the congregational churches that were to regain popular support from the Protestants. While its façade is more sober than the exultant Baroque churches put up as the movement gained momentum, the interior glorifies the new militancy in gleaming bronze, gold, marble and precious stones. Perhaps inevitably, the church's richest, almost overwhelming ornament is the **altar of St. Ignatius Loyola,** covering the tomb of the Jesuits' founder (in the left transept) with a profusion of lapis lazuli. The globe at the top is said to be the largest piece of this stone in the world.

In gentler contrast, the church of **Sant'Ignazio** stands in an enchanting Rococo stage-set of 18th-century houses. Inside, Andrea Pozzo (himself a Jesuit priest and designer of the saint's tomb at the Gesù) has painted a superb *trompe l'œil* ceiling fresco (1685) depicting St. Ignatius' entry into paradise. Stand on a buff stone disk in the nave's centre aisle for the full effect of the celestial dome apparently rising above the transept.

The **Pantheon** (Piazza della Rotonda) is the best preserved monument of ancient Rome and rivals the Colosseum in its combination of quiet elegance and sheer massive power. Emperor Hadrian, its builder (around A.D. 120), achieved a marvel of engineering with its magnificent coffered dome, over 43 metres (142 ft.) in interior diameter (larger than St. Peter's), borne by an intricate portico of pink and grey granite columns and arches. Bronze that once embellished the entrance was taken away to make Bernini's canopy for the high altar in St. Peter's.

This "Temple of all the Gods" today contains the tombs of Renaissance deities such as Raphael and architect Baldassare Peruzzi and of kings Vittorio Emanuele II and Umberto I.

Caravaggio admirers will find some of his greatest masterpieces in the neighbourhood: the St. Matthew trilogy in the fine Baroque church of **San Luigi dei Francesi,** and the moving

Capture Rome's golden glow from the gardens of the Janiculum.

Madonna of the Pilgrims in the Renaissance church of **Sant'Agostino**.

Pause now at a café in that serenest of city squares, the **Piazza Navona**. Nowhere in Rome is the spectacle of Italian street life more pleasantly indulged, thanks to an inspired collaboration of Roman genius across the ages. The elongated piazza was laid out around A.D.

90 by Emperor Domitian as an athletics stadium, *Circus Agonalis*—a sporting tradition continued in the Renaissance with jousting tournaments. The 17th century contributed its sublime Baroque décor, and today, sages on the city council safeguard it as a pedestrian zone. In the centre, Bernini's **Fountain of the Four Rivers** *(Fontana dei Fiumi)* celebrates the great rivers of the

Americas (Río de la Plata), Europe (Danube), Asia (Ganges) and Africa (Nile). Romans who delight in Bernini's scorn for his rivals suggest that the Nile god covers his head rather than look at Borromini's church of **Sant'Agnese in Agone** and the river god of the Americas is poised to catch it in case it collapses. In fact, the fountain was completed several years *before* Borromini's splendid—and structurally impeccable—façade and dome. Popular tradition suggests the church was built on the ruins of a Roman brothel where St. Agnes was stripped before being martyred.

The boisterous fruit and vegetable market on the **Campo de' Fiori** gives way in the afternoons to political meetings, admonished by the statue of philosopher Giordano Bruno. The Inquisition burned him alive here in 1600 for his preposterous idea that the universe was infinite, with many more galaxies than ours. An even more famous death occurred at the nearby Piazza del Biscione, more precisely the restaurant Da Pancrazio, site of Pompey's Theatre where Julius Caesar was assassinated.

Only with a special appointment can you visit the glorious **Palazzo Farnese,** built by Antonio da Sangallo the Younger, Michelangelo and Giacomo

Della Porta, now the French Embassy. Only the inner courtyard of Rome's finest Renaissance palace is accessible to the public, but its grand portico and the handsome stuccoed vestibule leading to it make it well worthwhile. With a French diplomat friend, you may get in to see the ceremonial dining room's fabulous frescoes by Annibale Carracci. Since 1870, the French pay a rent of one lira every

year and provide a palace in Paris as Italy's embassy—very nice, too, but not exactly Michelangelo.

Narrow streets south-east of the Campo de' Fiori take you to the **Jewish Ghetto** near the ruins of the ancient Roman Theatre of Marcellus *(Teatro di Marcello),* architectural model for the Colosseum. A permanent feature of Roman life for over 2,500 years but forced into a ghetto

Behind Campo de' Fiori, artisans will fix anything for you.

only in the 16th century, a small Jewish community still lives around the Via del Portico d'Ottavia. The hefty neo-Babylonian synagogue (built in 1904), with a small museum of Jewish history next door, is down by the river.

55

Classical Rome

The nucleus of classical Rome is around the Colosseum, with the Forum to the north-west and the Baths of Caracalla to the south. Don't be daunted—even the best-informed scholars find the monumental relics difficult to decipher—the mystery itself is more than half the charm of these vestiges of a vanished world. Take them in your stride, slower and more relaxed than ever when it comes to walking the ruins. Avoid the midday sun in the shadeless Forum and finish your visit with a picnic and siesta on the Palatine. Even if you're not an archaeology buff who wants to understand the meaning of every stone, it's worth at least an hour or two to stand among the debris of empire and wonder whether Fifth Avenue, Piccadilly, the Champs-Elysées or Red Square will look any better 2,000 years from now.

It says something about Rome's essential earthiness that, more than any inspirational church or opulent palace, it's the **Colosseum**—what Byron called "the gladiator's bloody circus"—that is the symbol of the city's eternity. Built in A.D. 80 by 20,000 slaves and prisoners, the four-tiered elliptical arena seated 50,000 spectators on stone benches. Flowing in and out of 80 arched passageways known as *vomitoria,* aristocrat and plebs alike came to see blood: bears, lions, tigers and leopards starved into fighting each other and against criminals, war captives and Christians. Gladiators butchered one another to the crowds' cries of *Jugula!* ("Slit his throat!")

For their churches and palaces, popes and princes have stripped the Colosseum of its precious marble, travertine and metal. They have left in the arena's basin a ruined maze of cells and corridors that funneled men and beasts to the slaughter. The horror has disappeared beneath the moss and what remains is the thrill of the monument's endurance. As an old Anglo-Saxon prophecy goes: "While stands the Colosseum, Rome shall stand; when falls the Colosseum, Rome shall fall; and when Rome falls, with it shall fall the world."

The nearby **Arch of Constantine** celebrates the 4th-century emperor's battlefield conversion to Christianity. Unperturbed by their depiction of pagan rituals and sacrifices, a cost-conscious Senate took fragments from monuments of earlier rulers, Trajan, Hadrian and Marcus Aurelius. Only a few reliefs, over the two outer arches, show the newly Christian Constantine.

With an exhilarating leap of the imagination, you can stand

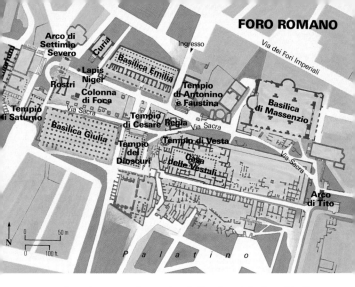

Arco di Settimio Severo

Curia

Lapis Niger

Rostri

Colonna di Foca

Basilica Emilia

Ingresso

Via dei Fori Imperiali

Tempio di Antonino e Faustina

Basilica di Massenzio

Tempio di Saturno

Via Sacra

Basilica Giulia

Tempio di Cesare

Regia

Via Sacra

Tempio dei Dioscuri

Tempio di Vesta

Casa delle Vestali

Via Sacra

Arco di Tito

N

0   50 m

0   100 ft.

P a l a t i n o

among the columns, arches and porticoes of the **Roman Forum** and picture the hub of the great imperial city, the first in Europe to house a million inhabitants. Earthquake, fire, flood and the plunder of barbarians and Renaissance architects reduced the area to a muddy cow pasture until the excavations of the 19th century. Today, a detailed plan and the portable sound-guide rented at the entrance (on the Via dei Fori Imperiali) will make sense of the apparent confusion and help you trace the layout of palaces, temples and market halls.

Part of the **Curia,** home of the Roman Senate, still stands, in-cluding its original marble floor. Steps nearby lead underground to the **Lapis Niger,** a black marble pavement laid by Julius Caesar over the presumed grave of Romulus, the city's founder. To the south of it are remains of the Basilica Julia law court and the **Rostra** orators' plat-form from which Mark Antony informed the people of Caesar's assassination. Countless Renais-sance and Baroque sculptors have drawn inspiration from the friezes on the **Arch of Septimius Severus** (honouring a 3rd-cen-tury emperor who died in York, England).

The **Temple of Saturn** doubled as state treasury and centre of

57

the merry December debauchery known as the Saturnalia, pagan precursor of Christmas. In the circular **Temple of Vesta,** the sacred flame perpetuating the Roman state was tended by six Vestal Virgins who, from childhood, observed a 30-year vow of chastity on pain of being buried alive if they broke it. At the end of the Via Sacra, the **Arch of Titus** commemorates the sack of Jerusalem in A.D. 70.

Most impressive monument of the Imperial Forums, built as an adjunct to the Roman Forum in honour of Julius Caesar, Augustus, Trajan, Vespasian and Domitian, is the 30-metre-high (98-ft.) **Trajan's Column** (A.D. 113). Celebrating Trajan's campaigns against the Dacians in what is today Rumania, the minutely detailed friezes spiralling around the column constitute a veritable textbook of Roman warfare. St. Peter's statue replaced the emperor's in 1587.

South of the Roman Forum, the **Palatine Hill** is Rome's legendary birthplace and today its most romantic garden, dotted with toppled columns among the wild flowers and spiny acanthus shrubs. Only rows of cypress trees and summer pavilions remain from the more formal botanical gardens laid out here in the 16th century by the Farnese family. From grassy knolls, enjoy the fine view back over the

Colosseum or southward over the great **Circus Maximus,** where chariot races were held for crowds of up to 200,000.

A kilometre south of the Colosseum, the huge 3rd-century **Baths of Caracalla** *(Terme di Caracalla)* were built for 1,600 people to bathe in considerable style and luxury. Imagine the still impressive brick walls covered in coloured marble, some of which you can see today adorning the fountain basins of the Piazza Farnese in front of the French Embassy (see p. 54). The baths and gymnasia were of alabaster and granite, profusely decorated with statues and frescoes. Public bathing was a prolonged social event as merchants and senators passed from the *caldarium* hot room to cool down in the *tepidarium* and *frigidarium.* Now the stage for spectacular open-air operas in the summer, the *caldarium* is vast enough for processions of elephants, camels and four-horse chariots.

South of the baths begins the **Old Appian Way** *(Via Appia Antica),* over which the Roman legions marched on their way to Brindisi to set sail for the Levant

Even without her head, the Forum's vestal virgin remains demure.

and North Africa. On either side lie the ruins of sepulchres of 20 generations of patrician families. The chapel of Domine Quo Vadis marks the site where St. Peter, fleeing Nero's persecution in Rome, is said to have encountered Christ. Further along the Via Appia are the **Catacombs of St. Callixtus,** a vast underground Christian cemetery, notably containing graves of 3rd-century popes.

The Vatican

The power of Rome endures both in the spirituality evoked by every stone of St. Peter's Basilica and in the almost physical awe inspired by the splendours of the Vatican palace. At their best, the popes and cardinals replaced military conquest by moral leadership and persuasion; at their worst, they could show the same hunger for political power and worldly wealth as any Caesar or centurion. A visit to the Vatican is an object lesson for faithful and sceptic alike.

Named after the hill on which it stands and which in the Middle Ages was surrounded by a malarial swamp, the Vatican has been a papal residence for over 600 years, but a sovereign state independent of Italy only since the Lateran Pact of 1929.

If you have the time, try to visit St. Peter's and the museums of the Vatican palace on separate days. The riches here pose the city's biggest threat of fatigue and visual overload. In any case, it's a good idea to divide your visit in two with a relaxed lunch. But check opening times: the Vatican museums are usually open all day around Easter and in the summer months, but close at 2 p.m. the rest of the year.

Best of all, have a picnic and siesta in the nearby gardens of the **Janiculum Hill** *(Gianicolo)* where, in the more stormy times of the Risorgimento, as an equestrian statue proclaims, Garibaldi fought one of his fiercest battles.

To appreciate the unique panorama of St. Peter's and its square, take your courage in both feet and walk. Start out by crossing the Tiber to the **Castel Sant'Angelo,** which was originally Hadrian's mausoleum built in A.D. 139. Its name derives from Pope Gregory's vision of the Archangel Michael—now represented by a statue on top—heralding the end of a plague in 590. (If you're walking *all* the way, take the pretty Sant'Angelo Bridge, adorned by ten Bernini angels.) It was 6th-century barbarians who commandeered the massive round pile as a fortress, using ancient statues as missiles to hurl on the heads of their enemies below. Linked to the Vatican by a thick-walled passage, it served as a hideout for popes in times of danger, notably Pope Clement VII, who holed up here for a month during the sack of Rome by Habsburg troops in 1527 (see p. 29). Philosopher Giordano Bruno and sculptor-goldsmith Benvenuto Cellini were imprisoned in the dungeons, which can be visited on a guided tour of what is now a museum of Renaissance art, furnishings and weapons.

In **St. Peter's Square** *(Piazza San Pietro),* his greatest creation, Bernini has performed one of the world's most exciting pieces of architectural orchestration. The sweeping curves of the colonnades reach out to the unending stream of pilgrims from Rome itself and the whole world, *urbi et orbi,* to take them into the bosom of the church beyond. In a rare opportunity for concentrated effort by one man on such a gigantic project, Bernini completed the 284 travertine columns, 88 pilasters and 140 statues of the saints in just 11 years, from 1656 to 1667. Stand on either of the stone disks set in the pavement on each side of the red granite Egyptian obelisk to appreciate the harmony of the quadruple rows of Doric columns, so perfectly aligned that they seem like a single row. The purity of Bernini's work here refutes the popular conception of Baroque as being nothing but overblown extravagance.

The great risk of the Renaissance lay in what would happen if too many of those geniuses got involved in the same project. For instance, **St. Peter's Basilica.** Largest of all Catholic churches and by any standards a grandiose achievement, it inevitably suffers from the competing visions of all the architects called in to collaborate—Bramante, Giuliano da Sangallo, Raphael, Baldassare Peruzzi, Michelangelo, Giacomo Della Porta, Domenico Fontana and

---

Seeing the Pope

When he's not in Bogotá or Bangkok, it is possible to see the pope in person at the Vatican. He normally holds a public audience every Wednesday at 11 a.m. (5 p.m. in summer) down in St. Peter's Square. An invitation to the Papal Audience Hall may be obtained from the Pontifical Prefect's Office (open Tuesday and Wednesday mornings) through the bronze gates in St. Peter's Square. A visitor's bishop at home can arrange a private audience.

On Sundays at noon, the pope appears at the window of his apartments in the Apostolic Palace (right of the basilica, overlooking the square), delivers a brief homily, says the Angelus and blesses the crowd below. On a few major holy days, the pontiff celebrates high mass in St. Peter's.

Carlo Maderno, each adding, subtracting and modifying, often with a pope looking over his shoulder.

From 1506 to 1626, it changed from the simple ground plan of a Greek cross, with four arms of equal length, as favoured by Bramante and his arch-enemy Michelangelo, to the final form of Maderno's Latin cross extended by a long nave, as demanded by the popes of the Counter-Reformation. One result is that Maderno's porticoed façade and nave obstruct a clear view of Michelangelo's dome from the square.

The church's dimensions are impressive: 212 metres (695 ft.) exterior length, 187 metres (613 ft.) inside length; 132.5 metres (435 ft.) to the tip of the dome [diameter 42.45 metres (139 ft.)].

As you go in, notice the keys of St. Peter inlaid in the doorway paving. Set in the floor by the centre door is the large round slab of red porphyry where Charlemagne knelt for his coronation as Holy Roman Emperor in the year 800 (see p. 22).

You'll find the basilica's most treasured work of art, Michelangelo's sublime **Pietà**—Mary with the dead Jesus on her lap—in its own chapel to the right of the entrance. The artist was 24, young and justly proud enough to append his signature (the only surviving example), visible on the Madonna's sash. Since a religious fanatic attacked it with a hammer, the statue is protected by bullet-proof glass.

But reverence can also cause damage: on a 13th-century blackened bronze **statue of St. Peter,** attributed to Florentine architect-sculptor Arnolfo di Cambio, the lips and fingers of countless pilgrims have worn away its toes.

Beneath the dome, Bernini's great **baldacchino** (canopy), cast out of bronze beams taken from the Pantheon's porch (see p. 52), protects the high altar, built right over St. Peter's tomb and reserved for the pope's mass. In the apse beyond, the Baroque master gives full vent to his exuberance with his bronze and marble **Cathedra of St. Peter,** throne of the apostle's successors. It is crowned by a *gloria* in which the dove of the Holy Spirit is lit up on sunny days from a window at the back.

It should come as no surprise that, as the greatest patron that painters, sculptors and architects have ever known, the Catholic Church should house in its "headquarters", one of the world's richest collections of art. The **Vatican Palace** contains eight museums, five gal-

Mass under the great baldacchino is reserved for the pope.

leries, the Apostolic Library, the Borgia Apartments, Raphael Rooms and the Sistine Chapel. Shuttle buses run regularly from St. Peter's Square to the museum entrance.

If you want at all costs to avoid the Sistine's day-long crowds, go straight there first thing in the morning (don't forget your binoculars for details on the ceiling). In any case, you can't miss it—arrows point the way. But there are many marvels to see en route.

With the booty from the ruthless dismantling of ancient monuments to make way for the Renaissance city in the 16th century, the **Pio-Clementino Museum** has assembled a wonderful collection of Roman and Greek art. Most celebrated is the tortured *Laocoön* group (from Rhodes, 1st century B.C.–1st century A.D.), only recently returned more closely to its pristine state by the removal of one son's pathetically outstretched arm added by over-zealous 16th-century "restorers".

Pope Julius II took a calculated risk in 1508 when he called in a relatively untried 25-year-old to the interior decoration of his new apartments. The result was the four **Raphael Rooms** *(Stanze di Raffaello)*. In the central Stanza della Segnatura are the two masterly frescoes, *Disputation over the*

Holy Sacrament and the *School of Athens,* confronting theological and philosophical wisdom. The *Dispute* unites biblical figures with historical pillars of the faith such as Pope Gregory and Thomas Aquinas, but also painter Fra Angelico and the divine Dante. At the centre of the *School,* Raphael is believed to have given the red-coated Plato the features of Leonardo da Vinci, while portraying Michelangelo as the thoughtful Heraclitus, seated in the foreground.

In stark contrast to Raphael's grand manner, look out for the gentle beauty of Fra Angelico's frescoes in the **Chapel of Nicholas V** (signposted as *Cappella del Beato Angelico)*. The lives of Saints Lawrence and Stephen are depicted in delicately subdued pinks and blues.

The richly decorated **Borgia Apartments** contain, in addition to Pinturicchio's frescoes with portraits of lusty Pope Alexander VI and his notorious son Cesare and daughter Lucrezia, the modern religious art collection of Paul VI. The latter includes Rodin bronzes, Picasso ceramics, Matisse's Madonna sketches and designs for ecclesiastical robes and, perhaps unexpectedly, a grotesque Francis Bacon pope.

Nothing can prepare you for the visual shock of the **Sistine Chapel** *(Cappella Sistina),* built for Sixtus IV in the 15th century. Even the discomfort of the throngs of visitors (silence requested) seems to yield to the power of Michelangelo's ceiling, his *Last Judgment,* and the other wall frescoes of Botticelli, Pinturicchio, Ghirlandaio and Signorelli. In this private chapel of popes, where the cardinals hold their conclave to elect a new pope, the glory of the Catholic Church achieves its finest artistic expression.

The chapel portrays nothing less than the story of man, in three parts: from Adam to Noah; the giving of the Law to Moses; and from the birth of Jesus to the Last Judgment. On Michelangelo's **ceiling,** you'll make out the celebrated outstretched finger of man's creation, the drunkenness of Noah, the turmoil of the Flood, but most overwhelming of all is the impression of the whole—best appreciated looking back from the bench by the chapel's exit.

On the chapel's altar wall is Michelangelo's tempestuous **Last Judgment,** begun 23 years after the ceiling, when he was 52 and imbued with deep religious soul-searching. An almost naked Jesus dispenses justice more like a stern, even fierce classical godhero than the conventionally gentle biblical figure. The artist's agonizing self-portrait can be made out in the flayed skin of St. Bartholomew, to the right below Jesus.

Amid all the Vatican's treasures, the 15 rooms of the **Picture Gallery** *(Pinacoteca Vaticana),* in a separate wing of the palace, sometimes get short shrift. This collection of ten centuries of paintings should not be overlooked and art-lovers may even want to devote a separate visit. Among the most important are works by Giotto, Fra Angelico, Perugino, Raphael's *Transfiguration* (his last great work),

---

Man at Work

As might be imagined, painting the Sistine ceiling wasn't easy. Michelangelo, sculptor in marble with only a little oil-painting behind him, had never before done a fresco (wall-painting on damp plaster). Preferring his inexperience to their incompetence, he fired his seven assistants in the first couple of weeks and continued alone for four years, from 1508 to 1512. Contrary to legend, he did not lie on his back, but painted erect on tiptoe, bent backwards "like a Syrian bow", with Pope Julius II climbing the scaffolding to check on progress and threatening to throw him off his platform if he didn't hurry up.

"I'm not in a good place," he wrote to a friend, "and I'm no painter."

Leonardo da Vinci's unfinished *St. Jerome*, Bellini's *Pietà* and Caravaggio's *Descent from the Cross*.

The neighbourhood south of the Vatican, **Trastevere**, literally "across the Tiber", has long been renowned as the most popular quarter of Rome. Here, ordinary people who, like the Cockneys in London consider themselves the original citizens, uphold ancient traditions and customs. It is good to wander among the narrow streets and markets to sample the authentic life of the city, highlighted by the July *Noiantri* ("We Others") street festival of music and fireworks down by the river.

Inevitably, "popular" and "authentic" became chic and the ambience is now somewhat diluted by a certain smart set moving in—and raising the rents. But the true Trasteverini hang on, mainly in the area immediately around **Santa Maria in Trastevere**, reputedly the oldest church in the city. Its foundation may date back to the 3rd century, but the present structure is the work of Pope Innocent II, himself a Trasteverino, around 1140. A wonderful Byzantine-influenced **mosaic** of Mary enthroned with Jesus decorates the domed ceiling of the apse. The liveliest fruit and vegetable market is to be found on **Piazza di San Cosimato**.

Other Museums

The **Borghese Gallery** (undergoing extensive restoration) is housed in a handsome Baroque villa inspired originally by Hadrian's Villa at Tivoli (see p. 68), but with its Italian formal gardens now transformed into an English-style landscaped park. This great collection includes outstanding sculptures by Bernini and paintings by Raphael, Correggio, Titian, Caravaggio, Botticelli, Rubens, Dürer and Cranach.

The **Capitoline Museums**, in the palaces of the Campidoglio, have extensive collections of sculpture excavated from ancient Rome. In the Palazzo dei Conservatori is the most celebrated piece, the superb Etruscan bronze **She-Wolf** *(Lupa Capitolina)*, symbol of the city. The wolf dates from around the 5th century B.C., but the little Romulus and Remus that she is suckling are Renaissance additions by Pollaiuolo. The **Picture Gallery** *(Pinacoteca Capitolina)* has important Venetian works by Bellini, Titian, Tintoretto, Lotto and Veronese, as well as a fine Rubens *Romulus and Remus* and Caravaggio's *Fortune Teller*.

The **Palazzo Barberini** (Via delle Quattro Fontane), another architectural battleground for arch-rivals Borromini and Bernini, is worth a visit as much for its splendid Baroque décor as for its collection of paintings. They come together in the palace's Great Hall with Pietro da Cortona's dazzling ceiling fresco, *Triumph of Divine Providence.* Notable in the collections are a Fra Angelico triptych, Raphael's *La Fornarina,* and works by Titian, Tintoretto and El Greco.

Other Churches

It's impossible even to count all the churches worth visiting in Rome, many of which it's most enjoyable to stumble on by accident. We suggest just three in easy reach of the Via Cavour thoroughfare leading from the main railway station *(Stazione Termini).*

Originally built in the 4th century on the Esquiline Hill site of a Roman temple to the goddess Juno, **Santa Maria Maggiore** is the largest of the churches dedicated to the Virgin Mary and a great favourite with pilgrims. They come, especially at Christmas time, to admire relics of the **holy crib** from Bethlehem. In the Oratory of the Crib *(Oratorio del Presepio),* are the moving 13th-century sculptures of Joseph, the Three Kings, the ox and the ass by Arnolfo di Cambio (Mary and the child Jesus are 16th-century additions). The most spectacular art treasure of the church is its gorgeous 5th-century **mosaics,** 36 Old Testament scenes high on the walls

(don't forget the binoculars) and a triumphant Mary and Jesus enthroned over the high altar. The coffered Renaissance ceiling glitters with the gold of the first shipments from the Americas.

In a nearby side street, **Santa Prassede** is unprepossessing from the outside but enchanting in the intimacy of its interior. The delicate 9th-century mosaics of Jesus and four angels make the **Chapel of St. Zeno** the city's most important Byzantine monument. To the right of the chapel is a fragment of rare jasper said to come from the column to which Jesus was tied for his flagellation. Notice, too, the fine mosaic of Jesus and the New Jerusalem over the chancel.

San Pietro in Vincoli (St. Peter in Chains) might not attract a second look (and might even prefer it that way, given the hordes of visitors) if it didn't contain one of the greatest of Michelangelo's sculptures, his formidable **Moses.** Intended for St. Peter's Basilica as part of Michelangelo's botched project for Julius II's tomb, the statue of the great biblical figure sits in awesome majesty at the centre of the monument. You can imagine how grandiose the original plan must have been when you realize from his sideward stare that Moses was supposed to be just a corner figure facing the centre. The horns on his head continue a traditional medieval mistranslation of the Hebrew for halo-like rays of light. On each side, the comparatively passive figures of Jacob's wives, a prayerful Rachel and melancholy Leah, were Michelangelo's last completed sculptures.

LAZIO

The excursions to be made today into the Lazio hinterland around Rome are those that ancient Romans themselves made to vacation homes by the sea or nearby lakes.

Tivoli

Follow the old Roman chariot road (repaved) of Via Tiburtina 30 kilometres (19 mi.) east of the capital to the haunting ruins of **Hadrian's Villa** *(Villa Adriana),* near the picturesque town of Tivoli, at the foot of the Sabine Hills. Sprawling across 70 hectares (173 acres), this retirement hideaway of the great emperor-builder was designed to recapture some of the architectural marvels of his empire, especially the Greece he loved above all else—a travel notebook for his old age. Barbarians and museum curators have removed most of the villa's treasures, but a stroll through the remaining pillars, arches and mosaic fragments in gardens running wild among the olive trees, cypresses and pines can be marvellously evocative of a lost world. To get a clear sense of the original, start with the villa's excellent scale model. The monumental baths, separate Latin and Greek libraries, Greek theatre, temples and pavilions together make up the home of a man who drew no distinction between the pleasures of mind and body. In the centre, the enchanting **Villa dell'Isola,** a pavilion surrounded by a little reflecting pool and circular portico, epitomizes all the magic of the place.

In Tivoli itself, overlooking the Roman plain, the **Villa d'Este** is a 16th-century counterpart, celebrating all the extravagance of the late Renaissance. The house, home of Cardinal Ippolito II d'Este, plays second fiddle to the joyous theatre of its gardens: alleys of cypresses and soaring fountains (500 in all, including Bernini's *Bicchierone),* grottoes, waterfalls and reflecting pools.

Alban Hills and Castel Gandolfo

The region immediately southeast of Rome is known locally as the Castelli Romani (Roman Castles) for the fortified hilltop refuges built during the medieval

Cooling off is a special joy behind the fountains of the Villa d'Este.

civil wars. Today, it's just the summer heat that drives the Romans out on day-trips to the vineyards of the Alban hills and lakes. The country villages of **Frascati, Grottaferrata, Marino** and **Rocca di Papa** make delightful stops, not least of all for a cool glass of their estimable white wine, especially during the autumn grape-harvest festivals.

The pope has his summer palace at **Castel Gandolfo,** on the shores of Lake Albano. He holds audience on Wednesdays from mid-July to early September and blesses the thousands of pilgrims on Sundays at noon. In the mellow microclimate of the nearby **Lake Nemi,** strawberries are grown all year round, served—with cream or lemon juice—in Nemi's village park.

The Beaches

For a swim in the Mediterranean or to nurture a suntan, Rome's closest beaches are Ostia and **Fregene,** the latter cleaner and more pleasant. But **Ostia** has the added attraction of the ruins of ancient Rome's seaport, set among lovely pine forests on the coastal plain.

North of Rome off the Via Claudia, a cooler, more secluded swim is to be had in the crystal-clear waters of **Lake Bracciano,** surrounded by olive groves and beaches of reeds and black volcanic sand.

Tarquinia and Northern Lazio

The A12 *autostrada* and the old Via Aurelia (which ends up in Arles in French Provence) take you to **Tarquinia.** Most important of the original 12 towns of the Etruscan confederation, the town dominated Rome in its heyday of the 7th and 6th centuries B.C. Today, the paintings and sculptures found in its **necropolis** of over 5,700 tombs provide fas-

cinating evidence of the brilliant
Etruscan civilization. Visits to
the tombs, outside town, are
organized from the **National
Museum,** housed in the fine
15th-century Gothic-Renaissance
Palazzo Vitelleschi as you enter
Tarquinia. The museum exhibits
sarcophagi, Etruscan and imported Greek vases and some of
the best wall-paintings, in reconstructed tombs. Displayed in a
room by itself, the prize of the

*They serve strawberries all the year
at Nemi, south of Rome.*

collection is the *Winged Horses*
sculpture from Tarquinia's Ara
della Regina Temple.

Tuscania is a quiet little fortified town, recovering now from
an earthquake in 1971 which
luckily did not harm its two
Romanesque churches on the

eastern outskirts (the tourist office on Piazza Basile will get you the keys). Built from the 8th to the 12th centuries, **San Pietro** stands at the back of a grassy courtyard with Etruscan sarcophagi, beside two crumbling medieval towers. The sober interior has Byzantine-style frescoes, an 11th-century altar canopy and a **crypt** built on Etruscan and ancient Roman pillars. The Romanesque tower and rose window of **Santa Maria Maggiore's** façade have a similar simple beauty.

Drive up to **Montefiascone** for the lovely view from its Rocca dei Papi gardens over Lake Bolsena. The church of San Flaviano at the bottom of the town's hill has some richly sculpted capitals on its massive columns.

In the restful charm of its medieval quarters, **Viterbo** makes a good overnight stop. The oldest neighbourhood, with narrow streets and little market squares, is around the Via San Pellegrino. On the equally attractive Piazza San Lorenzo, the Palazzo Papale has an impressive 13th-century Gothic loggia, opposite the Cathedral's intriguing mixture of Gothic campanile (bell tower) and Renaissance façade with a Romanesque interior.

ABRUZZI NATIONAL PARK

As a tonic for polluted lungs and street-weary limbs, plunge into the cool fresh air and mountain greenery of this exhilarating nature reserve (via the Pescina exit on the A25 *autostrada.)* The Abruzzi plateau is the highest in the Apennines, excellent for climbers and hikers, and the national park protects magnificent forests of beech, maple and silver birch trees. Wildlife is abundant: brown bear, wolves, rare Abruzzi chamois, foxes, badgers and red squirrels. Birdwatchers can see golden eagles, yellow-billed Alpine choughs and little firecrests, while even the most cloth-eared city-slicker might catch the drumming of a woodpecker.

This Is It

In the days before guide books began giving stars to hotels and restaurants, Bishop Johannes Fugger of Augsburg sent out an advance man for his trip to Rome to mark the inns where the wine was good. The code word was "est"— roughly "this is it". The fellow raved over the wine of Montefiascone, exclaiming: "Est, est, est!" The bishop drank and he drank and he drank, right into his grave. You'll find the tomb in San Flaviano's third chapel on the left, with its merry Latin inscription explaining the delicious cause of death. Est, Est, Est *is what they've called the wine ever since.*

After a ramble in the Abruzzi, relax on Lake Scanno.

Enter the park near the wild 1,400-metre-high (4,600-ft.) **Passo del Diavolo** (Devil's Pass) overlooking the Fucino valley and, to the north, affording a spectacular panorama of the Gran Sasso d'Italia plateau, the Apennines' rooftop. Nine kilometres (6 mi.) south at **Pescasseroli** is the park administration Visitor's Centre, at which you can get camping permits and maps for hiking. A ski resort in

winter, the town also has a nature museum, botanical garden and small zoo. Drive east to **Villetta Barrea** with its attractive villas bordering the lake.

Outside the park lie the pretty lake and popular summer resort of **Scanno,** where the village women still wear the handsome but rather austere regional costume.

SARDINIA *(Sardegna)*

The Mediterranean's second largest island (Sicily being the largest) is worth a holiday all to itself—and much more detailed treatment than we give it here. But for those who want in a few days to get just a feel for its atmosphere as part of a first-time visit to Italy, we suggest some seaside resorts, trips along the coast and a couple of excursions into the hinterland.

Prehistoric man dotted the island with his mysterious cone-shaped *nuraghi* houses and watchtowers before it was colonized by Cretans, Phoenicians, Carthaginians and Romans. Later, the island became part of the commercial empires of Pisa, Genoa and the Spanish and was annexed in 1718 by the dukes of Savoy. Malarial mosquitoes and repressive feudalism restrained the island's development until the 19th century, since when it has undergone a rapid industrialization balanced today by renewal of its cattle farming.

Cagliari

The island's capital and main port is a largely modern city, but with a Spanish flavour to its older quarters up on the hill. The **Archaeological Museum** includes important bronze statues of warriors and priests found in prehistoric tombs. The much renovated **Cathedral** has two superbly carved 12th-century pulpits, originally commissioned for the cathedral in Pisa. Before heading for the open road, try the savoury local cuisine, combining Spanish-style fish stews and Genoese pasta dishes.

The winding **Cagliari-Muravera road** across the plunging ravines of the Sarrabus mountains to the east coast is one of the most spectacular drives on the whole island.

Continue up the coast to Lanusei and head inland across the rugged **Gennargentu mountains,** covered with dense forests of cork oak and chestnut trees. Another regional delicacy: hot melted cheese with honey.

Further north, just off the Nuoro-Dorgali road is the secluded site of **Serra Órrios**, a well-preserved prehistoric village (signposted *Villaggio Nuragico).* A short walk along a marked path through the fields takes you to a group of dry stone houses with two temples and circular ramparts in a lovely setting of eucalyptus and olive trees. Archaeologists have located some 7,000 of these *nuraghi* structures around the island, most of them flattened cone towers believed to be parts of fortified citadels.

Snug houses shelter below Castelsardo's craggy fortress.

Costa Smeralda

The glittering Emerald Coast on the north-east tip of the island is one of Italy's smartest resort areas, with beautiful beaches, grand hotels, sports complexes and marinas for yachts and motor launches. It stretches round bays and rocky inlets from Olbia in the east to the promontory of La Maddalena.

Porto Cervo is the coast's fashionable centre, but **Baia Sardinia** competes with its craggy coastline. More exclusive is the little luxury resort island and fishing village of **La Maddalena,** a 15-minute ferry-ride from Palau. It is in fact the principal island of an archipelago of 14, most of them little more than a pile of rocks.

Linked to La Maddalena by a 7-kilometre (4-mi.) causeway, the isle of **Caprera** was the last home of Giuseppe Garibaldi, military leader of the Risorgimento movement for Italian unity (see p. 34). The house where he died in 1882 (his tomb is nearby) is now a **museum,** practically a sanctuary, where devout patriots refer to him not by name, but as "the Hero", *l'Eroe*.

The north coast road makes an enjoyable excursion along the dunes and pine groves lining the Gulf of Asinara. The fortress-town of **Castelsardo** stands high on a spectacular promontory overlooking the gulf. Inside its 16th-century cathedral, you hear the sea crashing on the rocks directly below its foundations. At **Porto Torres,** visit the important 11th-century Pisan Romanesque church of San Gavino. It has no façade, but its interior has a noble simplicity. Some of the pillars come from an ancient Roman temple, with two Corinthian capitals serving as a lectern.

Alghero

This quiet little seaside resort on the north-west coast has a pleasant Catalan flavour to its older quarters around the cathedral. Take a sunset stroll along the 16th-century Spanish ramparts.

There's good fishing to be had in the nearby bay of Porto Conte, and the Palmavera *nuraghi* citadel is well worth a visit. On the bay's south-western promontory is the fascinating **Grotta di Nettuno** (Neptune's Grotto). Guided tours of these subterranean caverns with their dramatic stalactites and stalagmites are organized by boat from Alghero or on foot directly at the site, down a rather steep stairway in the cliffs. It's a freshwater grotto fed by an underground river. The stalactites grow down at the rate of one centimetre every 100 years, faster than the stalagmites rising to meet them from the cave floor.

TUSCANY AND UMBRIA

Light is the secret of the region's magic. In that apparently miraculous collision of imagination and intellect that sparked the Renaissance in 15th-century Florence, its painters and architects had the constant inspiration of the dramatic changes in Tuscan light from dawn to dusk. And more than anywhere else in the country, Tuscany and Umbria present that ideal green Italian landscape, dotted with pink stone hilltop towns, where cypress-tree sentinels watch over the olive groves and vineyards.

Florence lies at the heart of the northern Apennines, in a basin of the Arno river which runs out to Pisa. Siena, its proud historic rival, dominates the Tuscan hill towns to the south, while the university town of Perugia and the Assisi of St. Francis are the keys to Umbria's luminous beauty.

With some careful timing, modern visitors can capture a glimpse of that miracle of light. Arrive early in the morning for your first look across the hills to the grey-stone towers of San Gimignano, but come to Siena's Piazza del Campo at sunset. Pisa's dazzling white marble is at its best in the noonday sun, but late afternoon is the blessed moment for the brilliant façade of Orvieto's cathedral.

FLORENCE *(Firenze)*

First-time visitors may want to stay in the thick of the fray, but veterans often prefer to enjoy the treasures of Florence by driving in from a vantage-point like Fiesole (see p. 97) or other nearby hill-town. Despite the magnificence of its monuments and museums, the city, particularly in the heat of summer, is less amenable to "hanging around" in than Venice, and the people, in their courteous but cool reserve, are less seductive than Romans or Neapolitans.

Our itineraries divide the city's heart into four quarters: from the Duomo north to San Marco; from the Piazza della Signoria, the Palazzo Vecchio and the Uffizi east to Santa Croce; from Mercato Nuovo west to Santa Maria Novella; and south of the Arno around the Pitti Palace and the Piazzale Michelangelo.

From the Duomo to San Marco

The **Duomo** (Cathedral), officially Santa Maria del Fiore, proclaims the inordinate but certainly justified civic pride of the Florentines. It was started in 1296 and the imposing green, white and rose marble façade was completed only six centuries later.

The first of its glories is the free-standing **Campanile**, based on a design by Giotto. The 81.5-metre (267-ft.) bell-tower is decorated on its lower sections by hexagonal bas-reliefs sculpted by Andrea Pisano and Luca della Robbia from Giotto's drawings. Characteristic of the city's civic consciousness, they portray the Life of Man from Adam's creation to the rise of civilization through the arts and sciences —music, architecture, metallurgy and the like—pursued so earnestly by the Florentine guilds that commissioned the work. Originals of Donatello's sculpture for the third-storey niches are kept in the cathedral museum, **Museo dell'Opera del Duomo** (Piazza del Duomo, 9), most notably statues of the prophet Habakkuk and Abraham with Isaac. Also in the museum, Michelangelo's unfinished **Pietà** of the dead Jesus in his mother's arms emphasizes the agony rather than the pathos portrayed by the *Pietà* in

St. Peter's in Rome (see p. 62). Michelangelo originally conceived the group for his tomb and represented himself in the figure of Nicodemus. Flaws in the marble so enraged the artist that he hurled a hammer at it, destroying Christ's left leg—the left arm has been restored and the rather insipid Mary Magdalen was added by a pupil.

Brunelleschi's masterpiece, the cathedral's grandiose redbrick **cupola**, with its eight white stone ribs curving to the marble lantern at the top, is the city's symbol, visible not only all over Florence but also from far beyond in the Tuscan hills. Completed in 1434, it measures 45.5 metres (149 ft.) in diameter and the 463 steps to its top (entrance inside the church, in the north aisle) climb in comfortable stages to reveal glimpses of the surrounding city, different views of the cathedral's interior and fascinating close-ups of the dome's structure. (Brunelleschi's original wooden model is displayed in the cathedral museum.) Look out, too, for Ghiberti's **bronze shrine** below the high altar.

In the third bay on the north aisle is Paolo Uccello's statue-like **equestrian painting** of the 14th-century English mercena-

Florence's cathedral is ever the central focus of city life.

ry Sir John Hawkwood (unpronounceable for Italians, so known as Giovanni Acuto). After brilliant performances in the 100 Years' War in France, Sir John obtained what modern-day footballers would call an "independent transfer" to Florence as a *condottiere*. His "fee" included tax-exemption, state funeral and cathedral monument.

The octagonal 12th-century Romanesque **Baptistery** of San Giovanni (St. John) is celebrated for the magnificent bas reliefs of its **bronze doors.** The oldest, facing south and telling the story of John the Baptist, were designed by Andrea Pisano in 1330. A century later, Lorenzo Ghiberti won the competition to design the great north and east doors, devoted respectively to the life of Jesus and scenes from the Old Testament. Michelangelo said the latter, facing the Duomo, were good enough to adorn the entrance to heaven and they have been known ever since as the *Doors of Paradise.* Among the losing candidates was Filippo Brunelleschi, who thereafter devoted himself entirely to architecture. (In the Bargello, pp. 87–88, you can compare his bronze model with Ghiberti's.) Byzantine-style **mosaics** inside the cupola include scenes from the *Creation, Life of St. John* and a *Last Judgment.*

Something of the might of the Medici family can be sensed in their massive palace, north-west of the cathedral, the 15th-century **Palazzo Medici-Riccardi.** Now Florence's prefecture, the formidable edifice, with its rough ashlar stone façade smoothing out in the upper storeys, set the style for the city's Renaissance palaces. The ground floor originally had an open loggia at the corner for the family banking business. After a rest in the quiet little garden of orange trees beyond the main courtyard, visit the upstairs chapel for Benozzo Gozzoli's 15th-century **fresco** of the *Journey of the Magi to Bethlehem.* It portrays the Medici clan led by the white-clad Lorenzo the Magnificent in what is in fact an allegory of the Greek patriarchs' procession to an oecumenical council with Pope Pius II in Florence.

Just across the square is the family church of **San Lorenzo** designed by Brunelleschi. Funds ran out before Michelangelo's planned façade could embellish the austere barn-like exterior. Inside, you'll see the Medici family arms set in the floor in front of the altar. Brunelleschi is at his most elegant in the **Old Sacristy** at the end of the left transept, decorated with four Donatello wall-medallions.

Adjoining the church but with a separate entrance are the **Medici Chapels** *(Cappelle Medicee),* monuments to the splendour and decadence of the dynasty. The **Princes' Chapel** *(Cappella dei Principi)* is a piece of 17th-century Baroque bombast in oppressive dark marble, for which the altar was not completed, appropriately enough, till 1939. At the end of a corridor, the summit of Medici power is celebrated in Michelangelo's superb **New Sacristy,** conceived as a pendant to Brunelleschi's in the church. Lorenzo the Magnificent and brother Giuliano lie in simple tombs beneath the sculptor's *Madonna and Child,* flanked by lesser artists' statues of the family saints Cosmas and Damian. Michelangelo's greatest work here is reserved for two minor members of the family, Lorenzo's grandson, Duke of Urbino, portrayed as a pensive Roman soldier above two allegorical figures of Twilight and Dawn, and his son, the Duke of Nemours, more warrior-like above figures of Night and Day.

For a moment of peace, wander through the handsome **Laurentian Library** *(Biblioteca Laurenziana)* to the left of the church entrance. Michelangelo designed the wooden desks displaying illuminated manuscripts in a collection ranging from Egyptian papyri to manuscripts of Napoleon.

The Dominican Monastery of **San Marco** provides the exquisite setting for a museum largely devoted to the paintings of Fra Angelico (1387–1455), who lived here as a monk. Off the cloister, with its ancient cedar tree, are some of his finest works, notably a *Descent from the Cross* altarpiece from the church of Santa Trinità and miniatures of the life of Jesus. In the small refectory is a stately Ghirlandaio mural of the *Last Supper,* a popular subject for monastic dining rooms. In the monks' cells upstairs, the frescoes of the man Italians call Beato (Blessed) Angelico were intended to be inspirational rather than decorative. His celebrated *Annunciation* faces the top of the stairs—compare the simpler version in cell 3—while other outstanding works include the mystic *Transfiguration* in cell 6 and *Jesus Mocked* in cell 7. The Prior's Quarters in the second dormitory (cells 12, 13 and 14) were the home of fire-and-brimstone preacher Girolamo Savonarola from 1481 till his death in 1498 (see p. 29). You can see some of his belongings, a portrait by fellow-monk Fra Bartolomeo and the picture of his burning at the stake.

As a museum conceived primarily for students of Florentine painting from the 13th to 16th centuries, the **Accademia Gallery** (Via Ricasoli, 60) is an important adjunct to the Uffizi (see pp. 84–87). But the major interest is in the seven statues of the **Michelangelo sculpture hall.** Six of them are unfinished—four *Prisoners, St. Matthew* and a *Pietà*—but each is a fascinating revelation of how Michelangelo releases their power from the marble. At the end of the hall, the great *David* (of which a mediocre copy stands in the Piazza della Signoria) provides the perfect object lesson of the finished product, a hero infused with all the contained energy needed to hurl that stone at Goliath.

In the **Piazza Santissima Annunziata,** Brunelleschi produced a consummate piece of Renaissance urban planning and pioneering example of the piazza as stage-set. He designed the graceful colonnade of nine arches for the **Spedale degli Innocenti,** hospital for foundlings, symbolized by the charming little babes in Andrea della Robbia's roundels above the arches. Michelozzo's later Santissima Annunziata church, together with the 17th-century fountains and equestrian statue of Grand Duke Ferdinando, preserve the harmonies of the master's overall design.

Piazza della Signoria to Santa Croce

Flanked by the city's most elegant shoe shops, the quarter's main street retains the tradition of its medieval name, Via de' Calzaiuoli (stocking- and shoe-makers).

If the tall rectangular block of **Orsanmichele** looks to you more like a grain-silo than the church it's supposed to be, that's because it was once both. Florentines always liked combining faith and business and rebuilt the oratory to St. Michael in the 14th century to house a wheat exchange, with arches in place of the present ground-floor windows and a granary upstairs. For 14 niches overlooking the streets, the guilds commissioned **statues** of patron saints from Florence's greatest talents, a landmark in Renaissance sculpture. Look out for Ghiberti's vigorous bronze of the city's patron *St. John* (east wall, on the Via de' Calzaiuoli) and *St. Matthew,* the bankers' tax-collector-turned-Apostle (west); Donatello's *St. George,* the armourers' dragon-killer (north, a bronze cast of a marble original in the Bargello) and *St. Mark,* whose vividly sculpted robes do credit to the linen-drapers he protects (south); and Nanni di Banco's outstanding conspiratorial group of *Four Crowned Martyrs* for the sculptors' own guild of stonemasons and woodworkers (north). In the interior is Andrea Orcagna's elaborate 14th-century Gothic **tabernacle** with a *Madonna* painted by Bernardo Daddi.

Piazza della Signoria is Florence's civic centre. Site of the town hall (*Palazzo Vecchio* or *della Signoria*) since 1299, the square bustles in all seasons, not least because it leads to the richest of Italy's art museums, the Uffizi. At the south end of the square is the 14th-century arcaded **Loggia della Signoria** or dei Lanzi, transformed from the city fathers' ceremonial grandstand into a guardroom for Swiss mercenary *Landsknechte*. It shelters Benvenuto Cellini's bronze masterpiece, **Perseus** brandishing the severed head of Medusa. In one inspired moment, the Renaissance braggart has combined the legendary technical wizardry he loved to show off as a goldsmith with undeniable sculptural beauty.

Also in the Loggia, the spiralling *Rape of the Sabines* of Giambologna (actually a Flemish artist named Jean de Boulogne) is another piece of dazzling virtuosity.

In a piazza that is a veritable sculpture garden, more statuary graces the orator's platform along the town hall's sober façade. To the left is a copy of Donatello's *Marzocco*, Florence's heraldic lion, next to his bronze of *Judith and Holofernes,* which always made the Medici uneasy with its theme of a tyrant decapitated. Directly beneath the palace tower, as a counterpart to Bandinelli's clumsy *Hercules and Cacus,* is a copy of Michelangelo's *David.* Standing against a hostile world of cruel Philistines, Florentines loved to identify with the beauty and courage of the poetic young giant-killer.

A commemorative stone (near the Baroque fountain) in the piazza marks the spot where Savonarola was executed (see p. 29).

In gentle contrast to Arnolfo di Cambio's austere Italian Gothic exterior of the **Palazzo Vecchio** or Palazzo della Signoria, Vasari added ornate stucco and frescoes to the first inner courtyard for a Medici wedding in the 1560s. A delightful Verrocchio bronze cherub tops the porphyry fountain in the

---

Keeping the Gods Safe

Almost as beautiful as the statue of Perseus are the little figures of Jupiter, Minerva, Mercury and Danae around the base. To keep Duke Cosimo's wife, Eleonora of Toledo, from taking them for her private apartments—"they'll risk being spoilt down in the piazza," she said—Cellini soldered them firmly to the pedestal. But the art custodians of Florence have now decided the Duchess was right, replaced them with copies and put Cellini's originals in the Bargello.

centre. Upstairs, the **Salone dei Cinquecento** was built in 1495 for Savonarola's short-lived Republican Council before serving as Duke Cosimo's throne room and, three centuries later, the chamber of Italy's first national parliament. The décor celebrates Florentine power—Vasari frescoes of victories over Siena and Pisa and Michelangelo's *Victory* statue, designed originally for Pope Julius II's tomb, is set here to honour the Grand Duke of Tuscany. On the second floor, the **Sala dei Gigli** (Hall of the Lilies) is brilliantly decorated in blues and golds with vivid Ghirlandaio frescoes of Roman and early Christian history. It adjoins the **Chancery** *(cancelleria)* where Niccolò Macchiavelli served as secretary to the Florentine Republic. Any world-weary thoughts inspired by the old cynic's portrait and bust are quickly dispelled by the original of Verrocchio's cherub cuddling a dolphin like a baby doll.

The **Uffizi** museum of Italian and European painting stretches in a long U-shape from the Palazzo Vecchio down to the Arno river and back. Duke Cosimo had Vasari design it in 1560 as a series of government offices (hence its name), a mint for the city's florin and workshops for the Medici's craftsmen.

That makes a lot of museum, but a great one that it would be sad to renounce through visual fatigue. We won't burden you with guilt by telling you "not to miss" this or to "be sure" to see that, but just signal some of what really is worth seeing. See all or only half a dozen, stop for an occasional peek out the window over the Arno and Ponte Vecchio bridge—and rendezvous later at the museum's roof-garden café above the Loggia dei Lanzi.

Constant reorganization often makes it hazardous to specify room numbers, but the paintings are exhibited chronologically from the 13th to the 18th century. Here are some of the highlights:

Giotto breathes a warm humanity into his *Madonna Enthroned* (1300) that distinguishes it from the more formal pictures of the subject by Cimabue and Duccio in the same room. See also Giotto's Madonna polyptych. Some 30 years later, the *Annunciation* triptych of **Simone Martini**, with Mary shying away from archangel Gabriel, has the characteristic elegance and poetry of his Siena school.

Paolo Uccello shows a dream-like, almost surrealist obsession with his (unsolved) problems of perspective and merry-go-round

Giotto brought a new humanity to images of the Madonna and Child.

horses in his *Battle of San Romano* (1456). It contrasts with the cool dignity of **Piero della Francesca** in his *Federigo da Montefeltro* and wife *Battista* (1465), portrayed against their Urbino landscape.

In his graceful *Allegory of Spring* (1478) and the almost too famous but undyingly delightful *Birth of Venus,* **Botticelli** achieves an enchanting mixture of sensuality and purity. His Flemish contemporary, **Hugo van der Goes,** is more down to earth in the realism of his *Adoration of the Shepherds,* which influenced Florentine painters like **Ghirlandaio**—compare here his *Adoration of the Magi.*

In the *Baptism of Christ* (1470) of **Verrocchio,** you can see the earliest identified work of his pupil, **Leonardo da Vinci** —the background landscape and the angel on the left, beautiful enough to reduce his companion angel to wide-eyed jealousy and Verrocchio to giving up painting for sculpture. Leonardo's *Annunciation* of a few years later already shows his characteristic gentle tone and feeling for precise detail, and the *Adoration of the Magi,* even as an underdrawing left unfinished by his departure for Milan (1481), reveals his revolutionary power of psychological observation.

The northern European rooms include a splendid *Portrait of His Father* (1490) by **Albrecht Dürer;** *Adam* and *Eve* (1528) by **Lucas Cranach;** *Richard Southwell* by **Hans Holbein;** and a moving *Mater Dolorosa* by **Joos van Cleve.**

In the mystic *Holy Allegory* (1490) of **Giovanni Bellini,** we can appreciate the typical Venetian serenity even without understanding its symbols.

The only **Michelangelo** in the Uffizi is the *Holy Family* roundel (1504), his earliest painting, decidedly sculptural in the group's solid plastic qualities. Without Michelangelo's strength and torment or Leonardo's complexity, the third of Italy's three Renaissance giants, **Raphael,** brings his own powers of clarity and restraint to the *Madonna of the Goldfinch* and a revealing *Self-Portrait.*

Titian has a superbly sensual *Venus of Urbino,* less Greek goddess than the prince's mistress she probably was, and an equally disturbing *Flora* (1515). Some are also upset by the eroticism of **Parmigianino** in his strange but undeniably graceful *Madonna with the Long Neck* (1534)—just look at those elongated fingers, too—a masterpiece of the sophisticated and subsequently decadent Mannerism that followed the High Renaissance.

There is an intriguing ambiguity to the half-naked peasant

youth posing as a *Bacchus* for **Caravaggio**, but nothing complicated about the robust sexiness of the **Rubens Bacchanale**. And compare Caravaggio's mastery of *chiaroscuro* (the play of light and dark) in the service of realism in his violent *Abraham and Isaac* (1590) with the more contemplative style of **Rembrandt** in his *Old Rabbi* (1658) and other portraits.

Time for that refreshment on the roof-garden.

For a change from all this fine art, try the **Science History Museum** (*Museo di Storia della Scienza*, Piazza dei Giudici, 1), where you'll find Galileo's telescopes and his (pickled) middle finger and an Edison phonograph.

Designed in the late 13th century by Arnolfo di Cambio but with a neo-Gothic façade added in 1863, the church of **Santa Croce** (east of the Uffizi) has an important series of Giotto **frescoes.** The pathos shines through the heavily restored paintings of St. Francis in the Bardi Chapel, to the right of the apse, and St. John in the Peruzzi Chapel next door. In a chapel in the left transept, the wooden **Crucifixion** by Donatello (1425) is in affecting naturalistic contrast to the Renaissance idealism of the time.

The church is also revered by Florentines as the last resting place of many great Italians. Galileo, Machiavelli, Ghiberti and composer Rossini are all buried there. **Michelangelo's tomb** (right aisle, second bay) was designed by Vasari, with symbolic statues of Painting, Sculpture and Architecture mourning beneath a bust of the artist (89 when he died). Michelangelo wanted the tomb surmounted by the *Pietà,* now in the cathedral museum (see p. 78), but the Florentines nearly didn't even get his body: they had to smuggle it out of Rome in a bale of sacking. For Dante, they have to be content with a cenotaph, as Ravenna, his burial place, refuses to part with his remains.

At the back of the cloister of Santa Croce's Franciscan monastery adjoining the church, Brunelleschi's **Pazzi Chapel** is a little gem of Renaissance elegance. Its spaciousness is enhanced by geometric patterns of dark stone against whitewashed walls. And Brunelleschi prefers Luca della Robbia's subdued glazed ceramic roundels to Donatello's too competitive wall medallions in the Old Sacristy of San Lorenzo. The most cherished treasure in the Santa Croce **Museum** is Cimabue's 13th-century *Crucifixion,* rescued and painstakingly restored after the town's 1966 flood.

The ominous 13th-century fortress of the **Bargello** (Via del

Proconsolo, 4) was Florence's first town hall and very unpleasant prison under the jurisdiction of the Police Chief or *Bargello*, before becoming the National Museum of sculpture. The old armoury is now the **Michelangelo Hall,** greeting you with a most unhappy bust of the master by Daniele da Volterra. Michelangelo's works here include a marble bust of *Brutus*, a *Virgin and Child* marble roundel and an early *Drunken Bacchus* (1499) —compare Sansovino's more decorous *Bacchus* of 20 years later. Among the Cellini **bronzes** is an imposing bust of his master, *Duke Cosimo*. The **General Council Hall** is dominated by the works of Donatello: his vigorous *St. George* intended for the Orsanmichele (see p. 82), two statues of *David,* doubting in marble, naked and restless in bronze, and the stone *Marzocco* lion, the town's symbol from the Palazzo Vecchio. You can also see the two bronze panels submitted for the Baptistery doors competition by Brunelleschi, the loser, and Ghiberti, the winner (see p. 80). On the second floor is a Verrocchio *David,* for which his 19-year-old pupil Leonardo da Vinci is believed to have been the model.

Geometric designs embellish Brunelleschi's Pazzi Chapel.

From Mercato Nuovo to Santa Maria Novella

Start out from the centre, on the Via Calimala, the heart of medieval Florence on the street of the drapers' guild taken over today by the colourful **Mercato Nuovo** (the Straw Market). Here, around a 16th-century loggia enclosing the bronze statue of a wild boar known as the *Porcellino,* you can buy a straw hat against the Tuscan sun and a basket to carry off the cheap and not so cheap jewellery, leather goods and embroidery.

West on the Via Porta Rossa is the 14th-century **Palazzo Davanzati**, its stern, fortress-like exterior still provided with rings at ground level for tethering horses and on upper stories to hold torches and lanterns for festive occasions. Inside, on the first floor, is a museum of Florentine domestic life from the 14th to 16th centuries, with furniture, utensils and ceramics, at their most attractive in the Sala dei Pappagalli (Parrots' Hall) with its *trompe l'œil* tapestries frescoed on the walls.

The church of **Santa Trinita** has a late 16th-century Baroque façade with a Gothic interior. Ghirlandaio decorated the Sassetti Chapel (far right of the high altar) with frescoes of St. Francis, and the *Adoration of the Shepherds* on the altar is considered his masterpiece.

Florence's most elegant shops continue the Via de' Tornabuoni's centuries-old tradition of aristocratic luxury. On the 15th-century **Palazzo Strozzi,** look out for the intricate wrought-iron lanterns by the much sought-after and expensive craftsman Niccolò Grosso, known as *Caparra* (Mr Down Payment) who coined the philosophy later attributed to Hollywood: "If you want something for nothing, you get what you paid for."

The 13th-century Dominican church of **Santa Maria Novella** is the finest of Florence's monastic churches. Leon Battista Alberti added the graceful white and green marble façade in the 15th century. The church is rich in artistic treasures, but its most prized, indeed one of the city's greatest paintings, is the **Masaccio Trinity** (left aisle, third bay). Above a pair of stoic kneeling donors, Mary and John stand on either side of the crucified Jesus upheld by his Father, while the dove of the Holy Spirit hovers between them, the whole forming an inspiring triangle under the coffered ceiling of a Renaissance chapel. Painted in weird, rather gruesome counterpoint below is a skeleton (perhaps one of the donors) and the inscription in Italian: "I was once that which you are and what I am, you will also be."

The Ghirlandaio **frescoes** of the lives of the Madonna and St. John, for the chancel behind the altar, kept the master's whole workshop busy from 1485 to 1490, and a 13-year-old apprentice named Michelangelo Buonarroti picked up some tips for his work a few years later on the Vatican's Sistine Chapel.

The Filippo Strozzi Chapel (right of the altar) is decorated with Filippino Lippi's **frescoes** of saints Philip and John, rich in colour and anecdotal detail: notice in the monumental *Exorcism of Demons in the Temple of Mars* three bystanders holding their nose at the smell.

In the Gondi Chapel (left of the high altar), the Brunelleschi **Crucifixion**, one of his few sculptures (1410), brings to the human body a characteristic idealized harmony, compared with Donatello's more personal piece in Santa Croce (see p. 87). Of another age, at once austere and serene, is the Giotto **Crucifixion** (1290) in the Sacristy (left transept).

Through an entrance left of the church, escape the bustle of the piazza in the Dominicans' 14th-century **cloister** *(Chiostro Verde)*, with Paolo Uccello's frescoes of the *Flood* now in the refectory.

North of Santa Maria Novella, spare a glance for the simple, clean-lined architecture of the **Stazione Centrale** (main railway station), built in 1935 in Mussolini's heyday but somehow defying the prevailing monumental bombast of the Fascist regime that you can see in Milan's monstrosity.

Heading back down to the river, have a restful drink in the plush neo-Renaissance bar of the Excelsior Hotel (Piazza Ognissanti), even—or particularly—if you're not staying there. Then cross the square to the **Ognissanti** (All Saints Church), 13th-century but with a Baroque façade of 1637. In Ghirlandaio's *Madonna of Mercy* (right aisle 2nd bay), portrayed immediately to the right of Mary, is the Florentine banker-navigator Amerigo Vespucci, who gave his name to the continent of America. Botticelli is buried in a chapel (right transept), his *St. Augustine* adorning the church, while in the **refectory** in the adjoining cloister, you'll find Ghirlandaio's *Last Supper*.

South of the Arno

There's nothing very romantic about the muddy green waters of the Arno river, with its broad *lungarni* embankments built in the 19th century to protect from flooding, but it does have two splendid bridges.

The **Ponte Santa Trinita** destroyed in 1944 has been rebuilt with the original 16th-century masonry scooped from the bottom of the river, including statues of the *Four Seasons*. Bartolomeo Ammanati's three lovely elliptical arches follow drawings by Michelangelo.

The **Ponte Vecchio,** intact since 1345, was Florence's first and for centuries only bridge.

War and Flood

In the 20th century, the Arno river has meant nothing but trouble. To slow the Allied advance in August, 1944, the Germans blew up all Florence's bridges except the Ponte Vecchio. And in case their enemy planned to drive vehicles across this ancient foot-bridge, they blocked approaches by destroying buildings within a radius of 200 metres.

On November 4, 1966, the river burst its banks and flooded the city, destroying and damaging over 1,000 paintings and 500 sculptures as well as countless precious books and manuscripts in its libraries. In places like the Bargello's Michelangelo Hall (see p. 88), you can see wall marks recording the flood level—3 metres (10 ft.) and more. But this was the golden Age of Aquarius and from all over the world, the sixties' art-loving brothers and sisters of the flower children poured into the city to help with the rescue operation spearheaded by Florence's own proud citizenry.

The boutiques with their back rooms overhanging the river were built from the 16th to 19th centuries. Vasari provided a covered corridor for Duke Cosimo to keep out of the rain when crossing from his Pitti Palace to the Uffizi. The duke didn't like the smell of the bridge's original butcher shops and had them replaced by the goldsmiths and jewellers whose descendants of-

fer you their high-quality wares today. Their most famous ancestor, Benvenuto Cellini, has his (1900) bronze bust in the middle of the bridge.

In Renaissance times, the quarter south of the Arno was an aristocratic preserve where the Medici held court. Today, their palace is a popular museum and the gardens of their private festivities are a public park.

Cross the Ponte Vecchio to the sprawling **Pitti Palace,** its dauntingly heavy and graceless façade belying the ornate and colourful interior. Duke Cosimo's wife, Eleonora of Toledo, acquired the palace from the Pitti merchant family in 1549 as the Me-

Little houses cling to the rear of Ponte Vecchio boutiques.

dici's official residence, which passed briefly in the 19th century to the king of a united Italy.

Its museums take you into the rich world of the Medici, much as they left it. The **Pitti Gallery** *(Galleria Palatina)* is quite simply, quite opulently, the family art collection. The paintings are displayed just as the dukes themselves hung them, two-, three- and four-high, by personal preference rather than in historical sequence. The richly decorated halls are named after the themes of their 17th-century frescoes—Venus, Hercules, Prometheus. Like any collection of family pictures, there's a preponderance of portraits, though here the aunts and uncles tend to be princesses and cardinals.

And the Medici's taste and means did permit a considerable number of masterpieces.

Titian displays his masterly use of colour and light in *The Concert* (Hall 5, Venus), a haunting portrait of *The Englishman* and bare-breasted *Magdalen* (Hall 6, Apollo).

Early proponent of "make love, not war," **Rubens** shows Venus restraining Mars in his vivid *Consequences of War* and portrays himself on the far left of his *Four Philosophers* (Hall 7, Mars).

Raphael is well represented by a stately *Veiled Woman* (Hall 8, Jupiter), a classic *Madonna of the Chair* and *Maddalena Doni,* deliberately imitating the pose of Leonardo da Vinci's *Mona Lisa* (Hall 9, Saturn), and *Pregnant Women* (Hall 10, Iliad).

Caravaggio contributes a typically disturbing canvas, an ugly *Sleeping Cupid* with distinct intimations of death (Hall 32, Education of Jupiter).

Up on the next floor, the **Modern Art Gallery** is devoted to 19th- and 20th-century Italian art. Most interesting are the *Macchiaioli* school of Tuscan pre-Impressionists who met at Florence's Caffè Michelangelo in the 1860s, seeking a new freedom from academic art that paralleled the political liberation of the Risorgimento. Giorgio de Chirico and Eduardo de Pisis are among the more important 20th-century painters exhibited.

Left of the main Pitti entrance, the **Silverware Museum** *(Museo degli Argenti)* has 16 profusely ornamented rooms of family treasures—gold, silver, jewels, beautiful 16th- and 17th-century amber and ivory, crystal and porcelain and Baroque furniture. The **Carriage Museum** *(Museo delle Carrozze),* in a wing on the far right of the palace, and the **Royal Apartments** *(Appartamenti Monumentali),* upstairs, right of the main entrance, show an opulent, truly palatial life that the Pitti's dour exterior never let you suspect.

Time for a rest in the shade of the cypresses, pines and holm oaks of the palace's **Boboli Gardens**. To the modern eye, they form a Renaissance and Baroque theme-park dotted with loggias, cool fountains, grottoes with artificial stalactites, and myriad statues of gods, nymphs and grotesques (the word derives from the Boboli grottoes).

Directly behind the palace, the Amphitheatre, shaped like a Roman circus, was the scene of the Medici's most extravagant fêtes and masked balls. In the middle of the nearby Pond of Neptune *(Vasca del Nettuno),* the burly sea god wields his trident in petrified parody of one of the Boboli's gardeners.

After the Pitti's riches, the unadorned white façade of the Augustinian church of **Santo Spirito** is a sobering antidote. Brunelleschi's design was never completed but the interior preserves the spatial clarity of his Corinthian-capitalled colonnades. In the right transept is a strikingly theatrical *Madonna Enthroned* by Filippino Lippi.

Across the church's tree-shaded piazza—popular for its pleasant market—is the **Cenacolo di Santo Spirito**, formerly the monastery's refectory with some 14th-century frescoes of the *Last Supper* and *Crucifixion* by Andrea Orcagna.

The church of **Santa Maria del Carmine** is an essential stop on any artistic pilgrimage to Florence. The church itself is an unprepossessing reconstruction after a devastating fire of 1771, but the Brancacci Chapel with the great **Masaccio frescoes** survived intact. The painter died at 27 after only 5 years of known creative activity (1423–28), working with his mild-mannered friend Masolini on scenes from Genesis and the life of St. Peter. Compare Masolino's sweet and harmonious Adam and Eve in his *Original Sin* (chapel entrance, upper right) with Masaccio's agonizing figures in the *Expulsion from the Garden of Eden* opposite to appreciate one of the early Renaissance's most dramatic statements. Florence's greatest artists, Michelangelo at their head, came to sketch Masaccio's trail-blazing use of light and visual depth as instruments of emotional impact, particularly striking in the broad sweep of his *St. Peter Paying the Tribute Money.* The chapel frescoes were completed in the 1480s by Filippino Lippi, who painted the side walls' lower panels.

Drive up the beautiful winding Viale dei Colli for a wonderful last panoramic view of the city dominated by the cupola of the Duomo from the vast **Piazzale Michelangelo** (with yet another copy of his *David*). While you're there, visit the charming Roman-

95

esque church of **San Miniato** up the hill behind the square. Antonio Rossellino's monumental 15th-century marble **tomb** of the Cardinal of Portugal, in a chapel off the left aisle, is notable for two beautiful genuflecting angels on the sarcophagus which greatly influenced Michelangelo.

TUSCANY *(Toscana)*

The original territory of the ancient civilization of the Etruscans has always been independent-minded, even aloof, in its attitude to Rome and the other regions. For the serious Italophile, its beauty and riches deserve weeks, months, even years of attention, but no first visit would be complete without at least one week here.

After an indispensable side-trip from Florence to Fiesole, our itineraries go west to Pisa and Lucca before turning south through the hills to Siena.

Fiesole

Just 8 kilometres (5 mi.) north-east of Florence (30 minutes on the number 7 bus from the Duomo), the road winds up a wooded hillside, revealing at each bend ever-changing views of Fiesole's gardens and villas

These monks find a haven of peace at the church of San Miniato.

before you and the monuments of the great city below.

Stop on the way at **San Domenico di Fiesole** for its 15th-century church and two important works by Fra Angelico, a *Madonna and Saints* in the first chapel on the left and a *Crucifixion* in the monastery refectory. Just off to the west is the pretty church of Badia Fiesolana, once the town's 10th-century Romanesque cathedral redesigned by Brunelleschi in the 1450s.

Only some wall fragments remain of the former Etruscan stronghold in Fiesole itself, but there are extensive Roman ruins, including a well-preserved **theatre,** still in use, which seats 2,500 spectators.

Car-drivers can negotiate the winding old side-road **Via Vecchia Fiesolana** for glimpses of handsome villas half-hidden among the cypresses and olive trees. The town centre, Piazza Mino da Fiesole, with its austere cathedral, is the starting-point for some exhilarating hill walks, the best being the steep lane leading west to the **San Francesco** monastery.

Pisa

The town, like the tipsy stubbornness of its Leaning Tower, is one of the world's blessed wonders. In its heyday from the 11th to the 13th century, it created a commercial empire down the

Tyrrhenian coast and in Corsica, Sardinia, Sicily, Syria, Palestine and Egypt. Its riches built that gleaming white marble complex of religious edifices known as the Campo dei Miracoli (Field of Miracles), left unscathed by the invasions and wars of succeeding centuries.

Conquering a flat, ungrateful landscape with serene, other-worldly harmony, this assembly of buildings in the **Piazza del Duomo** celebrates the whole cycle of life from baptistery, cathedral and campanile to the monumental cemetery of the Campo Santo.

The **Duomo** was built from 1063 to 1118 to honour Pisa's victory over the Saracens in Sicily. With oriental and Byzantine decorative elements reflecting the Pisan Republic's overseas interests, its four-tiered arcaded façade over three porches is a masterpiece of grace and delicacy. Architect Buscheto didn't hesitate to write in Latin (in the far left arch) "This marble church has no equal". Inside, there was no reason either for Giovanni Pisano to show false modesty about his superbly sculpted 14th-century **marble pulpit** (left aisle), depicting scenes of Old Testament prophets and New Testament apostles.

Thanks to its unstable subsoil, the **Leaning Tower** *(campanile)* is out of alignment by about 5 metres (15 ft.). Give or take a micromillimetre or two depending on annual subsidence, that means the 8-storeyed belfry stands 55.65 metres (182.6 ft.) high on its north side and 54.8 (179.8 ft.) on the south. Scientists are forever seeking new solutions for propping it up, but at its present rate of slippage, you still have another 200 years to see it standing more or less upright. Take the 294-step spiral staircase for a view over the Campo dei Miracoli and across the Arno river to the sea.

The lovely circular **baptistery** is topped by a traditional statue of John the Baptist. Inside, left of the baptismal font and altar, is Pisa's greatest work of sculpture, a hexagonal **marble pulpit** by Nicola Pisano, father of Giovanni who designed the cathedral pulpit. The 1260 carving of biblical themes has clear links to French Gothic sculpture, while drawing on models from Roman and Etruscan sarcophagi—a Herculean Daniel and a Mary inspired by heads of Juno and Phaedra.

In the 13th-century cloistered cemetery of the **Campo Santo** (Holy Ground), note the Gothic tabernacle enclosing a *Madonna*

Everyone likes to give the Leaning Tower a helping hand.

and Saints. Within the cloister, in the north gallery is a striking **fresco** of the *Triumph of Death* (1360) showing how humble and aristocrat face the same destiny.

Away from the Campo dei Miracoli, in a Benedictine monastery down by the Arno, the **San Matteo Museum** houses sculpture from the Baptistery and Cathedral as well as a gentle Simone Martini *Madonna and Child* and Masaccio's *St. Paul* (part of a polyptych split up between London, Naples, Berlin and Liechtenstein).

Lucca

The "sights" of this town take scarcely a day, but the seductive tranquillity within its old ramparts is such that people end up staying for weeks. Peace of mind has always been a priority here. In the stormy 15th and 16th centuries, Lucca's prosperous silk merchants preserved the peace by intercepting enemy armies and paying them to bypass the town. It has been particularly rich in musicians, most notably Boccherini and Puccini, and hosts a series of music festivals throughout the summer.

Begin with a stroll around the nicely preserved **ramparts,** along the Passeggiata delle Mura, for a good overall view.

The fine 14th-century cathedral, **Duomo San Martino**, has a Pisan-style arcaded façade with a *Descent from the Cross* carved by Nicola Pisano over the north door. Inside, to the right of the entrance, is a 12th-century equestrian sculpture of *St. Martin and the Beggar,* with a distinctly ancient Roman flavour. In the left transept, see the graceful 15th-century **tomb** of Ilaria del Carretto by Sienese sculptor Jacopo della Quercia.

North-west of the cathedral, you'll find an even more beautiful adaptation of the Pisan Romanesque style in the church of **San Michele in Foro,** less encumbered on its site of the old Roman Forum. The arcaded façade varies the patterns of its columns—sculpted, striped, scrolled, chevroned—in pink, green, black or white marble. With binoculars, you can spot up on the third tier of arches (3rd from the right) the heads of Risorgimento heroes Garibaldi and Cavour.

To capture something of the town's medieval character, explore the **Via Guinigi,** with its handsome 14th-century palaces, and the towered houses of **Via Fillungo,** leading to the Roman amphitheatre, now the Piazza del Mercato. Nearby, the façade of the church of **San Frediano** has a 13th-century mosaic of the *Ascension.* In the interior (4th chapel on left aisle), look for Jacopo della Quercia's marble altar.

Chianti

The best introduction to the Tuscan hill country is a tour of the famous **vineyards** that grace its southern-oriented slopes. The grapes that qualify as *Chianti Classico,* distinguished by a coveted black rooster label, grow in the region between Florence and Siena, most of them along the N222 Via Chiantigiana. The liveliest, most colourful time is during the autumn grape harvest, *la vendemmia,* but tasting—and buying at the vineyard—goes on all year round.

Start out at San Casciano in Val di Pesa, 17 kilometres (11 mi.) south of Florence, with a bonus for art-lovers of a Simone Martini *Crucifixion* and other Sienese works in the church of La Misericordia. South-east across to the N222, you find the characteristic landscape of vineyards interspersed with equally renowned olive groves as you approach Greve, a major wine centre on the river of the same name. (Americans pay homage to a monument to local boy Giovanni da Verrazzano, navigator-explorer of New York Bay.) The wine-route continues through Castellina with its 15th-century castle and ancient town gate. Then on to **Radda**, where you should peep in at the Piccolo Museo del Chianti, and Gaiole in Chianti, one of the best centres for tasting and a place to linger.

San Gimignano

The haunting silhouette of this medieval Manhattan, a skyline bristling with rectangular towers, and its lovingly preserved historic centre make it the most magical of Tuscany's hill-towns. (One of the most photogenic views is from the north, on the road from Certaldo, home and last resting-place of Boccaccio.) There were 72 towers—erected as symbols of its merchants' power and prestige—until the town's Florentine conquerors ordered them dismantled in the 14th century. Just 14 remain.

The most important are clustered around three adjoining **squares:** the triangular Piazza della Cisterna, the old banking centre named after the city's 13th-century travertine well, surrounded by elegant palaces; Piazza del Duomo, grouping church and town hall as the centre of civic and religious power; and the Piazza delle Erbe market-place with twin Salvucci towers.

The 13th-century town hall, **Palazzo del Popolo,** houses the civic museums. The **Pinacoteca** includes an emotionally intense *Crucifixion* by Coppo di Marcovaldo and a Taddeo di Bartolo painting of St. Gimignano, in which you can see what the towers of the medieval city looked like. Visit the interior of the 12th-century Romanesque

Collegiata (collegiate church ranking just lower than a cathedral) for its dramatic Barna da Siena **frescoes** of New Testament scenes along the right aisle. In sharp contrast, the Ghirlandaio **frescoes** in the Santa Fina Chapel (at the end of the right aisle) are a series of sophisticated social portraits. Against the east wall, flanking the church entrance, are wooden statues of Mary and the Archangel Gabriel by Jacopo della Quercia.

For a fine view of the surrounding country, climb up to the ruins of the **Rocca** citadel.

Volterra

This fortified town perched high on its hill works a sober charm among the buff-stone 13th-century edifices of its Piazza dei Priori and adjacent Piazza San Giovanni. The **Palazzo dei Priori** (1208) is the oldest of Tuscany's typical town halls, with a two-tiered tower, battlements and mullioned windows. It stands opposite the massive triple-arched **Palazzo Pretorio**, medieval police headquarters. The two squares are separated by the austere 12th-century cathedral and octagonal baptistery. The latter's baptismal font has bas-reliefs by Andrea Sansovino.

Siena's Gothic cathedral exudes grace and elegance.

Away from the centre, you can trace the town's ancient beginnings in the **Etruscan Guarnacci Museum** (Via Don Minzoni, 15). The collection includes sculpted stone, alabaster and terracotta funeral urns dating back to the 6th century B.C. One gaunt statue, *Ombra della Sera* (Evening Shadow) is an uncanny 2,000-year-old precursor of a modern Giacometti.

Siena

A city of rich russet browns and ochres, Siena is as delightfully feminine as greystone Florence is imposing in its masculinity. Contrasts with its old rival to the north are striking and inevitable. Whereas the nucleus of Florence was built to a strict Roman city plan of straight streets intersecting at right angles, Siena has all the Tuscan hill-town's hap-hazard organic forms, straggling up and down a forked ridge of not one but three hilltops.

Similarly, while Florentine art developed its formidable intellectual and emotional power, the tone of Sienese painting —Simone Martini, the Lorenzettis, even the Mannerist Sodoma—remained gentle and delicate, bathed in the light and colour of its surrounding coun-

tryside. But as its obstinately independent spirit has shown, even after the Florentine conquest of 1555—a spirit epitomized by its lusty Palio tournament—the town is not without vigour.

But go easy on those steep streets, rest awhile in the cool courtyard of a great banker's palazzo, enjoy the spicy cuisine with a good local Chianti. And take time out between two siestas to see some of Tuscany's most exhilarating monuments. Siena is good for tired blood.

Start at the grand sloping fan-shaped **Piazza del Campo**, site of the old Roman forum and arena

---

Riding for the Palio

The Palio horse races held on July 2 and August 16 are part of a traditional pageant dating back to the 15th century and beyond. Colourful Renaissance-costumed pages and men-at-arms put on a procession and show of flag-throwing with emblems—eagle, snail, porcupine, goose, etc.—of the 17 parishes (contrade) of the city and surrounding communes. Ten of them compete in the climactic breakneck bareback horse race round the Campo for which a painted silk standard, the Palio, is the prize. (To avoid the sometimes harrowing crush down in the square, you may prefer to reserve a seat in a stand or a place on a balcony.)

---

of the Palio horse race. The piazza's red-brick herring-bone paving is divided by nine marble strips for the nine patrician clans that ruled the city at the end of the 13th century.

Over a late-afternoon coffee on the shady side (next to the tourist office), you can appreciate the painterly impact of the "burnt sienna" glowing in the arcaded Gothic **Palazzo Pubblico** opposite, with its splendid 102-metre-high (335-ft.) **Torre del Mangia** (climb to its first tier at 88 metres [288 ft.] for a view of the city). The loggia at the tower's base is a chapel *(Cappella di Piazza)* marking the city's deliverance from the plague of 1348.

The modern town hall offices are on the Palazzo's ground floor, but its upstairs chambers, frescoed by the city's foremost artists, have been transformed into a **Museo Civico** (municipal museum). The **Sala del Mappamondo** (named after a lost map of the Sienese world painted by Ambrogio Lorenzetti to trace the city's international banking interests) has two great Simone Martini **frescoes.** To the left is a stately *Enthroned Madonna* (1315) and to the right, *Guidoriccio da Fogliano* (1328, but whose authenticity has recently been disputed), depicting the Sienese captain's ride to a historic victory at Montemassi—in the nicely detailed Tuscan landscape, notice the little Chianti vineyard in the military encampment. In the **Sala della Pace** (Hall of Peace, council chamber of the Nine Patricians) the full force of Siena's civic pride strikes home in the Ambrogio Lorenzetti **frescoes** (1337–39). One wall is devoted to *Bad Government,* a gloomy portrait of Tyranny, badly damaged, and the other two to Siena's own enlightened *Good Government,* full of fascinating detail of town life—roof-builders, shoe shop, school, outdoor tavern, ladies dancing in the street—and hunters riding out to the surrounding countryside. A second floor Loggia is adorned with Jacopo della Quercia's 15th-century carvings for the city fountain Fonte Gaia (of which a poor 19th-century replica stands in the piazza).

South-west of the Campo, the **Duomo,** built from the 12th to the 14th century, is for many the greatest of Italy's Gothic cathedrals. The exterior's majestic polychrome and black- and white-striped marble panelling surrounding Giovanni Pisano's three intricately carved portals presents that quintessential Italian preference for pictorial qualities over *mere* architecture. And that gleaming colour is pure Siena. The interior continues the bands of black and white marble, while **inlaid marble paving** covers

the floor with 56 pictures of biblical and allegorical themes done over two centuries by some 40 artists, most notably Beccafumi, di Bartolo and Pinturicchio. Off the left aisle is the early 16th-century **Cardinal Piccolomini Library** vividly decorated by Pinturicchio's action-packed frescoes of the life of Pope Pius II (the cardinal himself became pope, Pius III, but lasted only ten days). In the left transept is a magnificent octagonal 13th-century **pulpit** carved by Nicola Pisano, with help from son Giovanni and Arnolfo di Cambio. Among the fantastic detail of the new testament scenes, notice the damned being eaten alive in the *Last Judgment.* The 17th-century Baroque Madonna del Voto Chapel (in the right transept) was designed by Bernini, whose statues of St. Jerome and Mary Magdalen flank the entrance.

In the **Cathedral Museum** *(Museo dell'Opera Metropolitana),* Giovanni Pisano's original sculptures for the Duomo's façade have strangely distorted poses because they were meant to be seen from below. Look out, too, for Duccio di Boninsegna's *Enthroned Madonna,* Simone Martini's *Miracles of St. Agostino Novello* and Pietro Lorenzetti's *Birth of Mary.*

Take a leisurely hour or two for the lovely Sienese paintings in the Palazzo Buonsignori's

Pinacoteca Nazionale. Besides the works of the 14th-century masters, Duccio, Pietro and Ambrogio Lorenzetti and Simone Martini, see Siena's 16th-century Mannerists, painting at a time when the Renaissance teetered on the brink of effete decadence: Beccafumi's dreamy *Birth of Mary* and a highly decorative *Christ at the Column* by Sodoma.

Montepulciano

On the route to southern Umbria, this is one of Tuscany's most attractive hill-towns—with an excellent local wine. Stroll along the Via di Gracciano and Via Ricci to see the town's noble Gothic and Renaissance palazzi. On the **Piazza Grande,** with a graceful town well decorated with griffins and lions in its centre, the 14th-century **Palazzo Comunale** is a particularly imposing expression of civic dignity. In the austere little **Cathedral,** see Taddeo di Bartolo's fine triptych on the high altar. Antonio da Sangallo, architect of many of the town's palazzi, built his masterpiece, the 16th-century church of **Madonna di San Biagio,** south-west of town, at the end of an avenue of cypresses overlooking the tranquil Chiana valley.

Monte Argentario

If you're taking the coast road to or from Rome, stop off at the fashionable seaside resorts on this pine-forested peninsula beside the town of Orbetello. The sandy beaches and yachting harbours of **Port'Ercole** and **Porto Santo Stefano** are favourite weekend destinations for Romans, but they're much quieter in the week. Take a boat excursion out to the pretty island of **Giglio**.

Chic Romans head up the coast to Port'Ercole's sheltered harbour playground.

UMBRIA

The region has a less spectacular reputation than Tuscany (and is blessedly less crowded), but it's highly appreciated both for its great artistic treasures and the dreamy rolling green landscapes that inspired them.

It was dominated in the past by the papacy, which conquered the Lombard dukes of Spoleto in the Middle Ages, Perugia in the 16th century and held sway until the unification of Italy. Apart from pilgrims streaming to St. Francis's Assisi and university students heading for Perugia, it has remained a very happy backwater.

Orvieto

Half the pleasure of this lovely town high on its rocky precipice is a first glimpse of it from afar (not so very different today from Turner's 1828 painting in London's Tate Gallery). For a good view, approach it from the south-west, on the S71 from Lake Bolsena, or look across from the medieval abbey La Badia (now a hotel), immediately south of town.

Connoisseurs come for the great white wine, art-lovers for the magnificent Gothic **Cathedral.** Try both at sunset and you'll die happy. Scores of architects worked on the church from the 13th to the 17th century, but its glory remains the gleaming gabled **façade,** with its four slender spired pilasters and rose-window above the beautifully scrolled porches. At the base of the two northern pilasters, look closely at Lorenzo Maitani's marvellous carved marble **bas-reliefs** of scenes from the Old Testament and the Last Judgment.

Grey and white bands of marble give the interior a spacious simplicity. Off the right transept, the **San Brizio Chapel** is frescoed on the ceiling by Fra Angelico—*Christ in Glory*—and by Luca Signorelli on the walls. To the left, Signorelli portrays himself and Fra Angelico as bystanders in the vivid *Preaching of the Antichrist* (identified here with Savonarola). The nude figures in the *Resurrection of the Dead* on the right wall are less convincing (described by Leonardo da Vinci as "sacks of nuts").

The **Cathedral Museum** in the Palazzo Soliano includes other works by Signorelli, a Simone Martini polyptych and sculpture by Nino, Andrea and Giovanni Pisano.

If you want to cool off, ex-

108

Orvieto's rocky perch made it an ideal medieval stronghold.

plore the monumental **Pozzo di San Patrizio,** a 16th-century well dug 63 metres (206 ft.) down into the volcanic rock on the north-east edge of the precipice. Well lit by 72 windows, two spiral staircases of 248 steps take you right down to the water level.

Spoleto

Its greatest tourist attractions are the summer music and theatre festivals, but the town's beautiful natural setting amid densely wooded hills also makes it a base for hikes into the countryside, especially the oak forest on Monteluco.

The sober Romanesque **Cathedral** with 17th-century additions is decorated with damaged but still graceful Fra Filippo

109

Lippi **frescoes** in its chancel. In the left transept, son Filippino designed the **tomb** for the licentious painter-monk who seduced Sister Lucrezia—and others—in Florence's Carmine monastery.

⚑ Assisi

The enduring popular appeal of St. Francis (1182–1226) has turned his native town into Italy's major pilgrimage destination, second only to Rome. Its basilica, like the peaceful medieval town-centre, is beautifully preserved and the centuries-old pilgrim trade manages to avoid the commercialism that blights other religious shrines.

Park as close as you can to the lower square (*Piazza Inferiore*) at the west end of town. The basilica of **San Francesco** is in fact two churches, one above the other, built on top of the saint's tomb in the crypt.

The **Lower Church** was begun in 1228, two years after Francis' death, and the frescoes were painted in the 14th century, but a Renaissance porch now precedes the Gothic side-entrance. The subdued light of the low vaulted nave evokes the sober piety of the Franciscan tradition. Simone Martini has decorated the **St. Martin Chapel** (first left) with exquisite frescoes, including a most aristocratic Jesus appearing in St. Martin's dream. Stairs in

the nave lead down to the crypt and St. Francis's **tomb**, rediscovered only in 1818, centuries after it had been concealed from Perugian plunderers.

The superb frescoes of the life of Jesus in the **Mary Magdalen Chapel** (third right) and of St. Francis's vows of poverty, chastity and obedience above the

---

A Saint

Francesco di Bernardone was the spoiled son of a rich family well-known for his rumbustious ways. But a sojourn in a Perugia jail at 23, followed by a severe illness, sobered him up. After a vision in the Chapel of San Damiano, he vowed a life of poverty in the service of the Church. He nursed lepers, converted bandits. He travelled to Spain, Morocco, Egypt and Palestine, but it was his impact on a troubled Italian population that mattered most to a Church beleaguered by heresy. Thousands responded to the simple eloquence of his preaching. They told how the example of his gentle life had tamed wild wolves and taught swallows to sing a sweeter song. In his religious ecstasy on Monte La Verna (near Arezzo), he was marked with Christ's stigmata—a phenomenon the most sceptical scholars have never placed in doubt. He was canonized St. Francis just two years after his death in 1226.

---

elegant Gothic high altar are attributed to Giotto or his pupils.

In the right transept, the famous Cimabue **portrait of St. Francis,** believed to be a close physical resemblance, shows him to the right of the enthroned Madonna. Over in the left transept, see Pietro Lorenzetti's noble *Descent from the Cross.*

In the **Upper Church,** Cimabue's works in the apse and transepts have turned black, looking like photo negatives because of the oxydized white lead in his paints, yet you can still feel the intensity of the crowd's anguish in his *Crucifixion.*

In the brilliantly illuminated nave, the faithful are exalted by one of the most grandiose series of **frescoes** in Christendom. The *Life of Francis* is movingly celebrated in 28 scenes along the lower tier (starting from the right transept), while 32 frescoes in the upper tier illustrate scenes from the Old and New Testament. Giotto's most fervent supporters say he designed the St. Francis series and himself painted numbers 2 to 11.

Penetrate the historic heart of Assisi along the **Via San Francesco,** with its 15th-century Pilgrims' Hostel *(Oratorio dei Pellegrini)* at number 11. Its frescoes are attributed to Perugino. The noble **Piazza del Comune** is the town centre, grouping medieval palazzi around the old Roman forum. A triumph of Christianity over paganism, the Corinthian-columned church of **Santa Maria sopra Minerva** was a Roman temple under Augustus.

The austere little **San Damiano** monastery, where Francis heard the good word, is 2½ kilometres (1½ mi.) south of town, maintaining the purest Franciscan tradition.

Perugia

Dominating the Umbrian countryside from its 494-metre (1,600-ft.) hill, the town is emphatically more secular, more profane than its Franciscan neighbour. But the imposing weight of its past is lightened by the lively cosmopolitan studentry of its two (Italian and international) universities. Constantly at war with Assisi in the Middle Ages, Perugia's belligerence is symbolized on the north side of town by the lovingly preserved **Arco Etrusco** (Etruscan—and partly Roman— triumphal arch) that remained part of the medieval ramparts.

And in the town centre, something of the old aggressive civic power is evoked in the formidable **Palazzo dei Priori** (Town Hall) towering over the Piazza 4 Novembre. But Nicola Pisano's intricately carved 13th-century **Fontana Maggiore** (Great Fountain) does hold its own. Earth tremors badly damaged the buff-stone Cathedral opposite.

The third floor of the Town Hall (entrance around the corner on Corso Vannucci) is given over to the **Galleria Nazionale dell'Umbria**, a splendid collection of Umbrian and Tuscan painting. It includes a Fra Angelico *Triptych* and Piero della Francesca's *Annunciation* and *Madonna with Angels*. But Umbria's pride and joy is the work of Perugino (1445–1523). Look out for his *Adoration of the Magi* and a *Madonna della Consolazione* as sweet and serene as the Umbrian landscape of which you'll catch a glimpse through the museum windows. Pinturicchio, master of narrative fresco, is represented by his *Miracles of the Saints*.

Next door on the busy pedestrian street of Corso Vannucci (Perugino was Pietro Vannucci's nickname), is the **Collegio del Cambio**, 15th-century hall and chapel of the bankers' guild. The vestibule is decorated with 17th-century Baroque walnut-panelling. In the **Audience Hall** (*Sala dell'Udienza*) is a delightful series of Perugino frescoes. The left wall is allegorical, devoted to the bankers' widely acknowledged virtues, *Prudence, Justice, Fortitude* and *Temperance,* while religious themes invoke their piety on the other walls. (*Fortitude*

and one of the Sibyls are attributed to Perugino's 17-year-old pupil, Raphael.)

For a real feeling of the old medieval town, dodge the chickens scampering across the brick paving of the tiny tunnel-vaulted **Via Volte della Pace**, incongruously linking the modern shopping street of Via Alesse to a parking-lot behind the cathedral.

At the south end of the Corso Vannucci beyond the Piazza Italia, the **Carducci Gardens** provide a restful view of the Umbrian countryside.

Gubbio

Some 40 kilometres (25 mi.) north of Perugia, this venerable fortress-town is not easy to get to and once you're there, it's hard on those who don't like climbing steep cobbled streets. But for anyone who cherishes the tranquillity of a totally unspoiled medieval atmosphere, Gubbio is a delight. The **Piazza della Signoria** paved in brick and stone is a fine vantage-point for viewing the rest of the city. Its 14th-century battlemented **Palazzo dei Consoli** is one of the grandest civic edifices in all Italy and from the tall arcade that anchors it to the hillside, you have a magnificent panorama of the surrounding country. Then climb (even higher!) to the cathedral and the Renaissance courtyard of the Palazzo Ducale.

THE NORTH-EAST

Throughout Italy's history, its north-east regions have linked the country to an exotic outside world of Byzantium and the Orient through Venice, and to the Alpine countries beyond the Dolomites, while the plains of Emilia-Romagna from Ravenna to Parma provide an anchor to the heartland of the Po valley.

The result is a rich variety of distinctive cities and colourful hinterland. The afterglow of Venice's empire is undimmed. Elegant Palladian villas grace its Veneto mainland from Padua to Vicenza. The glories of Verona extend from its grand Roman arena to the palaces of the medieval and Renaissance princes whose intrigues inspired Shakespeare. In Emilia-Romagna, the pride and creativity of the great city-states is still very much in evidence in the monuments and museums of Bologna, Ferrara and Parma. Stretch your muscles in the Dolomites, with its first-class winter sports and summer hiking, or soak up sun and sea in the Adriatic resorts around Rimini.

VENICE *(Venezia)*

These palaces, canals and lagoons claim a place apart in our collective imagination. As our 20th century ends, Venice remains a dreamworld, its myth more powerful than harsh reality. Even when it threatens to disintegrate into nightmare at times of winter flood or overcrowded summer, visitors can take refuge on a boardwalk across the waters or in a quiet corner away from the mob, and continue their dream. One of the city's many blessings is that there still are so many quiet and beautiful corners. Another, so obvious, but impossible to overemphasize, is the *absence of cars,* the simple joy of wandering around a town relieved of our by now built-in urban traffic-stress, of standing on a little humpback bridge far from the Grand Canal and hearing only the water lapping against the moss-covered walls or the occasional swish of a gondola. You may never want to break the spell and go back to the real world.

VENICE

Go in May or October, if you can—the crowds at Easter and from June to September can be truly horrendous. Venice at Christmas has become fashionable and the February Carnival very commercial. But whenever you go, don't try to do it in a day. Without the time to explore those hidden corners, you risk hating it for the rest of your life. Give yourself a min-imum of three days, time to get lost—ultimately, but perhaps re-gretfully, you'll get back to the main landmarks signposted with bright yellow arrows. The town has more than enough sights to see, but you can taste much of its pleasures before you even set foot inside the museums, churches and monuments. The only "must" is Venice itself, your own Venice.

🛍 Grand Canal

From the railway station or the car park of Piazzale Roma, you begin with a *vaporetto* waterbus along the Canal Grande, the most stunning main street in the world. Use this wonderful first contact with the city as your introductory tour.

Vaporetto no. 1 takes you to the historic centre of town, Piazza San Marco, but beware of the faster no. 2, it takes a short-cut across a loop in the inverted S-shaped canal, missing out three-quarters of the sights. Airport motor launches cross directly to San Marco from the

Gondolas pole along the Grand Canal to the Rialto Bridge.

Lido—just drop your bags off at the hotel and take the Grand Canal in the opposite direction, round-trip. (Save your gondola ride for when you're settled in.)

Along the Grand Canal's 3.8 kilometres (more than 2 mi.), varying in width from 30 to 70 metres (100–230 ft.), are the old trading offices and warehouses of its commercial heyday. Known locally as *ca'* (short for *casa*) as well as *palazzo*, the marble, brick and white limestone palaces range over 600 years from Venetian-Byzantine to Baroque and Neoclassical, but most of them are 14th- and 15th-century Flamboyant Gothic, Venice's "trademark" in architectural styles. Their sea-resistant limestone foundations stand on massive pinewood stilts driven 8 metres (26 ft.) into the lagoon bed.

Left Bank

The superb Renaissance **Palazzo Vendramin-Calergi**, where Richard Wagner died in 1883, is today the winter casino. The gilt has gone from the façade of the 15th-century **Ca' d'Oro** (Golden House), but it's still the town's most beautiful Gothic palace. Italy's most impressive post office, **Fondaco dei Tedeschi** was once the trading-centre of Czechs, Hungarians and Austrians as well as the Germans of its name. Just beyond, the shop-lined **Rialto Bridge** arches the canal at its narrowest point. The 18th-century **Palazzo Grassi** was recently restored for modern art exhibitions. The prefecture puts its bureaucrats in the fine Renaissance **Palazzo Corner** (or *Ca' Grande*), while gondoliers claim Othello's Desdemona lived in the lovely late-Gothic **Palazzo Contarini-Fasan**.

Right Bank

The 700-year-old **Fondaco dei Turchi** was a warehouse in the 17th century for the merchants of Constantinople, now the Natural History Museum. It stands next

---

Going, Going Gondola

The proud fleet of 10,000 gondolas of a century ago has dwindled to a few hundred, while the prices have gone in the opposite direction. Apart from commuters taking cross-canal ferry gondolas, Venetians leave the sleek and slender black craft to the tourists. Still handing on the business from father to son, the gondoliers in their straw hats and sailor's jumpers or striped T-shirts are as cheerful and witty as, say, any other taxi-driver, but they don't sing as often or as well as they used to. Exorbitant as they are, how will you explain to grandchildren, after the last gondolas have disappeared, that you visited Venice and never went in one?

Reflections on the Water

The water explains almost everything. When the Lombards swept east across the Po valley, the Venetians found their salvation literally in the sea—perched on an archipelago of isles and shoals. Ruled by an energetic oligarchy under an elected Doge or duke, the Serenissima *or Most Serene Republic of St. Mark turned its back on the hostile mainland and made a fabulous fortune with an empire stretching across the eastern Mediterranean and beyond to the silk and spice routes of Asia opened up by Marco Polo. Italy had no vital importance for Venice until overseas trade declined and new sources of wealth had to be sought in agriculture on the mainland.*

Protected by the lagoons, Venice needed no ramparts, its palaces could be light and decorative rather than the solid fortress-like residences of Florence. Fronting canals instead of streets, the façades are designed to take their colour from the water's reflection as well as the sunlight. While Florentine art impresses us with its mastery of form and line, the most striking qualities of Venetian painting, with the added influence of Byzantium and the Orient, remain that colour and light.

to the plain brick 15th-century **Megio** wheat granary, decorated only by battlements and the city seal of St. Mark's lion. The imposing 17th-century Baroque **Ca' Pesaro** houses the Modern Art Museum. Come back early in the morning to the **Pescheria** (fish market), 20th-century Neo-Gothic, but nicely done. The university has a department in the handsome 15th-century Gothic **Ca' Foscari**. The **Ca' Rezzonico** is itself a fine specimen of the 18th-century Venetian art for which it is now a museum. Beyond the wooden Accademia Bridge, the perspective is completed by the magnificent Baroque church of **Santa Maria della Salute**.

Around San Marco

Building-space on the water being what it is, Venice has only one real piazza, but in comparison, any other would have died of shame anyway. Gloriously open to skies and sea, **Piazza San Marco**—to locals, just "the Piazza"—embodies the whole Venetian adventure. Its airy arcades reach out to the 900-year-old basilica and turn a corner past the soaring campanile to the Piazzetta and landing stage of St. Mark's basin *(bacino),* gateway to the Adriatic. The odysseys of victorious commanders began and ended here.

Here, too, the republic fell in 1797, at the hands of Napoleon. While he was removing the four

117

bronze horses from the basilica along with other art treasures to ship back to Paris, he was said to remark that the Piazza San Marco was "the living-room of the world". He closed off the piazza's west end with an Ala Napoleonica (Napoleonic Wing), through which you enter the Museo Correr, devoted to paintings and documents of Venetian history.

Invasion of the Body Snatchers

Here's the story. It's 828 or thereabouts. A couple of merchants—Venice is full of them—hear that the Doge needs a prestigious holy relic, to bolster his position vis à vis the pope. "How about the evangelist Mark?" they ask. "We can get you the whole body." "Go for it," says the Doge.

They go to Alexandria, where Mark had been bishop, and sneak the body out of the mausoleum, after carefully refilling the evangelist's shroud with the remains of Claudian, a minor saint lying nearby. Clever, but not clever enough to fool the Egyptians, who search their ship. "Hallo, hallo, what's in that basket?" they ask. "See for yourselves," say the merchants, uncovering some slabs of meat. "Kanzir, Kanzir! (pork, pork)," cry the Muslim soldiers and flee in horror, leaving Mark's bones safely concealed beneath.

The north and south arms of the square, the 16th-century **Procuratie Vecchie** and **Procuratie Nuove,** were the residences of the republic's most senior officials. They are now lined with fashionable boutiques, jewellery shops and, most important for breakfast *cappuccino* and afternoon tea, two elegant 18th-century cafés. During the Austrian occupation, the enemy frequented Quadri on the north side, while Italian patriots met only at Florian, opposite. To this day, the latter has the favour of Venetians, but also of foreigners who want to avoid foreigners, which complicates things for Venetians. Out in the square, orchestras play "Palm Court" music. Pigeons chase seed-vendors chasing tourists chasing their children chasing pigeons. This is no living-room, Bonaparte, it's another great piece of Italian theatre.

The glittering façade of the **Basilica di San Marco** forms an exotic backdrop, illuminating Venice's role at the crossroads of eastern and western culture. What began in 830 as the Doges' chapel for the remains of the evangelist Mark, the city's patron saint, was rebuilt in the 11th century as a grandiose

St. Mark's Basilica is as rich in design as Venice's history.

Byzantine-Oriental basilica. Greek mosaicists were brought in to decorate the arches and domes. Five Romanesque portals correspond to the five Islamic-style domes covering the church's Greek cross ground-plan. Spired Gothic tabernacles enhance the teeming richness.

The **San Alipio portal**, first on the left, is the only one decorated with an original 13th-century mosaic, depicting the *Transfer of St. Mark's Body*. The mosaic also shows the basilica with the famous bronze horses brought from Constantinople after the Crusade of 1204. The ones over the triple-arched main entrance are copies. (Since their restoration, the originals are kept in the basilica museum.)

Just inside the church entrance, to the right, is the tomb of Doge Vitale Falier, for whom Mark's remains were brought to Venice. In the six small cupolas of the narthex (vestibule), 13th-century mosaics portray Old Testament scenes of Abel's murder, Noah, Abraham and Moses.

The glow in the interior from the mosaics, gently illuminated by high windows, and the soft brown patina of the once white

Byzantine and Romanesque styles blend in St. Mark's.

marble fully earn the name of "church of gold". The original **mosaics** on the five domes and the great barrel vaults separating them date from the 11th to the 15th century. Among the best are the 12th-century *Pentecost* dome in the nave and the central dome's 13th-century *Ascension*. Others have been heavily restored or replaced, not with true mosaics, but reproductions in coloured stone of drawings by such artists as Bellini, Mantegna and Tintoretto.

The **high altar** stands over St. Mark's tomb. Scholars can't decide whether the altar's carved alabaster-columned canopy is 6th-century Byzantine or 13th-century Venetian. They agree it's fine work. Beyond it is the **Pala d'Oro,** a great golden altarpiece dating back 1,000 years and bejewelled in its present form in the 14th century. Guides will tell you that there were once 2,486 precious stones, including 1,300 pearls, 400 garnets, 300 sapphires, 300 emeralds, 90 amethysts, 15 rubies. Give or take the few pilfered by Napoleon, it is still precious enough that crowds have to be kept down by charging an entrance fee.

On your way out, stairs right of the main entrance lead to the **Museum,** in which you can see the original four **bronze horses,** probably imperial Roman. From the loggia, you get a fine view over the Piazza San Marco, while galleries provide a privileged close-up of the basilica's mosaic ceilings.

North of the basilica, the 15th-century **Torre dell'Orologio** is one of those busy little clocktowers, all gilt and polychrome enamel, that activate statues, in this case two green bronze Moors, to clang out the hour, joined below, in Ascension week in May, by the three Magi and a trumpeting angel revolving around a gilded Madonna. You can watch the Moors from the roof terrace.

The beloved **Campanile** towers 98.6 metres (324 ft.) over the city, for 10 centuries its belfry, lighthouse, weather-vane and gun turret. Emperor Frederick III rode his horse up its spiral ramp. Criminals were suspended from it in wooden cages. In 1902, it cracked, crumbled and collapsed slowly into the Piazza. Ten years later, on its 1,000th anniversary, it was rebuilt a few tons lighter but much the same as before: *"com'era, dov'era"* ("as it was, where it was"). Its collapse hurt no one, but did crush Jacopo Sansovino's beautiful 16th-century **Loggetta,** equally lovingly restored as entrance to the campanile's elevator for a view high over the Adriatic and all the way north, on clear days, to the Dolomites.

Flanking the **Piazzetta** that leads to the Bacino di San Marco, opposite the Doges' Palace, Sansovino's exquisite white limestone **Libreria Sansoviniana** is the city's most perfectly realized Renaissance structure, fulfilling all the classical ideals of harmonious proportions. The Doric-columned arcade, inspired by the Roman Colosseum, supports an Ionic gallery carrying the eye up to the beautiful roof balustrade with its obelisks and statues of Greek divinities. Its **Marciana Library** contains some 750,000 volumes and manuscripts, including the poetry of Petrarch in his own hand, and Marco Polo's testament.

The two tall **columns** facing out over St. Mark's basin were brought from Constantinople in the 12th century. They are topped by statues of St. Mark's winged lion and the city's first patron saint, Theodore, with his dragon.

The **Doges' Palace** *(Palazzo Ducale)* was for 900 years the focus of Venice's power and pomp, evoked in the imposing elegance of its pink marble and white limestone façades with their airy arcades, loggias and balconies fronting the Piazzetta and the basin. Erected over an older Byzantine-style castle, the present 14th–15th-century Flamboyant Gothic building has three fine sculptural groups at its cor-

ners, the *Drunkenness of Noah* by the Paglia Bridge, *Adam and Eve* at the Piazzetta, and the *Judgment of Solomon* by the basilica.

The **Porta della Carta** (Gate of the Paper, where the doge posted his decrees) makes a magnificent entrance. The Gothic sculpture shows the doge kneeling before St. Mark's lion, flanked by *Prudence* above *Temperance* in niches on the left and *Fortitude* above *Charity* on the right.

(That book in the lion's paw that you see all over Venice is inscribed: *Pax tibi, Marce evangelista meus,* "Peace unto you, my evangelist Mark".)

It's a Doge's Life

The doges saw their authority wax and wane between that of absolute monarch and pathetic figurehead. Subject to the changing powers of the republic's oligarchic council, many were murdered, executed for treason or ritually blinded—traditional punishment for a disgraced ruler. Though elected by the council, many created virtual dynasties. When the revered Giustiniani family were reduced by battle and plague in the 12th century to one last male, a monk, he was hauled out of his monastery on the Lido and persuaded to sire nine boys and three girls to continue the line before being allowed to return to his vows of chastity.

In the inner courtyard the **Scala dei Giganti** staircase is so named for Sansovino's giant statues of Neptune and Mars. Visitors take the golden **Scala d'Oro** past the Doge's opulent private apartments to the spectacularly decorated council chambers on the third floor. Here, as in most of the city's palaces and churches, the walls are decorated with painted panels and canvases rather than frescoes, too easily damaged by the Venetian climate.

Look out for Veronese's *Rape of Europa* and Tintoretto's *Bacchus and Ariadne* and *Vulcan's Forge* in the **Anticollegio;** a masterly allegorical series by Veronese glorifying Venice in the **Sala del Collegio,** where foreign ambassadors were received; weapons and suits of armour in the **Armoury** *(Sala d'Armi).*

Highlight of the palace tour, back down on the second floor, is the huge **Sala del Maggior Consiglio** (Great Council Hall), where ordinary citizens in the Republic's most democratic days presented their complaints in person before the oligarchy reserved it for their secret deliberations, and the last doge presented his abdication to Napoleon. Of the 76 doges portrayed here, one is blackened out, Marino Faliero, beheaded for treason in 1355. Tintoretto's *Paradise*

adorns the entrance wall. Said to be the world's largest oil-painting, 22 by 7 metres (72 by 23 ft.), it was done, with the help of son Domenico, when the artist was 70. Look, too, for the brilliant colours of Veronese's oval ceiling painting of *Venice Crowned by Victory,* forerunner of the Baroque *tours de force* in perspective.

For those hoping to go from the sublime to the sinister, the palace **prisons,** neat and tidy today along their narrow corridor, become all too romantic with their 17th-century Baroque **Bridge of Sighs** *(Ponte dei Sospiri).* It's much too *pretty—* the Venetians just can't help it— for such a celebrated passage to doom that supposedly moved its users to sigh on their way to the torture chambers (now off-limits).

Stretch your legs along the **Riva degli Schiavoni** (Quay of the Slavs), named after the Dalmatian merchants who unloaded their goods here. The ghosts of Dickens, Wagner and Proust wander around the venerable Danieli Hotel, along with actor Marcello Mastroianni in flesh and blood.

Probably nowhere is so much spectacular painting on view in such a tiny space as in the **Scuola di San Giorgio degli Schiavoni.** This captivating building was the guildhall of the *schiavoni* who commissioned Vittore Carpaccio to decorate their hall. His nine pictures, completed between 1502 and 1508, cover the walls of the ground-floor chapel. Note also the wonderfully ornate wooden ceiling.

Just 4 minutes by *vaporetto* from the Schiavoni, on its own little island, is the church of **San Giorgio Maggiore;** its campanile offers the most photogenic **view** of the city and its lagoon. The 16th-century church is a rare ecclesiastical building by Andrea Palladio, the man whose classic designs have so dominated aristocratic residential architecture throughout Europe—and North America. His customary Corinthian-columned elegance prevails here, extended from the façade to an airy interior. Two superb Tintoretto paintings decorate the chancel, *Gathering of the Manna* and an otherworldly *Last Supper* in which Jesus administers communion while servants bustle to clear up the dishes.

Around the Accademia

With that egocentrism that Venice's admirers find so charming, and justified, the rambling **Gallerie dell'Accademia** is devoted almost exclusively to Venetian painting, from the 14th century of its emerging glory to the 18th century of its gentle decadence. We propose here only some of the collection's most representative highlights:

Room 1: the 14th-century *Coronation of the Madonna* of **Paolo Veneziano,** first of the city's great masters, already glows with characteristic Venetian colour and texture.

Room 2: **Giovanni Bellini,** youngest and most gifted member of the painter family, brings gentle humanity to his *Enthroned Madonna with Job and St. Sebastian* (1485).

Room 4: **Andrea Mantegna** makes his *St. George* a very cool dragon-killer, a most appropriate patron saint for England.

Room 5: **Giorgione's** *Tempest* (1505) is one of the museum's most cherished, most mysterious treasures, a girl calmly nursing her child in a landscape prickling with the electricity of the approaching storm.

Room 7: **Lorenzo Lotto,** troubled loner among Venice's 16th-century artists, portrays a *Gentleman in his Study* with subtle, sombre psychology.

Room 10: most important of Renaissance rooms. **Titian's** *Pietà,* a vibrant last work completed by pupil Palma il Giovane, was originally intended for his tomb in the Frari church (see p. 128); **Veronese's** *Feast in the House of Levi* was meant to be the Last Supper, until the Holy Inquisition complained about its "buffoons, drunkards, dwarfs, Germans, and similar vulgarities"; **Tintoretto** gives full play to his dark sense of drama in the *Miracle of St. Mark*.

Room 17: **Canaletto's** hugely popular 18th-century *vedute* (views) of Venice were aristocratic precursors of modern postcards; in such works as *Island of San Giorgio Maggiore,* **Francesco Guardi** sought more poetry and melancholy and died a pauper.

Room 20: **Gentile Bellini** breathes little life into the grand pageant of his *Procession on San Marco* (1496), but it remains a fascinating "photograph" of Renaissance Venice.

Room 21: **Vittore Carpaccio** depicts in nine canvases the bizarre *Story of St. Ursula,* a British princess, said to have led 11,000 virgins on a pilgrimage to Rome, all of whom were raped and slaughtered on their way back.

East along the Grand Canal, a breath of the 20th century awaits you at the **Peggy Guggenheim Collection** of modern art in the Palazzo Venier dei Leoni. Home of the American heiress until her death in 1979, this unfinished 18th-century palace provides a delightful setting for Picasso, Marcel Duchamp, Magritte, Kandinsky and Klee, but above all for her compatriots Jackson Pollock, Mark Rothko and Robert Motherwell. In the overgrown garden are sculptures by Giacometti, Henry Moore, and the collector's husband, Max Ernst. She herself is buried there.

Almost as familiar a silhouette as the San Marco campanile, the lovely octagonal domed church of **Santa Maria della Salute**—just *Salute* to its friends—is the masterpiece of Baldassare Longhena, built to mark the city's deliverance from a plague in 1630. For a Baroque edifice, the interior is remarkably sober, even chaste. Tintoretto's *Marriage at Cana* is on the wall opposite the entrance, while three of Titian's most vivid canvases decorate the **chancel:** *Cain and Abel, Abraham Sacrificing Isaac* and *David and Goliath,* their drama heightened by the perspective *di sotto in su* (looking up from below).

The **Zattere,** along the Giudecca canal, are quays for merchant and industrial shipping serving the Adriatic coast and eastern Mediterranean, a pleasant, uncrowded promenade. Behind the Stazione Marittima, where the big cruise-liners dock, seek out the church of **San Sebastiano,** a veritable monument to the genius of Veronese, whose home was nearby and who is buried in its left aisle. See his magnificent ceiling paintings of the *Story of Esther,* especially the great oval *Triumph of*

The silhouette of Santa Maria della Salute epitomizes Venice.

Mordecai, and the *Apotheosis of the Madonna* in the choir.

Over on the Grand Canal, the **Ca' Rezzonico** is a grand Baroque palace completed in the 18th century and now a museum dedicated to those sunset years of the Venetian Republic. When the last of the Rezzonico family disappeared, Elizabeth Barrett and Robert Browning bought the palazzo, and the poet died in a first-floor apartment in 1889. The extravagant ballroom, soaring allegorical frescoes like Giambattista Tiepolo's *Merit between Virtue and Nobility* in the "Throne Room" (actually for Rezzonico weddings) and others, more wistful, by Guardi, all catch the tone of a declining

Venice enraptured by its own legend.

All over the city, you'll find *scuole* that are not schools but old confraternities similar, minus their religious affiliation, to the Freemasons, Rotarians, Elks or Lions. North of Ca' Rezzonico, the **Scuola Grande di San Rocco** is Venice's richest confraternity, in a fine 16th-century chapter house next to its own church. Happily, Tintoretto was a member and created for the house some 50 paintings over a period of 23 years, a series comparable in grandeur to Giotto's frescoes in Padua or Masaccio's for the Brancacci chapel in Florence. In the Sala Grande, see the high drama of *Moses Striking Water from the Rock* and a fascinating *Temptation of Christ,* with Satan portrayed as a beautiful youth. Titian is something of an interloper here with a remarkable easel-painting of the *Annunciation.* Tintoretto's masterpiece in *chiaroscuro* effects is the grandiose *Crucifixion* in the Sala dell'Albergo. You'll find a self-portrait just right of the room's entrance.

The nearby brick and white marble Gothic Church of the **Frari** (full name Santa Maria Gloriosa dei Frari) is above all celebrated for the high altar adorned with Titian's jubilant *Assumption of the Madonna.* The master's only painting on such a massive scale is a triumph of primary reds, blues and yellows that irresistibly draw you up to the altar. Drag youself away to see his other work here, the *Madonna di Ca' Pesaro* (left aisle), in which St. Peter presents the Pesaro family to Mary. Venetian composer Monteverdi's tomb is in a chapel left of the altar, but Titian's own monumental tomb (in the right aisle) is a cold and ponderous 19th-century monstrosity. Donatello has sculpted a fine polychrome wood *John the Baptist* for his compatriots' **Florentine Chapel,** right of the altar.

Back on the Grand Canal again, Longhena's exuberant Baroque **Ca' Pesaro** is now the town's Modern Art Gallery, devoted principally to purchases from the Venice Biennale exhibitions. Italian artists—Futurists Giovanni Fattori and Telemaco Signorini and the Ferrara trio of Filippo de Pisis, Carlo Carrà and Giorgio de Chirico—are better represented than other Europeans, of whom Matisse, Klee and Ernst are the most notable.

Around the Rialto

The ancient commercial heart of the city, named after the 9th-century settlement on *Rivo Alto* (high bank), the **Rialto** spread over both sides of the Grand Canal. Here the oriental spices and silks were unloaded. The merchants went to the banks and the sailors to the brothels. Today, the action is in the food markets and boutiques. On the west bank, the **Pescheria** (fish market) bustles early in the morning, but the **Erberia** (fruit and vegetables) is worth a return visit in late afternoon when the barges are unloading their fresh produce at the Fabbriche Vecchie warehouses. Nobody knows for sure, but nobody dares dispute the locals' claim for the little 11th-century church of **San Giacomo di Rialto**—San Giacometto to them—as the town's oldest (decipher the Byzantine interior under its Baroque incrustations).

Coming from San Marco, follow the **Mercerie** on the east bank, an ever-busy shopping street, past the 16th-century church of **San Salvatore** (Titian fans pop inside for his *Transfiguration* over the silver reredos on the high altar and *Annunciation,* right aisle).

The 16th-century **Rialto Bridge** is no architectural gem—Antonio da Ponte wangled the contract over the likes of Michelangelo, Palladio and Sansovino —but it's still one of the liveliest spots in town. Until 1854, it was the Grand Canal's only bridge. Along the double row of shops with three lanes of pedestrian traffic, you'll find jewellery, clothing and shoes, a few treasures, but a lot of junk, too.

North-east of the bridge, past the Fondaco dei Tedeschi post office, seek out the little 15th-century church of **Santa Maria dei Miracoli.** Its refined façade of delicate inlaid coloured marble and intricately carved friezes has won it the name of "golden jewel box" *(scrigno d'oro),* its designer Pietro Lombardo more sculptor than architect.

It's worth mapping out carefully your visit to the **Campo Santi Giovanni e Paolo.** Follow the Calle Larga Giacinto Gallina to the Ponte del Cavallo humpbacked bridge for the all-important first view of the magnificent **equestrian statue** of Bartolomeo Colleoni dominating the square. With his last and greatest piece of sculpture brilliantly evoking all the fierce resolution of a *condottiere* riding into battle, Andrea Verrocchio need not regret abandoning painting to his pupil Leonardo da Vinci. (Verrocchio's clay model was cast in bronze shortly after his death by Alessandro Leopardi.) Colleoni willed his huge fortune to Venice on the understanding his monument would be on Piazza San Marco, but once dead, he had to settle for this spot, in front of the *Scuola* of San Marco, a very Venetian solution. The 13th-century Gothic church of **Santi Giovanni e Paolo,** compressed by Venetians into San Zanipolo, was the doges' funeral church.

129

Some 25 are buried here, many in masterpieces of monumental tombs. On the west wall, left of the entrance, is a fine Renaissance monument for Doge Pietro Mocenigo. In the choir is the 14th-century Gothic tomb of Doge Michele Morosini.

Returning to the Grand Canal, you'll find in the glorious **Ca' d'Oro** the quintessential decorative tradition of Venetian architecture, more successful in its compact form here than in the beautiful but sprawling Doges' Palace. Completed in 1440, its Flamboyant Gothic design has a flair and grace that bewitch you into imagining the long-gone gilt of its façade. Take another, more leisurely, boat-ride for the view from the canal. The treasures of its **Galleria Franchetti** of Renaissance art include Andrea Mantegna's *St. Sebastian* and fragments of the Titian and Giorgione frescoes that once adorned the Fondaco dei Tedeschi.

Off the Beaten Track

Among the corners of town far from the madding crowd, the old Jewish **Ghetto** (north-east of the railway station) is particularly peaceful and reveals a fascinating page of Venetian history. It was a local iron foundry, *ghetto* in Venetian dialect, which lent its name to this and scores of other enclaves for the forced isolation of Jewish communities throughout Europe. In 1516, some 900 Jews (rising to a peak of nearly 5,000 by the mid-17th century) were confined to what was then an island beyond the Cannaregio canal.

In the cramped quarters, they had to build the six- and eight-storey tenements you see today, twice as high as those permitted elsewhere. Some 20 Jewish families still live in the Ghetto.

On the island of the **Giudecca,** you'll find another of Palladio's great Venetian churches, the **Redentore.** The grace of its overall form is best viewed from across the canal, because, like St. Peter's in Rome, the dome disappears at closer quarters behind its elongated nave. The Giudecca takes its name either from the Jews *(Giudei)* who lived here in the 12th century or from the *Giudicati,* nobles banished here by ducal judgment. It's now a quiet refuge for fishermen, artists—and tourists seeking to escape the mob. The strange neo-Gothic fortress at the west end of the island is in fact an abandoned 19th-century grain mill, the **Mulino Stucky.**

Out in the lagoon, they have been manufacturing glass on the island of **Murano** since 1292, when the hazardous furnaces were moved away from the city centre. Today, its factories and shops are an undeniable tourist-trap, but the **museum** *(Museo Vetrario)* tracing the glass industry back to Roman times is worth a look. And many enjoy watching burly fellows blowing molten globules into cute little green giraffes. The island's quiet spot is the 12th-century Venetian-Byzantine church of **Santa Maria e San Donato,** with a good mosaic in the apse.

Fantastic masks such as these are time-honoured features of Venice's annual Carnival.

The island of **Burano** is a simple fishing village, true haven of tranquillity, old ladies making lace on the doorsteps of their brightly coloured houses, a few artists on the quay, no hustlers.

Hemingway's favourite old hangout, the romantically overgrown island of **Torcello,** beyond Burano, is one of the lagoon's oldest inhabited spots, very prosperous until emptied by malaria. The mosquitoes have gone but its superb **Cathedral** remains. Founded in the 7th century and reconstructed in 1008, it's probably the finest of the Venetian-Byzantine churches. In the apse there's a moving mosaic

of the Madonna above a frieze of the 12 Apostles. Notice, too, the fine Corinthian capitals on the slender Greek marble columns.

With its fine sandy beaches and smart hotels, the **Lido** is as restful as any fashionable seaside resort, but after a couple of days in Venice, its *cars* come as something of a shock. Nostalgics take tea in the Grand Hôtel des Bains to recall the decadent 1900s evoked there by Thomas Mann's novella (and Luchino Visconti's movie), *Death in Venice*.

VENETO

The Venetian mainland reflects some of the *Serenissima's* artistic glories, but the cities that came under its domination in the 15th century retain their individuality.

An *autostrada* links Venice to Padua, Vicenza and Verona for those in a hurry, but others should take the charming backroads.

The Brenta

When Venetian aristocrats gave up the high seas for a more leisurely life on the land, they built Palladian Renaissance villas and extravagantly frescoed Baroque country houses on the banks of the Brenta Canal between Venice and Padua. A romantic way to visit some of the best, is on the *burchiello,* a modern version of the rowing barge

that took the gentry, Casanova and Lord Byron to their trysts and parties in the country. (Get details from the city tourist office of the 8-hour trip, in either direction on alternate days, optional return by bus, from May to October.)

Otherwise, follow the canal along the pretty S11 country road to Padua. First stop, off a side road to Fusina, is Palladio's **La Malcontenta** (1571), to which a too flighty Venetian countess was sent to pine, malcontent, in exquisite isolation on the canal. The villa with its classical portico to catch the summer breezes was the architect's "visiting card" for scores of commissions, copied worldwide, especially in the cotton plantations of America's Deep South where elegant porch-living became an article of faith.

At nearby Oriago, the Palladian style can be seen in **Villa Gradenigo** and, at Mira, in the 18th-century **Villa Widmann.** The influence is clear even in the most spectacular of the Brenta villas, at Stra, the opulent **Villa Pisani** or Villa Nazionale. Built for the Pisani doges in 1756, with 200 rooms, Tiepolo frescoes in the ballroom, and vast park with pond, labyrinth and stables, it was bought by Napoleon in 1807 and subsequently hosted Tsars, Habsburg emperors and, for their first meeting in 1934, Hitler and Mussolini.

Padua *(Padova)*

This proud university town—Galileo taught physics here from 1592 to 1610—was a major centre of the Risorgimento reunification movement. Something of the old spirit remains at the handsome Neoclassical **Caffè Pedrocchi,** the activists' meeting place on a little square off bustling Piazza Cavour.

North along the Corso Garibaldi is the 14th-century **Scrovegni Chapel,** also known, because of its site among ruins of a Roman amphitheatre, as the Arena Chapel. As a penance for his father's usury, the patrician Enrico Scrovegni built the simple little hall in 1303 specifically for the great **Giotto frescoes,** beautifully preserved and indisputedly his. In 38 pictures arranged in three rows under a starry heavenly blue vault, Giotto tells the stories of Mary and Jesus. Among the most moving, look for the *Kiss of Judas,* the *Crucifixion* and the *Lamentation.* A monumental *Last Judgment* covers the entrance wall.

The entrance to Piazza del Santo south of the city centre is guarded by Donatello's grand **statue of Gattamelata,** the 15th-century condottiere Erasmo da Narni, perfect ideal of a Renaissance hero, whose "honeyed cat" nickname still mystifies historians. Behind him looms the 13th- and 14th-century **Basilica of Sant'Antonio,** known as Il Santo, named after the Portuguese-born Franciscan monk who died in Padua. The Romanesque façade makes a striking contrast with the six Byzantine cupolas and two minaret-like towers around a central Gothic cone-shaped dome. In the lofty Gothic interior, Donatello's sculptures at the **high altar** include a stoical *Crucifixion* and large bronze reliefs narrating St. Antony's miracles, notably the *Mule Adoring the Eucharist* and the healing of the *Irascible Son,* who cut off his foot in remorse at kicking his mother. The **Scuola di Sant'Antonio,** right of the church, has some Titian frescoes of the saint.

Vicenza

This is Andrea Palladio's home town and he has made of it a place in many ways more truly *serene* than the often more excitable Venice. At the centre, **Piazza dei Signori** is graced by his **Basilica** (1549), not a church, but the old Roman concept of a gathering place for the lawcourts of the Gothic Palazzo della Ragione that it encases with a colonnade and loggia. If you wonder what to think of it, Palladio's modest opinion was that it "ranked among the most noble and most beautiful edifices since ancient times, not only for its grandeur and ornaments, but

also its materials'' (hard white limestone). Inside is a museum of his designs and models.

The main commercial street is, inevitably, **Corso Palladio,** lined with the master's elegant mansions at nos. 42 and 165, and others by disciples. The 15th-century **Palazzo da Schio** (no. 147) is also known as Ca' d'Oro, after the famous Venetian Gothic palace. You'll find Palladio's best town palace where the Corso widens out into the Piazza Matteotti to give him more freedom for the wonderfully airy **Palazzo Chiericati.** Its Museo Civico houses works by Tintoretto, Veronese, Hans Memling and Van Dyck.

Set in a little garden, the audacious **Teatro Olimpico** is Palladio's last work (completed by Vincenzo Scamozzi in 1584). Facing an amphitheatre auditorium is a fixed décor of classical Roman statuary and columns with what look like three long streets leading away from the stage. It's quite a shock when you go through the archways and find the streets go back only a few feet, a simple illusion of perspective.

Take the N247 to Monte Berico and Palladio's most

Padua's market is held outside the Palazzo della Ragione.

celebrated building, the hilltop **Villa Rotonda.** Designed as a belvedere for Cardinal Capra in 1551, it's an exquisite piece of applied geometry, a domed rotonda set in a square surrounded on all four sides by simple Ionic-columned porticoes, offering different views of town and countryside with the changing light of day. Film-director Joseph Losey used the villa for his *Don Giovanni,* in which valet Leporello unrolls down the long staircase the list of his master's mistresses—1,003, *mill'e tre.*

Verona

A favourite of Roman emperors and the "barbarian" rulers that followed, the city likes to be known as *la Degna,* the Dignified, but it also has a very lively atmosphere, stimulated by its Adige river flowing swiftly down from the Dolomites. And perhaps by a memory of its fierce medieval history. The family feuds that inspired Shakespeare's *Romeo and Juliet* ended only with the 14th-century ascendancy of the tough Scaliger dynasty, in turn conquered by Venice in 1405.

The hub of city life is the vast Piazza Bra, with the town hall on its south side and the great **Roman Arena** dating back to A.D. 100. Only four of its outer arches survived an 1183 earthquake undamaged, but the inner arcade of 74 arches is intact. It seats 22,000. People in the top rows during the summer opera festival get a terrific view of the surrounding city.

Along the north side of the piazza, the Liston, a people-watcher's delight lined with smart cafés and restaurants, is *the* street for the Veronese bourgeoisie's evening stroll *(passeggiata)*. It leads to the boutiques, galleries and antique shops of the equally fashionable **Via Mazzini.**

Turn right at the end down Via Cappello for the 13th-century tavern that the local tourist industry understandably insists was **Juliet's House** *(Casa di Giulietta Cappelletti),* complete with balcony. Romantics arriving after closing time (6 p.m.) "with love's light wings o'erperch these walls; for stony limits cannot hold love out."

The **Piazza delle Erbe** along the ancient elongated Roman forum makes the prettiest of market-places. Its medieval houses and old umbrella-covered stalls surround a 14th-century fountain and a line of columns, one of which bears the lion of St. Mark, in old allegiance to Venice.

West of Piazza Bra, the massive brick 14th-century **Castelvecchio** fortress on the Adige river now houses an art museum. Its collections are principally of the Venetian school, notably Mantegna's *Holy Family,* a Giovanni Bellini *Madonna,* and Lorenzo Lotto's *Portrait of a Man,* attributed by some to Titian.

The austerely handsome 12th-century church of **San Zeno**

Famous for its skiing, Cortina d'Ampezzo is also popular with summer hikers.

Maggiore with superb bronze doors and imposing free-standing brick campanile is a rare jewel of Italian Romanesque architecture. (The 14th-century battlemented tower to the left is the remnant of an old abbey.) The dignity to which the town aspires is there in the simple interior, illuminated by the magnificent Mantegna **triptych** on the high altar.

DOLOMITES

The mountain landscape of Italy's eastern Alps is an exhilarating mixture of rich green Alpine meadows with jagged white limestone and rose-coloured granite peaks. Summer hiking in the largely German-speaking region of Alto Adige (Austrian South Tyrol till 1918) is a delight. Well-marked paths lead to farmhouses and rustic mountain-

restaurants where you can try the local bacon *(Speck)* or spinach dumplings *(Spinatknödl)* as a change from spaghetti—saves you carrying a picnic.

Bolzano *(Bozen)*

South Tyrol's historic capital makes a good base for hikes. It has a 14th-century Gothic **Church** with characteristically Austrian polychrome tiled roof. Inside is a fine 16th-century sculpted sandstone pulpit and marble high altar. Get your hiking equipment on the old arcaded shopping street, Via dei Portici *(Laubengasse)*. Then head north-east of town to the **Renon** *(Ritten)* plateau for wonderful views of the Dolomite peaks, reached by cableway and rack railway.

Cortina d'Ampezzo

The queen of Italian winter sports resorts has elegant hotels, smart boutiques and a bouncing nightlife. In its sunny sheltered basin high in the Boite valley of the eastern Dolomites, it provides excellent skiing facilities as well as skating and bobsleigh. It, too, is a favourite with summer hikers. Take the cable car to **Tofana di Mezzo** for an awesome view clear down to the Venetian lagoon. Equally spectacular are the panoramas from the **Belvedere di Pocol** and **Tondi di Faloria.**

EMILIA-ROMAGNA

The two regions were united at the time of the Risorgimento, with Emilia following the Apennines from Bologna to Piacenza while Romagna covers the eastern area of Ravenna and the Adriatic resorts around Rimini down to Cattolica.

Rimini

The Adriatic coast, of which Rimini is the chief resort, has wide sandy beaches, at some points stretching 300 metres (1,000 ft.) from the water's edge back to the dunes. Its lively hotels, beach clubs and myriad discos make Rimini a favourite playground for the sun-soakers, while the fishing port remains peaceful.

Inland, on the other side of the railway, is the old city that was Ariminium to the Romans. The 27 B.C. **triumphal arch** *(Arco d'Augusto),* anachronistically ornamented with medieval battlements, stands at the junction of the imperial highways from Rome, Via Flaminia and Via Aemilia (which gave the region its name). The **Ponte di Tiberio** bridge built over the Marecchia river in A.D. 21 is still in use. The unfinished 15th-century **Tempio Malatestiano** is an important Renaissance design of Leon Battista Alberti, incorporating elements of the Arco d'Augusto in the façade. More pagan temple than church, it served as a

mausoleum for the cultivated but cruel tyrant, Sigismondo Malatesta, and his mistress (later wife), Isotta degli Atti.

To the south of Rimini are the resorts of **Riccione,** very popular, and the quieter **Cattolica,** while **Cesenatico,** to the north, has a colourful fishing port.

🏛 Ravenna

For those who find it difficult to appreciate mosaics as we usually see them, in fading indecipherable fragments, the beautifully preserved mosaic decoration of Ravenna's churches, up to 1,500 years old, come as an exciting revelation. They stand at the summit of the art as orig-

Mosaic at Sant'Apollinare depicts theme of sacrifice.

inally practised by the Greeks and Romans.

Now some 10 kilometres (6 mi.) from the sea, the ancient capital of the western Roman Empire was once a flourishing port on the Adriatic. Emperor Honorius made it his capital in 402, followed by his sister Galla Placidia. Ruled in the early 6th century by Theodoric, king of the Ostrogoths, it was recaptured for Emperor Justinian and Byzantine culture left its mark for another two centuries.

139

You'll see something of the town's Venetian-dominated era on the graceful **Piazza del Popolo**, bordered by the 17th-century Palazzo Comunale—Venetian insignia on the piazza's two columns have been replaced by local saints Apollinaris and Vitalis. Next to the church of San Francesco, in a building of 1780, is the **tomb of Dante,** who died here, in exile, in 1321, with a fellow poet's epitaph: "Here I lie buried, Dante, exile from my birthplace, son of Florence, that loveless mother."

The oldest of the Byzantine monuments, in the northern corner of the city centre, is the 5th-century **Mausoleum of Galla Placidia.** Three sarcophagi stand in the cross-shaped chapel, but no one knows if her remains are in one of them. The deep blue, gold and crimson mosaics on the vaults and arches depict *St. Laurence,* the *Apostles* and the *Good Shepherd Feeding His Sheep* (over the entrance).

In the same grounds is the magnificent three-storey brick church of **San Vitale,** consecrated in 547. Its narthex is set at an angle to the main entrance (through a Renaissance porch). The octagonal construction provides the interior with seven

But Ravenna provides more than just food for the spirit.

exedrae or recesses, the eighth being the choir and apse. Try to come on a bright morning when the sun provides natural illumination for the mosaics. The Old Testament scenes, such as *Abraham Sacrificing Isaac* are more lively than the rigidly formal Emperor Justinian and Empress Theodora, with their court retinue, and Christ between two angels, St. Vitalis and, far right, Bishop Ecclesius holding a model of the church. The cloisters house a National Museum of Roman, early Christian and Byzantine sculpture.

You can see the art of mosaics still being practised in workshops along the nearby Via Giuliano Argentario.

Next to the cathedral, the 5th-century **Battistero Neoniano** (Baptistery of Bishop Neon) has a fine mosaic procession of the Apostles. It was originally a Roman bath.

East of the city centre, the early 6th-century church of **Sant'Apollinare Nuovo** was built by the Christianized Ostrogoth king Theodoric. In the nave, classic Byzantine mosaics show on the left, Ravenna's fortified port of Classe, from which a procession of 22 virgins follows the three Magi with gifts for Jesus on his mother's lap; on the right, from Theodoric's palace, 26 martyrs carry jewelled crowns.

Five kilometres (3 mi.) south of the town, protected only by a couple of cypresses from an incongruous wilderness of highways and bleak urban development, stands the lovely church of **Sant'Apollinare in Classe** (549), next to it, a splendid cylindrical 11th-century Romanesque campanile. In the apse of the Greek-columned interior is a delightful mosaic of St. Apollinaris, Ravenna's first martyr and bishop, surrounded by sheep, with Moses and Elijah in the clouds above him.

Bologna

The capital of Emilia-Romagna is a thriving town with a certain patrician atmosphere to its elegantly arcaded historic centre. It is the home of Europe's oldest university, established in the 11th century on the foundation of a renowned law school dating back even earlier, to the end of the Roman empire. Bologna also boasts of the diploma its Philharmonic Academy gave Mozart in 1770—though he might have done quite well without it. The town's revered place in Italian gastronomy compares to that of Lyon in France.

On the west flank of the handsome Piazza Maggiore, the massive medieval **Palazzo Comunale** with its Renaissance porch is a striking expression of Bologna's civic power. The 14th-century basilica of **San Petronio** ranks among the most imposing of Italy's Gothic churches. It has a fine **central portal** with reliefs of Old Testament scenes on its pilasters sculpted with great dignity and power by Jacopo della Quercia. Adam's pose in the *Creation* scene (top left) inspired the Michelangelo figure reaching out to God on the Sistine Chapel ceiling. The soaring vaults of the sober interior have the monumentality of French or German Gothic.

In the adjoining square, the 16th-century **Neptune Fountain** is one of the town's most popular symbols, for which Giambologna sculpted the bronze sea god surrounded by nymphs and cherubs.

A medieval atmosphere clings to the old houses in the tiny streets behind the Metropolitana cathedral to the north. At the end of the busy Via Rizzoli, the two **leaning towers** are all that remain of a whole forest of medieval status-symbols—like those of San Gimignano in Tuscany (see pp. 101–102). The 12th-century Torre degli Asinelli, 97.6 metres (320 ft.), is the taller, with 498 steps to its rooftop view.

You'll find the city's characteristic arcaded **palazzi** along the Via Zamboni leading past the university to the **Pinacoteca Nazionale.** The Pinacoteca's fine collection is devoted in large part to the Bologna school,

most notably the Baroque paintings of the Carracci family, of whom Annibale was the most gifted—see his *Annunciation* and *Madonna in Glory*. Look out for Raphael's important *Ecstasy of St. Cecilia* and Parmigianino's *Madonna di Santa Margherita.*

South of the city centre, the founder of the Dominican order is buried in the church of **San Domenico,** 13th-century but with many 18th-century Baroque modifications. The monk's marble **tomb,** *(Arca di San Domenico,* 6th chapel, right aisle) was designed by Nicola Pisano with additional works by Nicolò dell'Arca and the 20-year-old Michelangelo. He did the saints Petronius and Proculus, and the angel on the right—first and last time he ever put wings on an angel.

Ferrara

A half-hour's drive from Bologna on the *autostrada* takes you to this stronghold of the high-living d'Este dukes, archetypal scheming, murderous, lovable Renaissance villains. In their formidable **Castello Estense,** 14th-century moated fortress, guides tell delightfully dubious stories of what went on in the dungeons.

You get a sense of the dukes' grandeur among the Renaissance palazzi of the **Corso Ercole I d'Este,** part of a 15th-century urban expansion, *Addizione Erculea,* that was one of the most ambitious pieces of town planning of its age. The d'Estes' **Palazzo dei Diamanti** (12,000 pieces of diamond-shaped marble on its walls) houses the Pinacoteca Nazionale, with works of the Ferrara masters Cosmè Tura, Ercole de' Roberti, Garofalo and Dosso Dossi.

The triple-gabled 13th-century **Cathedral** still has its loggia of shops attached to the south wall. The cathedral museum exhibits two major works by Cosmè Tura, *St. George* and the *Annunciation,* and sculptures by Jacopo della Quercia, *Madonna of the Pomegranate* and *St. Maurelius.*

Parma

The home of two famous painters, Correggio and Parmigianino, has much more to offer than just that great cheese and ham. The **Piazza del Duomo** forms a wonderfully harmonious space for the graceful octagonal baptistery and the austere nobility of the 12th-century Romanesque **Cathedral** and its 13th-century campanile. Inside, on the ceiling of the central octagonal dome, are the grandiose Correggio **frescoes** of the *Assumption of the Virgin* (1530). In this, his masterpiece, Correggio has achieved, in the truest sense, exalting emotion without the sentimentality of Mannerist imitators.

The lovely 13th-century pink Verona marble **Baptistery** has superbly sculpted doors by Benedetto Antelami, who also carved most of the 12 statues of the months in the interior.

Behind the cathedral, the 16th-century Renaissance church of **San Giovanni Evangelista** also has in its dome a fine Correggio fresco of the *Vision of St. John on Patmos.* Look out, too, for the Parmigianino frescoes in the 1st, 2nd and 4th chapels on the left aisle. In the 16th-century Renaissance church of **Madonna della Steccata** (Via Garibaldi), Parmigianino painted the frescoes of the *Foolish and Wise Virgins* on the arch above the high altar.

In the charming **Camera di San Paolo** (Via Melloni), you'll find the Benedictine convent's private dining room for the highly unconventional abbess, Giovanna da Piacenza. She commissioned Correggio to decorate it in 1518 (his first work) with mischievous *putti* angels and a very pagan view of Chastity as symbolized by the goddess Diana.

The **Galleria Nazionale** (on Piazzale Marconi) exhibits more excellent works of Correggio and Parmigianino, and a sketch of a young girl, *Testa di Fanciulla,* by Leonardo da Vinci.

THE NORTH-WEST

Lombardy, Piedmont and the Ligurian coast together make up the country's most prosperous region. Industry and commerce have made the fortune of its three great cities—Milan, Turin and Genoa. If the latter has drawn on the riches of the seas, Milan and Turin, in close contact with France and Germany across the Alps, have had the added underpinning of a flourishing agriculture in their Po valley hinterland. The lords of this constant economic expansion also called on the greatest artists both from Italy and beyond, from Jan Van Eyck to Leonardo da Vinci.

The region has won world recognition in the vanguard of the arts, of modern design in clothes and furniture, and of the automobile and communications industries.

For relaxation, the Italian Riviera east and west of Genoa alternates a rugged coastline with fine sandy beaches. Hugging the slopes of Mont Blanc (Monte Bianco), Courmayeur is Italy's oldest ski resort. North and east of Milan are the romantic lakes Como, Maggiore and Garda.

MILAN

Quite happy to leave the politics of national government to Rome, this is clearly the country's economic and cultural capital. Despite its prestigious museums and magnificent cathedral, tourists do not think of Milan as an obvious holiday destination (though some do make the pilgrimage just for Leonardo da Vinci's *Last Supper*). But anyone interested in contemporary Italian life will want to hang out a few days in its cafés and restaurants, elegant shopping avenues and side-street art galleries. If the main railway station is a monstrous reminder of Mussolini, the Pirelli skyscraper opposite is a more graceful symbol of the new era. With its vivacious residents, fashion-conscious and self-assured to the point of pushy, this is *the* modern city of Italy.

Lighting a candle for a moment of meditation in Milan Cathedral.

144

Around the Duomo

Nowhere does a cathedral more dominate a major city centre. Almost non-stop throughout the day, but especially at that magic moment of the *passeggiata,* the **Piazza del Duomo** is one of the liveliest squares in all Europe. People gather around the cafés, kiosks and shopping arcades, the young discussing music and clothes, their fathers arguing politics and business, and everybody talking football.

And all in the shadow of the **Duomo,** most grandiose of Italy's Flamboyant Gothic cathedrals. Teams of Italian, French, Flemish and German architects and sculptors contributed to this astonishing cathedral, begun in 1386. For the best view of that awesomely rich façade, finished in 1813, and bristling silhouette

of marble pinnacles and statues, stand in the courtyard of the Palazzo Reale south of the cathedral. (It houses the Cathedral Museum, which displays fine examples of Gothic sculpture from the façade.) The cathedral's interior is a vast and noble space, showing its north European influence in the soaring columns and a decoration of **stained glass windows**, from the 15th century to the present day.

Give yourself plenty of time for a spectacular walk out on the **roof.** The elevator entrance (clearly signposted outside the cathedral) is in the right transept. Wander high above the city turmoil under the flying buttresses and around the statues (2,245 in all) and pinnacles (135), up to the roof-ridge for an unbeatable view of the city. To go down, take the staircase (158 steps) for some fascinating close-ups of the cathedral's construction.

West of the Piazza del Duomo, tucked away between the busy Via Orefici and Via Mercanti, is the last vestige of the medieval city, **Piazza Mercanti.** The 13th-century seat of communal government on its south side, Palazzo della Ragione, has a fine Romanesque equestrian relief of a *podestà*

It took 500 years to complete the cathedral's Gothic façade.

(chief magistrate). It stands opposite the elegant porticoed Palazzo dei Giureconsulti (1564).

Leading north from the Piazza del Duomo, the huge cross-shaped shopping arcade of the **Galleria Vittorio Emanuele** is a splendid monument in steel and glass to the expansive commercial spirit of the 19th century. Today, cafés, restaurants, bookshops, boutiques and the tourist office bathe in its unabashed neo-Renaissance décor.

In the winter, the Galleria provides a sheltered, albeit draughty, passage from the Duomo to another holy of holies, the 18th-century **La Scala** theatre, high temple of opera. Even if you can't be there for an opera (opening with a gala to end all galas every sacrosanct December 7), attend a concert there or at least visit the little museum (left of the theatre), if only for a chance to see the sumptuous Neoclassical auditorium with its six tiers of balconies and galleries.

Milan's most prestigious thoroughfare is **Via Monte Napoleone,** an august parade of Neoclassical palazzi and luxury shops. Narrow side streets such as Via Borgospesso, Via Sant'Andrea and Via Bagutta take you into a more tranquil 18th-century world, now graced by art galleries, antique shops and the town's smarter *trattorie*.

Around Castello Sforzesco

The massive brick fortress, the **Castello Sforzesco,** north-west of the city centre, was rebuilt in its present form in the 15th century by Duke Francesco Sforza. The bulk of the solid square structure stands around a vast courtyard, Piazza d'Armi. Beyond, in the handsome old residential quarters of the Corte Ducale, is the entrance to the Castello Sforzesco **art museums,** devoted to sculpture, painting *(Pinacoteca),* ceramics, furniture and archaeology. In collections that include important works by Giovanni Bellini, Mantegna, Titian, Correggio and Tintoretto, pride of place—and a room to itself—goes to Michelangelo's last work, the unfinished Rondanini *Pietà* (1564). Working on it until six days before his death, the sculptor chiselled a pathetic Mary struggling to hold up the dead Jesus, strange throwback to medieval sculpture for his last tussle with recalcitrant stone.

Behind the castle is a delightful English-style **park** for a rest away from the city and even a dream of tropical lands among the exotic fish of the municipal Aquarium in one corner.

Reflections merge past and present in a boutique window.

Even without Leonardo da Vinci's masterpiece in the adjoining refectory, the church of **Santa Maria delle Grazie** (Via Caradosso, south-west of the Castello) would be worth a visit as a jewel of Renaissance architecture. Adding to an earlier late Gothic design, Donato Bramante—Pope Julius II's chief architect in Rome—fashioned in 1492 a magnificent red brick and white stone chancel *(tribuna)*. The graceful lines of the rectangular choir and 16-sided cupola are best viewed from the little cloister that Bramante built on the north side. Inside the church, stand in the choir to appreciate the full majesty of the dome.

Leonardo da Vinci's **Last Supper** *(Cenacolo)* is being lovingly resuscitated in the little Dominican refectory to the left of the church. Despite centuries of deterioration and clumsy restoration since it was completed in 1497, there is enormous psychological impact in Leonardo's depiction of the trauma for each of the disciples when Jesus declares: "One of you will betray me." Almost as awe-inspiring as the painting itself is a glimpse of the immense effort going since 1979 into the painstaking centimetre-by-centimetre recovery of the fragmentary but still powerful traces of the "real Leonardo". We can now see, for example, that Philip (third to the right) has an expression of acute grief rather than the simpering pathos left

---

Autopsy of a Masterpiece

The great culprit in the disintegration of the Last Supper *was not so much Milan's infamous humidity or modern pollution as Leonardo himself—or at least the understandable demands of his genius.*

For this summit of his life's work, Leonardo did not want to suffer the restrictions of fresco —painting onto damp plaster. A fresco was painted section by section without modifying once dry, thus denying him the chance to add that overall shadowy sfumato effect that gave his paintings their psychological depth and subtlety. Nor would the sustained effort demanded by a fresco's damp plaster permit him, as was his habit, to leave the painting when inspiration deserted him, to go and work on something else.

So Leonardo preferred a tempera with oil and varnish on an ideally dry surface, in fact a disastrous choice for the damp climate. Deterioration was already noted in 1517, when Leonardo was still alive. By the time fellow artist Giorgio Vasari saw it a generation later, there was "nothing visible but a muddle of blots". It's a miracle that 400 more years of dust and smog have left anything at all.

by "restorers" who presumed to improve on the original.

For another aspect of Leonardo da Vinci's talents, visit the **Science Museum** *(Museo della Scienza e della Tecnica)* in the nearby Via San Vittore. Among the rooms devoted to the history of science and technology, one gallery is reserved for **Leonardo's inventions,** displayed as models constructed from his notebooks. You'll see his aircraft, a machine for making screws, hydraulic timber-cutter, revolving bridge, various machine-tools and a system of map-making by aerial views long before any aircraft, even his, was operational.

At the eastern end of Via San Vittore, beyond a noble atrium courtyard, the church of **Sant' Ambrogio** is the city's most revered sanctuary, built from the 9th to the 12th century. It stands on a foundation that dates back to the time of St. Ambrose (340–397), first bishop of Milan and one of the Church's four founding fathers (with Peter, Paul and Jerome). Its sober five-bayed façade is characteristic Lombard Romanesque, flanked by a 9th-century campanile and taller 12th-century tower topped by a modern loggia. In the interior, left of the centre nave, notice an 11th-century **pulpit** standing on a Christian sarcophagus of the Roman era. Under a canopy carved with Roman-esque-Byzantine reliefs, is the **high altar,** richly encased in bejewelled and enamelled plates of gold and silver.

The Brera and Other Museums

The handsome 17th-century palace of the Jesuits is now the **Pinacoteca di Brera,** one of the country's foremost art museums. In its fine arcaded courtyard, notice a bronze statue of Napoleon, remarkable rare example of the emperor with no clothes. (It was he who turned the Brera into a national gallery with confiscations from the Church and recalcitrant nobles.)

Among the highlights: two paintings by Giovanni Bellini of the *Madonna and Child* and a highly personal *Pietà;* Veronese's *Jesus in the Garden;* Tintoretto's dramatic *Discovery of St. Mark's Body;* and an impressive *Christ at the Column* by Donato Bramante.

Mantegna has a touching *Madonna,* but his masterpiece here is the *Dead Christ,* achieving a gripping emotional effect with its foreshortened perspective. Piero della Francesca's celebrated *Montefeltro altarpiece* (1474) is his last work.

The gentle beauty of Correggio's *Nativity* and *Adoration of the Magi* and Raphael's stately *Betrothal of the Virgin* contrast with the earthier inspiration of Caravaggio's *Supper at Emmaus.*

The non-Italian artists include El Greco, Rubens, Van Dyck and Rembrandt. In the modern collection, look out for Modigliani, Boccioni, de Chirico, Carrà and de Pisis.

The **Biblioteca Ambrosiana** (Piazza Pio XI) was the 17th-century palace and library of Cardinal Federigo Borromeo. Its principal treasure is Leonardo da Vinci's luminous *Portrait of a Musician* (1485), unfinished but at the same time the best preserved of the master's few surviving works. You can see his pervasive influence on Milanese artists in the decorative paintings of Bernardino Luini and a fine *Portrait of a Young Woman* by Ambrogio de Predis. Nothing sweet about Caravaggio's *Bowl of Fruit*—the worm is in the apple and the leaves are withering. Travellers on their way to or from Rome will be especially interested in Raphael's cartoons (preparatory drawings) for his *School of Athens* fresco in the Vatican.

The **Poldi-Pezzoli Museum** (Via Manzoni 12) is a small, formerly private collection. Its prize pieces include Piero della Francesca's *San Nicola da Tolentino,* Mantegna's *Madonna and Child,* a Botticelli *Madonna* and Antonio Pollaiuolo's lovely *Portrait of a Young Woman.*

LOMBARDY

This central part of the Po valley is only a fraction of the Italian lands conquered by the Lombards when they crossed the Alps from eastern Europe in the early Middle Ages. But it has proved the most fruitful, all too tempting to the acquisitive appetites of France, Spain and rival Italian duchies and city-states such as Venice, which pushed its Republic as far west as Bergamo. Natural fertility was enhanced by Europe's most advanced systems of irrigation, still operating in the medieval canals that you'll see on your way south to Pavia. Lombardy's rice, wheat and maize are the main basis of the nation's *risotto, pasta* and *polenta.*

On a more sentimental note, the three major lakes at the foot of the Lombardy Alps, Garda, Como and Maggiore, are perfect settings for mending broken hearts, breaking mended hearts and all romantic conditions in between.

Pavia

The Lombards' first capital, before Milan, is now a sleepy red-brick university town. Its principal attraction, the spectacular Charterhouse or **Certosa di Pavia** is in fact some 10 kilometres (6 mi). north of the city, a 30-minute drive from Milan. Built by Gian Galeazzo Visconti,

Duke of Milan, for his family mausoleum, the monastery's 15th-century church is a high point in the transition from Flamboyant Gothic to Renaissance. Even without the originally designed crowning gable, the sculpted marble **façade** makes a dazzling impact, with its statues of prophets, saints and apostles above the medallion reliefs of Roman emperors.

The Gothic interior is lightened by the brightly coloured paving and groin-vaulting. Among the chapels which were given Baroque finishings in the late 16th century, notice an exquisite Perugino altarpiece of *God the Father*. Right of the triumphant Baroque high altar, is a beautifully carved 15th-century lavabo (ritual basin) and a charming *Madonna and Child* by Bernardino Luini. In the right transept is the Visconti tomb, and a door leading to the lovely small cloister of russet terracotta, with a fine view of the church's galleried octagonal tower. Since 1947, Cistercians have taken over from the Carthusian monks but continue the manufacture of herbal liqueurs.

Bergamo

Rising out of the plain of the Po valley on its own steep little hill, 47 kilometres (30 mi.) east of Milan, the delightful town of Bergamo makes a welcome break in the monotony of the *autostrada*. The city has a proud soldiering history, giving the Venetian Republic a famous *condottiere,* Bartolomeo Colleoni (see p. 129), and the largest contingent in Garibaldi's 1,000 Red Shirts. The Città Bassa (lower city) at the foot of the hill, is the modern town of shops, hotels and restaurants—serving a savoury *risotto* they insist is superior to Milan's. **Piazza Matteotti** is the hub of the town's lively café scene, along the Sentierone arcades. Opposite is the Teatro Donizetti and a monument showing the Bergamo-born opera composer accompanied by the naked lady he is said always to have needed for inspiration.

Venetian ramparts still protect the historic **Città Alta** (upper city) up on the hill. The gracious **Piazza Vecchia** is surrounded by Renaissance public edifices, notably the **Palazzo della Ragione** with a medieval Torre del Comune—take the lift to the rooftop view over the Po valley to the Alps. The town's most venerable edifice is the 12th-century Romanesque church of **Santa Maria Maggiore.** Notice the finely carved monumental north porch and slender campanile. The Baroque interior has impressive 16th-century tapestries and inlaid wooden choir stalls and beautiful intarsia work

153

at the altar rail. Adjacent to the church is the Renaissance **Colleoni Chapel**, an ostentatious mausoleum in red, white and green marble.

A short walk from the Città Alta's Porta Sant'Agostino, the **Galleria dell'Accademia Carrara** has an important Mantegna *Madonna and Child* and interesting works by Bellini, Lotto, Raphael and Titian.

Lake Garda

On the west shore, the people of Salò, where Gaspare Bertolotti is regarded as originator of the violin, suggest his design was inspired by the contours of the lake. But Italy's largest lake is shaped more like a banjo, 52 kilometres (32 mi.) from the ruggedly romantic cliffs of the neck down to its broad "sound box", 18 kilometres (10 mi.) across, surrounded by rolling green hills. Graced with vineyards (notably Bardolino), lemon trees, olives and cedars, the lake enjoys mild winters and mellow summers.

At the south end, boat cruises start out from Peschiera, Sirmione and Desenzano, particularly recommended for dramatic views of the east shore's mountains and the beautiful **Punta di San Vigilio**, with its little church

and 16th-century Villa Guarienti. Begin your road tour out on the narrow **Sirmione** promontory. This fishing village and renowned spa resort affords a splendid view of the lake from the tower of the 13th-century castle, **Rocca Scaligera**. The drive itself, along the winding **Gardesana Occidentale** cut through the cliffs of the west shore, is spectacular.

Grape harvesting is a joy in Lake Garda's vineyards.

The resort-town of **Gardone Riviera** is much appreciated for its parks and botanical gardens and as a base for hikes back into the hills. Above the resort, in Gardone di Sopra, is a 20th-century "folly", **Il Vittoriale,** bizarre and disturbing residence of Gabriele d'Annunzio, poet, adventurer, fascist. Melancholy gardens of dark laurel and cypresses lead up to a mausoleum of the writer's sarcophagus flanked by those of his disciples.

It overlooks the prow of a World War I warship, the *Puglia,* hauled up the hillside as the crowning piece of his relics, for which the villa is a museum: two cars in which he drove to his war exploits and the aircraft from which he dropped propaganda leaflets over Vienna (see p. 37).

Lake Como

Embraced by green wooded escarpments, the lake favoured by some of England's most romantic 19th-century poets, Wordsworth, Shelley and Byron, retains a certain wistful atmosphere for the leisure hours of the Milanese. As at Garda, a mild climate nurtures luxuriant vegetation in the villa gardens and parks.

The lake divides into two arms on either side of the tranquil resort town of **Bellagio,** which juts out on a hilly promontory. Up on the heights above the town, the elegant 18th-century **Villa Serbelloni** stands in the middle of a beautiful park of rose trees, camelias, magnolias and pomegranates. (Not to be confused with the Villa Serbelloni luxury hotel down near the lake front.) You can take a bracing swim at the lido at the southern end of town. Lake cruises—and car-ferries—leave from the Lungolario Marconi.

The lake's south-west arm is the most attractive for your excursions. From Lezzeno, take a boat cruise to see the colourful grottoes, and look out for the waterfall at Nesso. **Como** itself is a factory town, but has a handsome Gothic-Renaissance cathedral crowned by a superb Baroque dome added in 1744 by Turin's great architect, Filippo Juvarra. It stands next to the

arcaded Broletto, 13th-century seat of municipal government.

The western shores of the lake are lined with gracious villas nestling in perfumed gardens. At **Cernobbio,** the 16th-century Villa d'Este is now a hotel where you can at least take tea as an excuse to stroll among the cypresses and magnolias. Between the genteel resort towns of Tremezzo and Cadenabbia, you'll find one of the lake's most

A garlanded maiden watches over the Isola Bella's garden-terraces in the middle of Lake Maggiore.

beautiful residences (open to the public), the 18th-century **Villa Carlotta.** There's a marvellous view of the lake from its terraced gardens, famous for the display of camelias, rhododendrons and azaleas in late April and May.

Lake Maggiore

The northern, more blustery end of the lake lies in Switzerland, but the rest shares the other lakes' mellow climate. The resort towns offer excellent opportunities for relaxation and sports on longer stays, but for short visits, you'll get a better idea of the lake on a boat cruise (3–4 hours, with a meal on board, from Stresa, Baveno or Pallanza) than by road.

Close to the western shore, the **Borromean Islands** *(Isole Borromee)* are celebrated for their Baroque palazzi and magnificent gardens. They are still the property of the Borromeo family that provided Milan with its greatest cardinals. The 17th-century palazzo on **Isola Bella** is decorated with admirable paintings by Annibale Carracci, Tiepolo, Zuccarelli and Giordano. The terraced gardens constitute one of the finest ensembles of the Italian formal style. View the lake from the uppermost of the ten terraces, by the unicorn statue that is the Borromeo family emblem. **Isola dei Pescatori** is a delightfully peaceful fishing village with tiny narrow streets, while **Isola Madre,** further out in the lake, is the largest of the islands and almost deserted, except for its palazzo and botanical garden inhabited by peacocks and pheasants among the palms and rhododendrons.

Stresa is the principal resort. The lakeside promenade, Lungolago, is famous for its flowers and bewitching view of the islands. Take the cable-car to the peak of the **Mottarone** at 1,491 metres (4,892 ft.) for its exhilarating view of the Lombardy lakes, the Alps and Po valley. A toll-road will also take you there via the Giardino Alpinia (Alpine Garden), displaying over 2,000 varieties of mountain plants.

PIEDMONT *(Piemonte)*

As its name suggests, this region of the upper basin of the Po river lies in the foothills of the Alps.

From the fall of the Roman Empire to the 19th century, it stood outside the mainstream of Italian history. Its royal House of Savoy walked a diplomatic tightrope between the rivalries of France, Switzerland, Spain and the German emperors until the fall of Napoleon. The new nationalism led Piedmont into the Italian orbit at the head of the Risorgimento unification movement, and the House of Savoy provided the first king of united Italy.

Close links to France have left their mark. A French patois is still spoken in hill villages and you'll notice bilingual street signs in the Aosta Valley (geographically part of Piedmont, but administratively separate). The country's most venerable ski resort, on the Italian side of Mont Blanc, is known as Courmayeur, not Cortemaggiore. The classical palaces and squares of Turin, Piedmont's royal capital, are in many ways closer in spirit to France than the rest of Italy. But whatever cooler Gallic ambience this may have created has been thoroughly "Italianized" by the steady influx of workers from the south for the steel, chemical, automobile and communications industries.

Turin *(Torino)*

Best known for its industry, most notably the giant Fiat automobile works, the proud Piedmontese capital is far from being a dull or dismal factory town. It has retained the checkerboard layout of its origins as a Roman *castrum*. Its rise to prominence in the 17th and 18th centuries was accompanied by Italy's first coherent urban planning and the classical and Baroque palaces and monuments give its main streets and squares a great dignity and panache.

The tone is set by the formal elegance of the **Piazza Castello,** dominated by Filippo Juvarra's richly articulated Baroque façade for the **Palazzo Madama.** The original medieval castle received its new name when transformed in the 17th century into the royal residence of Vittorio Amedeo I's widow, Maria Cristina. It now houses the **Civic Museum** *(Museo Civico di Arte Antica)* beside a splendid ceremonial staircase, also designed by Juvarra. The paintings include Jan Van Eyck's 14th-century miniatures for the *Book of Hours of the Duc de Berry,* Pontormo's *St. Michael* and a particularly handsome *Portrait of a Young Man* by Sicilian master Antonello da Messina. On upper floors are the royal collections of furniture, ceramics and carved ivories.

Across the square is the former royal chapel, the 17th-century church of **San Lorenzo,** designed by Turin's other great Baroque architect, Fra Guarino Guarini. Philosopher and mathematician as well as priest, he has created a marvellously intricate interior surrounding the octagonal space with 16 red marble columns. Arches rise to hold the central lanterned cupola formed by an 8-pointed star.

At the **Armoury** *(Armeria Reale),* take a look at the interesting collection of Asian and European weapons and armour dating back to Roman and Etruscan times. Then relax a while behind the Palazzo Reale in its **Royal Gardens,** designed by Louis XIV's Versailles landscape-architect, André Le Nôtre.

The late 15th-century **Cathedral** cherishes one of Italy's most celebrated relics, the shroud said to have enveloped Jesus on his descent from the cross, taking the imprint of his face and body. Kept in the **Chapel of the Holy Shroud,** *(Cappella della Santa Sindone),* it was brought to Turin in the 17th century after a journey 200 years earlier from Jerusalem to France via Cyprus. Measuring 4.1 by 1.4 metres (13 by 5 ft.), the sheet is kept in an iron-boxed silver casket placed in a marble urn on the altar. Modern scientific tests have not provided conclusive authentification, but even sceptics visit its black marble chapel, a masterpiece of Guarini's High Baroque, with its cone-shaped dome formed by a web of intersecting arches that rise to a 12-pointed star. From outside, the chapel's spire looks like a three-tiered pagoda.

The pride of Turin, as in so many Italian cities, is not in one monument but in a glorious square, the **Piazza San Carlo**, one of the most beautiful in Europe. The 17th-century palazzi make an exquisite setting for your late afternoon *passeggiata* along the arcades of shops and cafés, culminating in the graceful symmetry of two Baroque churches, Juvarra's Santa Cristina and its twin, San Carlo. Stretching north and south of the square is the town's most elegant shopping street and main axis, Via Roma.

North-east of the piazza, in the Palazzo dell'Accademia delle Scienze, is the **Egyptian Museum** *(Museo Egizio)* second in importance only to Cairo's. Its treasures include statues of the Pharaohs of 1500 B.C., of Tutankhamen and the god Amen-Ra, as well as a mummified crocodile, and artefacts of everyday life, combs, clothes, kitchen utensils, even food.

On the second floor, is the **Galleria Sabauda** (Savoy Gallery), with an important collection of Italian and European art. The Italian works include a Fra Angelico *Madonna and Angels,* Veronese's *Supper at Simon's House* and Pollaiuolo's *Tobias and the Archangel.* Among the European paintings are Jan Van Eyck's *St. Francis Receiving the Stigmata* and works by Roger Van Der Weyden, Van Dyck, Rembrandt, Hans Memling and François Clouet.

One of the city's more bizarre monuments is the **Mole Antonelliana,** with its swordfish-like 167-metre-high (547-ft.) granite spire, named after its engineer-designer Alessandro Antonelli. Planned originally in 1863 as a synagogue, it's now a beloved city symbol used for exhibitions and elevator trips to its panoramic terrace.

The designing talents of Fiat, Alfa Romeo, Bugatti and Ferrari (but also Benz, Peugeot and Ford) are celebrated out at the **Museo dell'Automobile** (Corso Unità d'Italia, 40), south of the city centre beside the Po river.

Take the pretty excursion up on a hill across the river to Sassi, 10 kilometres (6 mi.) east of Turin, to see Juvarra's Baroque masterpiece, the splendid domed **Basilica di Superga** and the hilltop view of the Alps and the Po valley. Kings of the House of Savoy are buried in the basilica's crypt.

Courmayeur

The 4,810-metre (15,781-ft.) peak of Mont Blanc (Monte Bianco) may be in France, but the Italian side of the mountain gets the better weather. The Aosta Valley's Courmayeur is as pleasant a base for hiking—and more strenuous mountain-climbing—in summer as it is for skiing in winter. Adepts recommend the mineral waters for whatever ails you—and a shot of *grappa* for whatever doesn't.

This is Italy's oldest ski resort and an Alpine Museum traces its history in the Casa delle Guide *(Maison des Guides)*.

One of the most spectacular excursions in the whole country is the 90-minute **cable-car ride** from La Palud, north of Courmayeur, to the Colle del Gigante, 3,354 metres (11,004 ft.) and Aiguille du Midi, 3,842 metres (12,606 ft.). This gives you a wonderful view across to the peak of Mont Blanc and the whole roof of the western Alps. (The Aiguille cable-car station is across the French border, so take your passport; nationals of non EEC countries need a visa.)

ITALIAN RIVIERA

The Ligurian coast that holidaymakers have dubbed the Italian Riviera has an ancient history of piracy and commerce, not always easily distinguishable. The great port-city of Genoa made the Mediterranean more or less safe for respectable traders and the rest of the coast settled down to some quiet fishing, sailing and harmless traffic in postcards and sun-tan lotion.

The picturesque, more rugged coast east of Genoa is known as the Riviera di Levante (Riviera of the Rising Sun), while the coast west to the French border at Ventimiglia is the Riviera di Ponente (Riviera of the Setting Sun), better known for the sandy beaches of its family resorts.

Genoa *(Genova)*

Hemmed in between the Apennine mountains and the sea, Genoa has tended, like historic rival Venice on the east coast, to turn its back on Italy to seek its fortune on the high seas. This may account for a cool reserve, almost aloofness, that some read even into the architecture of the tall houses in the straight and narrow streets behind the port.

With 28 kilometres (17 mi.) of docks, Italy's biggest port remains the key to the city's identity. For a close-up of the giant oil-tankers that have replaced the schooners of old, start your city tour with a motor-launch **harbour cruise** from the Calata degli Zingari quay between the passenger and cargo terminals.

Then, at the end of the main shopping street of Via XX Settembre, west of the Piazza De

161

Ferrari that constitutes the city's bustling modern centre, enter the historic quarters. **Piazza San Matteo** was the medieval home of the august Doria family, navigators and merchants who helped build the city's great commercial empire. Their arcaded houses, with grey and white striped façades (nos. 15–17) were built from the 13th to 15th century. The Romanesque-Gothic church of **San Matteo** has the same grey and white façade. In the crypt, you'll find the tomb of Andrea Doria, great 16th-century admiral who took Genoa into the Spanish camp against the French and became the city's virtual dictator.

The Renaissance and Baroque palaces of the **Via Garibaldi** are a unique testimony to the town's historic prosperity, many of them now banks or museums. The **Palazzo Bianco** (no. 11) makes a handsome setting for its collection of Genoese painters, Cambiaso, Strozzi and Magnasco, as well as works by Pontormo and Palma il Vecchio, and the Flemish school: Rubens, Gérard David and Van Dyck. The 17th-century Baroque **Palazzo Rosso** (no. 18), taking its name from the red façade, displays works by Veronese, Titian, Dürer, Rubens and Van Dyck.

Perhaps because his home town is ashamed of not financing his crazy trip to America, Genoa still has no decent monument to Christopher Columbus. Closest reference you'll find is on a ramp leading to the **Porta Soprana** medieval turreted gate on Piazza Dante, an obscure plaque indicating the house of the discoverer's father.

Riviera Resorts

Quite apart from its superb beaches, the coast is rich in colour and fragrancy—almond, peach and apricot blossoms in spring, groves of orange, lemon and eucalyptus trees, exquisite gardens of mimosa, roses and carnations.

Along the mostly rugged Riviera di Levante east of Genoa, by far the prettiest spot is **Portofino,** more fishing and sailing harbour than resort, though it does have some fine hotels back in the hills. Above the colourfully painted houses clustered around the harbour, take a cliff walk past the church of San Giorgio to the **lighthouse** *(faro)* at the end of the promontory for a superb view along the coast. The cliffs are clothed in a profusion of exotic vegetation, with occasional glimpses of imposing villas framed by cypresses, palm trees and cascades of bougainvillea.

It is possible to escape the crowds on the Italian Riviera.

Boat excursions will take you to other beautifully secluded fishing villages, such as **San Fruttuoso** and **Camogli**. By road, you can visit the charming little town of **San Rocco** and take a 40-minute walk over to Punta Chiappa, looking out over the whole Riviera.

Santa Margherita Ligure is a jolly resort town with lively cafés, discos and *trattorie*. The family resort of **Sestri Levante** has fine sandy beaches.

Most popular of all, down the coast beyond the naval city of La Spezia, are the beaches of **Viareggio,** favourite resort of the Tuscans and famous for its pine groves, mostly of the very welcome umbrella variety.

Cool off with an excursion inland to **Carrara,** where the marble quarries provided the

raw material of Italy's greatest achievements, the monuments of the Roman Empire and the Renaissance. The town is still full of sculptors, and Piazza Alberica is the scene of a summer sculpture competition—14 days to produce a masterpiece. Visit the still active **quarries** of Fantiscritti and Colonnata. The marble that Michelangelo chose for his *Moses* and *Pietà* is now hewn, at

$3,000 a cubic metre, for replicas at Caesar's Palace, Las Vegas, and tombstones in the Los Angeles Forest Lawn cemetery.

The Riviera di Ponente west of Genoa is an almost continuous chain of family resorts with broad stretches of fine sandy beaches. **San Remo** is the best known, with its casino and elegant promenade along the Corso Imperatrice. For time away from the beach, explore the narrow winding medieval streets of the **La Pigna** quarter, leading up to the 17th-century sanctuary of Madonna della Costa. From its terrace, you have a splendid view of the coast.

Nearby **Bordighera** is particularly proud of the palm trees along the Lungomare Argentina promenade. Since the 16th century, the town has had the exclusive privilege of providing Rome with its palm fronds for the Sunday before Easter.

Alassio completes this coast's trio of major resorts, justifiably proud of its gardens nurtured by a particularly mild winter. Take an excursion east to the quiet medieval town of **Albenga,** with its Romanesque-Gothic houses around the 11th- to 14th-century cathedral and early Christian (5th-century) baptistery.

Evening is the time for a drink on Portofino's harbour.

165

THE SOUTH

One of the great joys of the south is the extent to which it is still virgin land for the majority of Italy's visitors. It has its perennial favourites: the islands of Capri and Ischia in the Bay of Naples, the ruins of Pompeii, and the resorts of the Amalfi coast. Otherwise, southern Italy is overlooked by tourists almost as much as it has been by the national government since the 1871 reunification. Less prosperous than the north, it cannot offer the same wealth of modern hotel facilities. Monuments and museums have suffered from earthquakes, the last in 1980, and civic neglect. But things are improving fast and the compensations for the more venturesome visitor are considerable.

The chief pleasure of the south or *Mezzogiorno,* is the people. If the warm-hearted, outgoing, gregarious Italian in love with the music and sun of life is a delightful legend, your best chance of finding him, despite the harsh reality, is in the south. Despite dilapidation, cultural treasures survive—the Greek temples of Paestum and Sicily, Puglia's intriguing stone *trulli* houses, of prehistoric design, the Arab, Norman and Spanish architecture of Sicily's cathedrals and palaces, the Baroque riches of Naples. And beyond the ugly suburbs of the south's modern building speculation—hardly worse than in the north—is a countryside largely unspoiled: the Lattari Hills behind Amalfi, Puglia's Gargano peninsula, Sicily's rugged interior.

NAPLES *(Napoli)*

The very idea of this teeming, undisciplined town may intimidate the faint-hearted, but for those as enterprising and cheerful as the Neapolitans themselves, the rewards are rich. Indeed, two of its museums are among the most important in Europe, but they and the monuments play second fiddle to the street-life. In the outdoor theatre that is Italy, Naples is unabashed melodrama: around the port, the popular quarters of Spaccanapoli,

Shrines protect each street in Naples' old Spanish quarter.

even the more bourgeois neighbourhoods of Vomero and Posillipo. Spend hours in the restaurants. Whether the Chinese or the Italians invented noodles, Naples is where real *spaghetti* began and where the Spaniards brought Italy's first tomato.

The cautious tell you not to drive in Naples. Too crazy, they say. Crazy, certainly, and you may prefer walking or the bus on the first day. But once you get a taste of the town, try the inspired anarchy of Naples' traffic, where one-way signs are meaningless and red and green lights purely decorative. You learn an important lesson about life, exploring the outer limits of the possible, when you see a Neapolitan driver backing, shunting and slaloming his way out of a traffic jam without hurting a flea.

The face of Naples has been made and remade by its many earthquakes, permitting—imposing—transitions from Gothic to Renaissance and Baroque. Remember that today many of the city's churches, palaces and museums may be closed for ongoing reconstruction and restoration after the devastating earthquake of 1980.

The Port and Spaccanapoli

Traffic roars down the broad Corso Umberto I to the pivotal **Piazza Municipio** to serve the docks or spin off into the commercial district behind Santa Lucia, the teeming historic centre of Spaccanapoli or the residential districts of Vomero and Posillipo.

Towering over the long rectangular square on its south side is the massive dry-moated **Castel Nuovo.** Originally the 13th-century fortress of Naples' French ruler Charles d'Anjou, it was rebuilt in the 15th century as a palace for the Spanish kings of Aragon. Entrance to what is now administrative offices and a communal library is between two towers on the west side, away from the harbour, through a fine two-storey Renaissance **triumphal arch** crowned by a statue of St. Michael. Francesco Laurana's sculpted reliefs celebrate the ceremonial entry of King Alfonso in 1443.

The **port** is a vast enterprise of civil, commercial and military activities. Ocean liners dock at the great Stazione Marittima, ferries to the islands of Capri and Ischia (see pp. 175–176) leave from the Molo Beverello, while out in the bay you'll see huge oil tankers. Celebrated in song, the old popular harbour district of **Santa Lucia** is now lined with elegant hotels and restaurants contrasting with the formidable medieval Castel dell'Ovo out on the promontory. The sunset walk gives you a great view of the bay and Mount Vesuvius. At the Mergellina (western) end of the harbour, the fishermen bring their morning catch into Porto Sannazaro.

South of the Piazza Municipio, the Via San Carlo curves round to the 19th-century steel and glass shopping arcade of **Galleria Umberto I,** opposite the great Neoclassical temple of Neapolitan *bel canto,* the **Teatro San Carlo** opera house, built in 1737. The solemnly monumental colonnaded hemicycle of the **Piazza del Plebiscito** was laid out by Napoleon's marshal Joachim Murat when, as King of Naples, he occupied the Spaniards' **Palazzo Reale** on the east side of

the piazza. The rooms are still decorated and furnished with the Baroque pomp of the 17th and 18th century.

Leading north from the palace, the Neapolitans' favourite shopping street of **Via Toledo** is named after Viceroy Dom Pedro Alvarez de Toledo. It separates the Town Hall *(Municipio)* and broad commercial streets going down to the harbour from a checkerboard of narrow alleys to the west, a Spanish neighbourhood of the 16th century that is now a mass of tall crowded tenements badly hit by the 1980 earthquake.

Via Toledo takes you into the city's historic heart, **Spaccanapoli**

Thriving and Surviving

Two attitudes to this town are fatal. One is to see all Neapolitans as lovable fellows evicted from their tenements singing O Sole Mio. *The other is to imagine them all cut-throats waiting in doorways.*

Romantics are inevitably disillusioned by a town where the major art is the art of survival, overcoming the hardships of a chronically depressed economy with a maximum of ingenuity and optimism that leaves little room for sentimentality. The people will sell you anything you want and a lot that you don't. Sing O Sole Mio, *O.K., but for money. And if paranoiacs, as social psychologists in Naples*

have observed, find their suspicions "satisfied" by becoming easy prey for pickpockets or purse-snatchers, it's because their whole nervous demeanour almost begs the thieves to act. Some people, say the criminologists, are born victims.

Without waving your jewels in dark alleys, stay cool and self-assured and no harm will come. And when you've finished raging over the Gucci bag or Cartier watch you thought you'd haggled for so brilliantly, only to discover they're fake, you may doff your hat to the hustler's diabolical talent and the back-street industry behind him. Did you really need *that stuff?*

(around a Roman road that "splits Naples" into upper and lower districts). In an area stretching from the permanently traffic-jammed Piazza Dante, between Via San Biagio dei Librai and Via Tribunali and over to the Porta Capuana, the popular image of old Naples survives. Children and dogs splash each other in the ornate fountains. Jewellers, second-hand bookshops, fishmongers and teeming tenements jostle decaying Spanish Baroque palazzi commandeered as workshops for carpentry, leathercraft and more clandestine manufacture. A permanent festival of laundry hangs across the narrow streets. Gossip, business and vendettas fly between balconies, while ropes haul up baskets of vegetables, letters and pet cats.

For a sense of the neighbourhood's old splendour, start on **Piazza Gesù Nuovo**, with its characteristically extravagant Baroque Immacolata column *(guglia)* in the centre. Behind an embossed façade, the same architectural exuberance continues inside the Jesuit church. But the jewel here, on the south corner of the square, is the 14th-century church of **Santa Chiara**, built for the wife of Robert d'Anjou and retrieved from its 18th-century Baroque additions and 20th-century firebombing. The original rose window and elegant porch

survive and the French Gothic interior is beautifully restored. In the choir are the **sculpted tombs** of Marie de Valois (on the right) and Robert d'Anjou (behind the high altar). Through an entrance between the church and campanile, visit the lovely 14th-century **Cloister** *(Chiostro delle Clarisse)*, converted in 1742 into a country garden—a delightful haven of tranquillity.

Take the Via Tribunali to the Franciscan church of **San Lorenzo Maggiore**, with its Baroque façade incorporating the 14th-century marble porch, which was added after the earthquake of 1731. Inside, the sober French Gothic chancel, exceptional in Naples for its ambulatory around the nine chapels, contrasts with the Baroque chapel left of the choir.

The **Cathedral's** three handsome 15th-century portals are somewhat overpowered by the ugly 19th-century Neo-Gothic façade. Inside, left of the Baroque nave, go down to Naples' earliest known Christian sanctuary, the 4th-century Basilica of **Santa Restituta,** in which the original Roman columns survived the 1688 earthquake. At the end of the right nave is the 5th-century domed baptistery with remnants of some fine mosaics in the dome.

The eastern end of Spaccanapoli is dominated by the

Hohenstaufen emperors' medieval **Castel Capuano** (law courts since the 16th century) and a Renaissance city gate, **Porta Capuana,** flanked by massive towers from the Spanish ramparts. Between the gate and the fortress, a boisterous market offers a veritable open-air "museum" of counterfeit luxury brands of luggage, wristwatches, polo shirts and tennis shoes.

The Museums

The roguish image of the city's present might make it easy to forget the city's glorious past. Luckily, two truly magnificent museums preserve the region's treasures from the ravages of earthquake and theft. Inquire at

Neapolitans excel at colour displays to entice shoppers.

the tourist office (main railway station or Via Partenope 10a in Santa Lucia) about ever-changing details of opening times.

Originally a 16th-century cavalry barracks, the **Archaeological Museum** *(Museo Archeologico Nazionale)* is in no way a dry bundle of old bones and stones, but sheer pleasure for anyone even remotely interested in southern Italy's Greek, Etruscan and Roman past. All visits to Pompeii and Herculaneum should begin or end here. The collections display, beautifully, not only the paintings and mosaics buried there nearly 2,000 years ago by Mount Vesuvius, but a host of other sculptures from the region's villas and temples.

(As some pieces are exhibited on a rotation basis, you may want to identify those on display with the museum guide cataloguing them by number.)

The ground floor is devoted to **sculpture,** including many Roman copies of classics from Greece's Golden Age in the 5th century B.C. which are our only access to these lost masterpieces. The most famous of these is the *Doryphorus* (Spear-carrier) of Polycletus, second in fame among Greek sculptors only to Phidias. The Emperors' Gallery includes busts and statues of Julius Caesar, Augustus, Claudius and Caracalla.

The **Pompeii mosaics** and **Herculaneum bronzes** are on the mezzanine floor. The lively secular and pagan mosaics from Pompeii's patrician villas make a striking contrast with the rigid formality of church mosaics that we see elsewhere in Italy. They include *Clients Consulting a Sorceress* and *Strolling Musicians,* vivid little friezes of an octopus, a cat catching a quail and the huge exciting mural of *Alexander* driving Darius of Persia from the battlefield at Issus in 333 B.C. The **paintings** here are the best preserved of any from Roman antiquity—frescoes in brilliant blues, greens and the inimitable Pompeii reds. The most celebrated is the sophisticated portrait of *Paquius Proculus and his Wife,* but look out, too, for the elegant *Hercules and Telephus* and four delicate portraits of women, including *Artimedes* and the *Flower Gatherer.*

The **Capodimonte Museum** (currently undergoing extensive restoration) is housed, as its name suggests, in an 18th-century hilltop palace. The garden offers a welcome rest before and after a visit to the rich collections of Italian and European painting.

Highlights include: Simone Martini's *St. Louis of Toulouse Crowning the King of Naples;* a Masaccio *Crucifixion;* Perugino's *Madonna and Child;* a fine Lorenzo Lotto portrait of

Cardinal Bernardo de' Rossi; Giovanni Bellini's gentle *Transfiguration of Christ* standing serenely between Moses and Elijah; Mantegna's *Portrait of a Boy;* Michelangelo's drawing of *Three Soldiers* for his Vatican fresco of *St. Peter's Crucifixion;*

Naples' Archaeological Museum houses Pompeii's best paintings.

Parmigianino portraits of *Lucrezia* and the celebrated Roman courtisan *Antea;* an Annibale Carracci *Pietà* and *Mystic Marriage of St. Catherine.*

The Titian room contains half a dozen of his great works, among them a brilliant *Pope Paul III with his Farnese Nephews,* the artist's daughter *Lavinia Vecellio* and *Philip II of Spain.* The stark realism you'll

173

see in Caravaggio's *Flagellation* and the *Seven Works of Mercy* launched a whole Neapolitan school of "Caravaggeschi" displayed here: Caracciolo, Stanzione and the Spaniard Ribera.

Most notable among the museum's non-Italian painters are El Greco, Breughel *(Blind Leading the Blind* and the *Misanthrope),* Cranach, Holbein, Dürer and a Van Dyck *Crucifixion.*

Vomero and Posillipo

Much of Naples' middle class looks out over the city from the hilltop Vomero neighbourhood in geometrically laid out, tree-shaded streets respectably named after artists and musicians of the Renaissance and Baroque periods: Michelangelo, Giordano, Scarlatti and Cimarosa. On the south-east edge of the Vomero hill just below the massive Castel Sant'Elmo, the elegant Baroque Charterhouse **Certosa di San Martino** offers a haven of tranquillity in its white cloisters and monastery gardens. The 16th-century church is rich in Neapolitan Baroque paintings, notably by Caracciolo, Stanzione and Giordano. The monastery's museum traces the kingdom of Naples' long history in costumes, sculpture, paintings and prints. Both children and adults adore the monumental Christmas crib of 1818, a Neapolitan speciality presenting the characters of the Nativity accompanied by peasants and artisans.

The 19th-century **Villa Floridiana** houses a fine museum of ceramics from all over Europe and Asia. From its delightful gardens, famous for their camelias amid the pines, oaks and cedars, you have a superb view of the Bay of Naples.

The genteel **Posillipo** neighbourhood enjoys a privileged position on a promontory at the western edge of town. Drive around its gardens and villas, some of them romantically dilapidated but still graceful, such as the 17th-century Palazzo di Donn'Anna on the bay front.

CAMPANIA

The green and fertile region round Naples, between the Tyrrhenian coast and the western slopes of the Apennines, was originally colonized by the Etruscans and Greeks. The volcanic soil has produced a profusion of tomatoes, olives, walnuts, grapes, oranges, lemons and figs.

The succession of authoritarian rulers from the Middle Ages to the 18th century—Norman and Angevin French, German emperors and Spaniards—kept in place a feudal system that has left the region to this day socially backward compared with the north. Village festivals and processions bear witness to the heavy rural attachment to religion and even pagan superstition harking back to Roman times.

Holidaymakers favour the islands in the Bay of Naples and the resorts of the Amalfi coast. All in easy reach of the remains of Pompeii and Herculaneum, the Vesuvius volcano and, further down the coast, the Greek temples of Paestum.

Capri

Ferries or hydrofoils leave from Naples, Sorrento and Positano. Look out for the dolphins accompanying the ship across the Bay of Naples. With its fragrant subtropical vegetation, mountainous terrain and dramatic craggy coast, this still beautiful island manages to cater to the boisterous fun of the package tours while providing quiet hideaways for that blessed, cursed race we like to call the idle rich. Winters here are marvellously mild and deserted, but even in summer you can seek out the island's many enchanted corners away from the mob.

To drive your own car on the island, you need a special permit (not usually available at the height of the holiday season). At the main harbour of Marina Grande, take a minibus or the funicular railway up to the main town of **Capri.** Or rent a canopied limousine or taxi for the day, not cheap, but negotiable and worth the splash if you want to escape the crowds who swarm into the souvenir shops and pizzerias clustered around the pretty 17th-century domed church of Santo Stefano. Escape down the little paved road south of town to the peace of the shady Romanesque and Renaissance cloisters of the **Certosa di San Giacomo.** Take your siesta with a view over the cliffs of the south coast and port of Marina Piccola.

Dominating the western half of the island, the quieter resort town of **Anacapri** derives a sleepy charm from its white villas along narrow flowery lanes. A short walk from the Piazza della Vittoria takes you to Swedish doctor-writer Axel Munthe's famous **Villa San Michele.** The house is an intriguing mixture of Baroque furniture and Roman antiquities, but the main attraction is the charming garden with its trellised arches and terraces looking out over the bay. Back at the piazza, take the chair-lift for a soaring view of the whole island on your way up to the terraced gardens and chestnut trees of **Monte Solaro,** 589 metres (1,933 ft.).

The island's most popular excursion—prettiest by boat from Marina Grande, but also possible by road north-west of Anacapri—is to the celebrated cave, the **Blue Grotto** *(Grotta Azzurra).* Most effective at noon, the sun shining through the water turns the light inside the cave a brilliant blue, and objects on the white sand seabed gleam like silver. Duck your head as the rowboat takes you through the one-metre-high (3-ft.) cave entrance. The cave, 54 metres (177 ft.) long, 15 (49 ft.) high and 30 (98 ft.) wide, is believed from the man-made niches to have been a *nymphaeum,* a kind of watery boudoir for the Emperor Tiberius, who retired to Capri in the 1st century A.D.

Of the dozen villas that Tiberius built on Capri, the best preserved are the ruins of **Villa Jovis,** sprawling across an eastern promontory opposite the mainland. The spectacular view from the 297-metre-high (974-ft.) Salto di Tiberio precipice is said to be the last pleasure enjoyed by the emperor's enemies before they were hurled over the edge.

Ischia

Lying at the western end of the Bay of Naples—ferries or hydrofoils from Naples and Pozzuoli—the island has won the overwhelming favour of German tourists in the summer, thanks to thermal springs, fine sandy beaches and good facilities for watersports. Casamicciola Terme and Lacco Ameno are among the smarter spa resorts.

One of the best beaches, pockmarked with volcanic steam spouts, is the Lido dei Maronti on the south coast near the pretty little fishing village of Sant'Angelo. The island interior has a rich vegetation of vines, olive trees and exotic plants. Naturelovers can hike up the extinct volcano of Mount Epomeo 788 metres (2,585 ft.), starting from Fontana.

Pompeii

More than in any of the empire's colossal arenas, soaring aqueducts or triumphal arches, you'll find the reality of Roman life in the bakeries, wine-shops, groceries and brothels of Pompeii. The town that Vesuvius blotted out along with Herculaneum on August 24, A.D. 79 (see pp. 180–181) is still being meticulously excavated from its ashes. It was rediscovered in 1594 by an architect cutting a new channel for the Sarno river, but excavation did not begin till 1748.

To enjoy Pompeii to the full, try to divide your visit into two, early morning and late afternoon (there's practically no shade), with a siesta in between. Good rubber-soled shoes are essential. On-site guides will tell you some jolly but highly fanciful stories; more serious guides are available by advance arrangement through the museum *(Antiquarium).* Start at the Porta Marina

Divine messenger warns Pompeii too late of impending doom.

entrance on the south of the site, near the Villa dei Misteri railway station.

We'll point out the site's principal "monuments", but the magic is, as always, in the serendipity of making your own discoveries, both moving and frivolous. The tragic dimension remains, 19 centuries later, in the bodies of human victims or a pet dog in huddled or contorted postures found petrified under the cinders and reconstituted in plaster or transparent resin.

Even stronger is a sense of the everyday life of a moment earlier in the curbed streets with their smooth paving stones rutted by chariot wheels and pedestrian crossings on stepping stones.

The road from the main gate passes on the right the basilica law courts and stock exchange to reach the **Forum,** the town's main public meeting place directly facing Mount Vesuvius. Imagine a square looking originally something like Venice's Piazza San Marco, with two-storey porticoes running along three sides and the six-columned **Temple to Jupiter** flanked by ceremonial arches at the north end. (After earlier earthquake

177

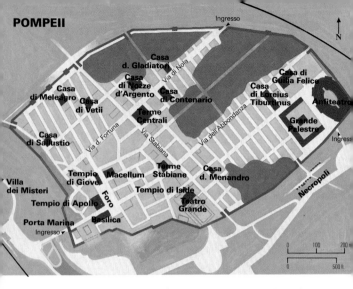

damage, the temple was used as the *Capitolium* and city treasury.) You can still see plinths from the square's statues of local and national celebrities and the white base of the orator's platform. In the northeast corner is the market *(macellum)*.

On the **Via dell'Abbondanza** running east from the Forum, those are ancient, not modern graffiti you find scratched and daubed in red on the walls of the houses and shops. Election slogans, insults, obscene drawings—our subway kids continue a venerable tradition. Prominent phallus signs often indicate a house of joy, with an arrow

pointing upstairs to where the action is, but sometimes they're just a shopkeeper's good-luck sign. Notice the oil and wine jars in the shops, the bakers' ovens and flour-grinding mills shaped like giant cotton-reels (excavators found a donkey lying by one he'd been turning when Vesuvius erupted).

At the **Stabian Baths** *(Thermae Stabianae),* you can see the separate men's and women's facilities, changing room, with clothes-locker niches, and three baths, cold, lukewarm and hot *(frigidarium, tepidarium* and *caldarium).* The **Teatro Grande** seated 5,000 spectators. Behind the stage was the gladiators'

House and Garden

Unlike the predominantly aristocratic Herculaneum, Pompeii's population of 25,000 was a mixture of patricians, nouveau riche *merchants, small shopkeepers, artisans and slaves. They made their money from commerce in wool and wine.*

The typical patrician house had two storeys, with servants and lodgers living upstairs. The family's living and sleeping quarters surround a first courtyard or atrium. Opposite the entrance is a main living room (tablinum) *backing onto the dining room* (triclinium). *This looks onto another courtyard or Greek-style porticoed garden* (peristylium).

barracks, where 63 skeletons were found. Their weapons, along with Pompeii's more fragile works of art, are exhibited at Naples' Archaeological Museum (see p.172), which provides an invaluable adjunct to your visit here.

At the far end of the Via dell'Abbondanza, visit two of the town's best villas: the **House of Loreius Tiburtinus,** for its beautiful peristyle garden of fountains, water channels and cascades, one of them with paintings of *Narcissus* and *Pyramus and Thisbe;* and the **House of Julia Felix,** big enough to have been perhaps a luxury hotel, with its own bath-house

and a handsome portico of slender marble columns around the peristyle. At the great **Amphitheatre** just to the south, you get a fine view back over the town from its upper tiers.

A short walk outside the main site to the north, the **Villa of Mysteries** *(Villa dei Misteri)* is Pompeii's most cherished artistic treasure. The "mysteries" are those depicted in **frescoes** of a woman's initiation into the Dionysiac cult. Archaeologists suggest that the scenes of dancing satyrs, flagellation and a woman kneeling before a sacred phallus indicate rites that the town preferred to keep at a decorous distance, in this splendid suburban villa.

Vesuvius *(Vesuvio)*

The old Roman name of Europe's most famous volcano means "Unextinguished" and there's no reason to change it. In the 1980s, it was 1,281 metres (4,203 ft.) high, having added 79 metres (259 ft.) with the big eruption of 1944 and subsequent smaller ones.

Barring risks from "unscheduled activity", you can peek inside the steaming crater. From the Ercolano *autostrada* exit, take the winding mountain-road's right fork for a short chair-lift ride to the summit. Exploiting the fertile volcanic soil, some vineyards still produce the esteemed *Lacryma Christi* white wine. The **Eremo Observatory** halfway up the mountain has been studying eruptions since 1845 and has an impressive display of relief plans, seismographs and geological specimens spewed out of the volcano. Inside the **crater,** look for the fumarole phut-phutting steam and hot gases. You also have a grand view back over Naples and its bay.

Blowing Its Top
The cone of Vesuvius actually "grew" out of the crater of another volcano, Mount Somma, exploding the latter's outer wall with the eruption that engulfed Pompeii and Herculaneum in A.D. 79. Molten lava at a temperature of 1400 ° Celsius (2552 °F.) burst from the volcano's magma chamber 5,000 metres (16,400 ft.) down in the earth's bowels but never got as far as Pompeii. The town was buried in gigantic showers of cinders and lapilli (volcanic pebbles). Herculaneum disappeared under a river of mud. Since 1631, when 3,000 people were killed at the foot of the mountain, there have been 23 noteworthy eruptions, the last three in 1906, 1928 and 1944. Astrologers tell gamblers to put their money on one more for this century, but seismologists suggest an earthquake is a "safer" bet.

Herculaneum (Ercolano)

You can combine your Vesuvius trip with a tour of one of the volcano's victims near what is now Ercolano. Herculaneum is smaller and perhaps less spectacular than Pompeii, but its very compactness and better preservation give a more immediate sense of the shape and ambience of a whole Roman town. While Pompeii was burned out by volcanic cinders, the mud swamping Herculaneum covered the houses in a protective crust that kept upper stories and even some of the woodwork still intact. The gardens have been lovingly replanted.

Rediscovered by well-diggers in the 18th century, the town is still being excavated, a delicate business as much of it is covered by modern buildings.

The entrance off the Corso Ercolano takes you around the site for a striking view across the town of terraced villas from which wealthy Roman landowners looked out to sea towards Ischia on the horizon. The streets (Cardine III, IV and V) have curbed pavements, lined with two-storey houses with balconies and overhanging roofs for shade.

At the southern end of Cardine V, the spacious **House of the Stags** (*Casa dei Cervi*) is named after its two marble sculptures of stags attacked by hounds. In one of the rooms off the garden is a statue of a shockingly drunken Hercules. In the middle of Cardine IV, the **House of Charred Furniture** *(Casa del Mobilio Carbonizzato)* has a marvellously preserved latticed divan bed and small table. Next door, the **House of Neptune** has lost its upstairs façade but the ground floor wine-shop with its narrow-necked amphoras on the shelves looks open for business. The inner courtyard has a lovely green and blue mosaic of Neptune with his wife Amphitrite.

The grandest of the villas, the **House of the Bicentenary** (excavated 200 years after the first "dig" in 1738) stands on the avenue Decumanus Maximus on the north-east edge of town. It has splendid marble paving and, etched in the wall of one of the smaller rooms, a controversial cross regarded by some as evidence of a Christian chapel, though others insist the emblem was not adopted until the conversion of Constantine three centuries later.

🎸 Sorrento and the Amalfi Coast

The coast curving along the southern arm of the Bay of Naples round the Sorrento Peninsula to Salerno is one of the most romantic in Italy. The sinuous coast road tames even the most audacious Italian driver overlooking the sheer drop of rugged cliffs and ravines. In olden days, only brigands and pirates ventured out here, their ruined redoubts still dotting the hillsides. Now, wild roses and camelias tempt lovers out onto jutting crags high above terraces of orange and lemon groves, vineyards, walnut and almond trees.

From the sirens that tried in vain to tempt Ulysses and his sailors onto its rocks to the sentimental songs of latterday minstrels, **Sorrento** has lost none of its popular enchantment. Surrounded on three sides by ravines above the sea, the pretty tree-shaded resort makes a perfect base for excursions along the coast. Its craftsmen are famous for their inlaid walnut woodwork. Compare their modern wares with their forefathers' Baroque furniture exhibited in the **Museo Correale,** in an 18th-century palazzo at the east end of town.

Positano spills down its hillside in a spectacular cascade of gleaming white houses dotted with gardens of oranges and lemons. Take the **cliff-walk** from the town's main beach, the broad Spiaggia Grande, to the long and narrower Spiaggia Fornillo. In the little church of Santa Maria Assunta, with the region's characteristic majolica-tiled dome, see the 13th-century Byzantine-style altar-painting.

Most charming and lively of the coast's resorts, **Amalfi** was once a powerful rival to the maritime republics of Pisa and Genoa, with trading posts in the 10th and 11th centuries in Palestine, Egypt, Cyprus, Byzantium and Tunis. Its two destinies come together in the **Piazza del Duomo** where open-air cafés and ice-cream parlours look up a long staircase to the Arab-Norman **campanile** and polychrome mosaic façade of the Romanesque **Cathedral**. It was built in the 9th century, with the façade added in the 13th, when the remains of St. Andrew were brought to its crypt from Constantinople. The interlacing Arab-Norman arches of the 13th-century cloister, **Chiostro del Paradiso,** make a handsome setting for the summer recitals of chamber music. Amalfi has excellent facilities for sailing and other water sports. Take a trip to nearby Conca dei Marini to visit the stalactites and stalagmites of the **Grotta di Smeraldo,** where the waters are as brilliantly emerald green as those of Capri's Grotta Azzurra are blue.

Set back on a high ridge behind Amalfi is the peaceful village of **Ravello,** once a hideout for Romans fleeing the Huns and Visigoths. Today it's a delightful resort of modest but elegant hotels and villas, notably **Villa Cimbrone,** where the fragrant gardens command a marvellous view of the Gulf of Salerno. The exotic flowers and palm trees of the **Villa Rufolo,** with its mysterious polychrome arcaded cloister, gave Richard Wagner inspiration for his last opera, *Parsifal.* "I've found the magic garden of Klingsor," he wrote, "the garden in which diabolically beautiful women bewitched the knights seeking the Holy Grail."

Paestum

A 40-minute drive south from Salerno, Italy has no more magnificent testimony of its Greek colonies than this complex of wonderfully preserved Doric temples dating back to the 5th and 6th century B.C. Standing alone in fields leading to the sea, their buff-stone columns take on a wonderful golden glow at sunset. Four temples loom over the forum and residential quarters of Poseidonia (as it was known before the Roman era). After the town was abandoned to malaria and Arab invaders in the 9th century, the monuments disappeared under wild vegetation until their rediscovery 900 years later. The most spectacular, directly opposite the entrance to the site, is the 5th-century **Temple of Neptune**. The

Peek among bougainvillea at a church on the Amalfi Coast.

roof has gone, but with its entablature and 36 columns still standing, it is, with Athens' Theseion, the best preserved of all Greek temples. To the south, the more dilapidated **Temple of Hera** (also known, mistakenly, as the Basilica) is a hundred years older. The northernmost **Temple of Ceres** was used as a church in the early Middle Ages, as attested by three Christian tombs.

PUGLIA

Known to many under its Roman name of Apulia, the region stretches from the "spur" of the Gargano peninsula to the heel of Italy's boot, endowed with a wild and unspoiled beauty over the gently undulating stony plateaus grazed by sheep and goats. Massive fortresses and fortress-like churches testify to the passage of the Normans and then the

German emperors in the Middle Ages. In among the groves of olive, almond and fig trees, the stones have been gathered up from time immemorial to build the smaller, but equally sturdy corbelled *trulli*.

The goddesses of Paestum have gone, but not their devotees.

Gargano

The peninsula's seaside resorts have good beaches among the pine groves, first-class camping and water-sports facilities with excursions and hikes into an attractive hinterland of rolling hills. Before starting out on the coastal circuit from Manfredonia, visit the 12th-century church of **Santa Maria di Siponto** (south-west of town), built over a 5th-century crypt.

Pugnochiuso is among the best of the beach resorts, along with **Vieste,** where Emperor Frederick II left you a castle from which to view the Adriatic, and the pretty fishing village of **Peschici** climbing up its rocky promontory.

Go inland through Vico to join the wild deer for picnics in the **Umbra Forest.** Perched on the Gargano heights south of the forest, **Monte Sant'Angelo** was a major medieval pilgrimage town, celebrated for its 5th-century sanctuary of **St. Michael** in a mountain cave which the archangel revealed to the Bishop of Siponto in a dream. The sanctuary inspired the building of the great French island-monastery of le Mont Saint-Michel after Bishop Aubert travelled to Gargano to collect a piece of St. Michael's red cloak. From a Gothic portico in the middle of town, beside the massive 13th-century **Campanile,** a staircase of 90 steps takes you down to the

185

sanctuary's 11th-century bronze doors. Notice to the left of the altar, the beautifully carved stone episcopal throne.

From the north coast resort of Rodi Garganico, you can take a 90-minute boat trip out to the pine tree covered **Tremiti Islands.** The biggest, San Domino, offers good camping and a holiday village organizing underwater diving and snorkelling.

Alberobello

This agricultural town is the centre of Puglia's famous *trulli,* the white-washed houses with ruddy or grey dry-stone roofs, cone-shaped, dotting the landscape like giant spinning tops turned

The drystone trulli *houses of Alberobello use prehistoric building techniques.*

upside down. The cone is formed by small limestone slabs set in a spiral without mortar to bind them. Though the region's oldest surviving *trulli* date back only to the 16th century, the construction technique is prehistoric, brought here perhaps from Greece or the Middle East. Many roofs are daubed with an ancient religious symbol, pagan, Christian, even Jewish (the menorah candlestick).

In Alberobello, two neighbourhoods of *trulli* houses, shops and churches, **Rioni Monti** and **Aia Piccola,** are protected as a *zona monumentale.* Shopkeepers are happy to let you climb up to their roof-terraces for a striking view across a whole forest of *trulli* domes. Out in the country in and around **Locorotondo** and **Selva di Fasano,** you'll find *trulli* farms, barns, grain-silos, even filling stations.

North-west of Alberobello, a *strada panoramica* along a ridge overlooking the Adriatic coast leads to **Castellana Grotte,** a group of spectacular caves 60 metres (190 ft.) underground. Take a guided tour of the translucent stalactites reaching down to fuse with stalagmites in glowing columns of red, green and pink. Besides the usual comparisons with temples, cathedrals and church organs, the strange formations remind people of old relatives and new lovers.

SICILY *(Sicilia)*

The Mediterranean's largest island is in many ways a country to itself and deserves a separate holiday to do it proper justice. Here, for anyone who has a few days to spare for a first impression, we'll just provide some highlights representative of its many facets: the capital Palermo, the ancient Greek settlements and, for a rest, the coastal resort of Taormina.

Palermo

This bustling capital deserves the necessary effort to get at its colourful past. Cleverly integrating designs of Arab and Byzantine predecessors, the Norman palaces and churches join the crumbling grandeur of Spanish Baroque façades in momentary triumph over the chaos of the modern port-city.

The intersection of Via Vittorio Emanuele and Via Maqueda is the town's historic centre, **Quattro Canti** (Four Corners), in a characteristic setting of Baroque churches (San Giuseppe and Santa Caterina) and monumental **Pretoria Fountain.** Behind the town hall, **Piazza Bellini** evokes Palermo's cosmopolitan history. The 12th-century church of **San Cataldo** with its three little red domes and Arabic inscriptions was originally built as a synagogue. Beside it, the Norman Gothic **Martorana** church, partly remodelled with a Baroque façade and porch, has a fine campanile of four storeys of slender mullioned windows. Inside the porch, 12th-century **mosaics** show, to the right, Jesus crowning Sicily's Norman king, Roger II, and to the left, his ad-

Normans carved this Romanesque capital in a Monreale cloister.

miral, Georges of Antioch, at the feet of the Madonna. In the nave are mosaics of Christ Pantocrator (Omnipotent Lord) with angels.

West along Via Vittorio Emanuele, the **Palace of the Normans** *(Palazzo dei Normanni)* turned the Arabs' 9th-century fortress into a royal residence, appropriate setting for the later brilliance and luxury of Emperor

Frederick II's Sicilian court (see p. 23). In the royal apartments, see the hunting mosaics in **King Roger's room** *(Stanza normanna),* but the jewel of the palace, indeed one of Norman architecture's greatest achievements in Italy, is the 12th-century **Palatine Chapel** up on the first floor. The noble Romanesque interior has a magnificent painted wooden ceiling

with Arabic honeycomb motifs and stalactite pendentives. The **mosaics** of the dome and apse depict Christ Pantocrator with the Evangelists and Jesus blessing Peter and Paul. The combination of figurative and intricate geometric designs was a collaborative effort of Syrian Muslim craftsmen with Byzantine Christians. To the right of the sanctuary is a fine pulpit on chevron-patterned Corinthian columns next to a tall, elaborately carved Easter candelabrum.

The pink-domed church of **San Giovanni degli Eremiti** (Via dei Benedettini) is another intriguing example of 12th-century Arab-Norman design. Its exotic character is enhanced by the twin-columned **cloister** overgrown with tropical plants, orange, lemon and palm trees.

Housed in a 17th-century monastery, the town's **Archaeological Museum** (Piazza Olivella) displays superb statues and sculpted *metope* (friezes) from the Greek temples of Selinunte (600–500 B.C.), on Sicily's south coast. The **Palazzo Abatelli Art Gallery** includes in its collection a gripping fresco of the *Triumph of Death* by an anonymous 15th-century artist, Antonello da Messina's exquisite *Annunciation* and Francesco Laurana's sculpture of *Eleonora of Aragon.*

189

Monreale

This hilltop suburb south-west of Palermo boasts Sicily's finest **Cathedral** (12th century). Go round to the back of the church to see its wonderful russet and brown stone chancel of interlacing arches, Gothic rose windows and Arab windows with pointed arches. In the grandiose interior, the 12th- and 13th-century mosaics of the nave and apse depict Old Testament scenes and Christ Pantocrator with saints, while the aisle mosaics narrate the miracles of Jesus. The more warmly human figures are believed to be the work of Venetian mosaicists, as opposed to the more rigidly formal Byzantine figures of Palermo's Palatine Chapel.

The beautiful cloister offers strangely mixed sensations: spiritual meditation along the arcades of delicate chevron-fluted columns and an almost sensual pleasure among the exotic flowers and trees and Arab fountain of its garden.

Agrigento

If you can make only one pilgrimage to the great Greek sanctuaries of Sicily, let it be to Agrigento's magical **Temple Valley** *(Valle dei Templi)* dating back to the 5th century B.C. The **Temple of Juno** with its sacrificial altar stands in majestic isolation high on a ledge at the eastern end of the Via Sacra. The **Temple of Concordia** is the best preserved, thanks to its subsequent use as a church in the 6th century A.D. But the golden glow of the

---

Chiaroscuro

Sicily is a fascinating study in light and shade. It may surprise visitors expecting in a sun-drenched island an equally sunny, happy-go-lucky disposition among its people. Somehow the experience of successive waves of Greek, Arab, Norman, German and Spanish rulers before entering the national Italian orbit has left its people more withdrawn than, say, the Neapolitans on the mainland. Like the thick, almost windowless walls that shield their dwellings against the summer heat, a cool, even sombre reserve

protects the people from the visitor's probing curiosity in the too-dazzling light of a Sicilian day. The joy is there, but private.

Evolving during the rule of the Spanish, in place of official justice, the Mafia exploited the Sicilian custom of settling personal wrongs among themselves and administered its own law and order, pocketing fines, punishing obstreperous enemies, rewarding obedient friends. After years of resenting mainland Italy as "foreign" and incompetent, Sicilian society is beginning, very slowly, to open up.

temples' Doric columns and the idyllic setting amid acacia and almond trees on a precipice overlooking the Mediterranean are enough to start you worshipping a whole pantheon of Greek gods. Nearby is the even older **Temple of Hercules.**

North of Temple Valley, next to the 13th-century Norman church of San Nicola, the **Archaeological Museum** has a fine marble sculpture of *Ephebus* (5th century B.C.), a gigantic *telamon*, a male figure used to hold up a temple roof's entablature, and some superb Greek wine vessels.

Syracuse *(Siracusa)*

The east coast Corinthian settlement founded in 734 B.C. was the most powerful of Greece's overseas colonies and, under Dionysius (405–367 B.C.), a direct rival to Athens. In its heyday, its population was nearly three times the size of today's 118,000. It was here in the 3rd century B.C. that mathematician Archimedes worked out his water displacement theory in the bath and ran naked into the street crying "Eureka!".

Syracuse's original settlement was the port-island of **Ortigia,** joined by causeway to the mainland. Two pillars surviving from the Greek Temple of Apollo stand like a gateway, but the Spanish era has given it a charming 17th-century ambience of Baroque houses with balconies supported by floral carvings and an occasional stone nymph. The graceful crescent-shaped **Piazza del Duomo** is the perfect place for breakfast surrounded by 17th- and 18th-century palazzi and the **Cathedral.** The church is in fact a Baroque elaboration of the Greeks' Temple of Athena (5th century B.C.), with its columns incorporated into the masonry of the outside walls. On the island's west side, the **Fontana Aretusa** is a freshwater spring with black and white ducks swimming in its semi-circular papyrus pond.

The principal excavated site, **Parco Archeologico,** is located on the north-west corner of the modern city. Rebuilt by the Romans to hold 15,000 spectators for their games, the **Greek Theatre** dates back to the 5th century B.C. when Aeschylus personally came over from his south coast home at Gela to supervise productions of his tragedies. A classical drama festival is held there in May and June. The nearby **Paradise Quarry** *(Latomia del Paradiso)* provided the city's building materials and is now a pleasant garden of oleander and orange trees. Its popular attraction is the cave known as **Orecchio di Dionisio** (Dionysius' Ear), carved from the rock.

Taormina

This attractive resort town, already very popular in antiquity as a vacation spot for the Greek bourgeoisie from Syracuse, commands a splendid view of the Mediterranean from its hillside villas and hotels. No Sicilian *passeggiata* is more celebrated than a promenade on the elegant shopping street of **Corso Umberto** and out along the **Via Roma** past the subtropical vegetation of the terraced gardens. With great views south along the coast and to the volcano of Mount Etna to the west, the **Greek Theatre** (3rd century B.C.) provides a wonderful setting for the summer classical drama—and a slightly surreal one for the Taormina film festival. Excursions further up the mountain take you to two medieval fortresses, on foot to **Castello di Taormina** and, by car along a winding road, to **Castelmola**, for grand views.

Mount Etna

Europe's tallest volcano is still very active, as you'll see from tell-tale yellow sulphur stains of mini-eruptions as you approach the crater. The summit stood at 3,343 metres (10,975 ft.) above sea level in 1985, but varies according to the eruptions' destruction or lava deposits. Because of the erratic nature of the eruptions, approaching the crater is no easy business. The routes by bus, special Land Rover and cable-car from Taormina or Catania change from year to year, lava permitting. Inquire at local tourist offices and travel agencies before setting out. In any case, the last stretch to the crater itself is on foot, so take sturdy shoes and warm clothing—it's cool and windy up there, even in summer. From October to May, the summit is covered in snow.

The volcanic soil produces a rich crop of citrus fruits—oranges, tangerines and lemons—as well as figs, almonds, grapes and olives. The slopes are remarkably sweet-smelling for a volcano, with forests of eucalyptus and umbrella pine among the oak and pistachio. Higher up, you get a whiff of sulphurous gases hissing from the small craters pockmarking the barren moonscape of the summit. When the Rifugio Sapienza, 1,881 metres (6,172 ft.), is in use, an overnight stay on the volcano makes it possible to reach the summit at sunrise for a spectacular view both into the **crater** and back over the Sicilian coast to the Italian mainland. Otherwise, try to be there at sunset.

The tiled stairs of Caltagirone ease the steep climb.

WHAT TO DO

While you're wandering around the country's myriad palazzi and churches, ancient ruins and modern museums, you may occasionally wonder what the *Italians* are doing—and feel a great urge to join them. If the ephemeral idea of *la dolce vita* didn't outlive the early 60s and even then was the preserve of a happy few, today's widening prosperity has resurrected and expanded the Italians' propensity for the sweet life.

Their mania for sport is contagious, elegant shops all too seductive, and the time-honoured theatricality extends from grand opera and flamboyant discos to traditional carnivals and colourful religious processions.

SPORTS

It would be an understatement to describe the Italians as sport-crazy, at least as far as spectator sports are concerned. For millions, Sundays are less sacred for mass in the morning than football in the afternoon. In a country with just a century of national unity and the scalding experience of Mussolini's fascism, sport seems almost the only activity which can inspire in Italians any semblance of patriotic fervour.

Witness the crowd's ferocious, unashamedly chauvinistic partisanship at Rome's international open tennis championships or the Davis Cup. On a day when Italy is involved in an international football match, streets all over the country are deserted—until the cars come out honking for a frenetic victory parade or the men shuffle on foot to the Piazza del Duomo for a funereal post-defeat commiseration and recrimination.

You can observe the **football** (soccer) phenomenon, with the *tifosi* (fans) in full cry, in all the major cities, the most celebrated teams studded with top foreign stars being in Turin (Juventus and Torino), Milan (A.C. and Inter), Florence (Fiorentina), Genoa (Sampdoria), Rome and Naples.

Cycling races are still popular—especially the round-Italy *Giro d'Italia* in June—though they badly need a new world-class champion to arouse a fervour comparable to that for football. You can watch World Cup **skiing** at Cortina d'Ampezzo and Val Gardena. **Bocce,** the bowls game similar to French *boules* or *pétanque,* is played wherever there's a patch of tree-shaded sandy gravel and a bar *(osteria)* close enough at hand to serve a glass of wine or *grappa.*

Heading for a hike in the Alps above Piedmont's Aosta Valley.

SPORTS

Motor racing fans can watch the Grand Prix of Italy at Monza, near Milan, or Imola, near Bologna.

On the beaches of the Adriatic coast, the Italian Riviera, Sardinia and Sicily, **swimming** is a pleasure that needs a few words of warning. Conditions of water pollution change from year to year, but observe the obvious general rule of thumb of avoiding a dip in the immediate vicinity of major industrialized port-cities: Genoa, Naples and Palermo. Look out for red flags warning about dangerous undercurrents; and for small children check that beaches are patrolled by life-guards. Remember, for many smart resorts like the Venice Lido or Sardinia's Costa Smeralda, to budget for beach umbrellas and deckchairs.

For water sports at the resorts, you can usually hire equipment on the spot for **snorkelling** and **wind-surfing** (particularly good on the lakes). The Italians are great experts at **scuba-diving** and have skilful (and handsome) instructors. You may well come across archaeological finds— ancient anchors, wine-jars, even

Sports enthusiasts find a cool way to play volleyball.

sculpture—which *must* be reported to local municipal authorities. It's not difficult to get hitched up to a motorboat for **water-skiing**.

Sailing is great sport around Sardinia and Sicily, but also on the Argentario peninsula (see p. 107).

Offshore **fishing** is popular all along the coasts, notably for tunny (tuna) off western Sicily, for swordfish on the east coast and spear-fishing at Bordighera. For freshwater fishing in the inland lakes and rivers, you should get a permit from the local municipality.

Hiking is the simplest and most exhilarating way of seeing the countryside, up in the Do-lomites or the Alps, around the lakes and the Abruzzi National Park. Remember good shoes, light but solid, and some warm clothing. You can hire horses for **riding** at resorts like Sestri Levante, Alassio, San Remo. To explore the country on horse-back from the major inland cities, inquire at the A.N.T.E. (National Association of Equestrian Tourism), Largo Messico 13, Rome.

Golf players can usually play on local private courses with proof of their home club membership. Venice has an 18-hole course at the Lido's Alberoni. On the Riviera, try Rapallo, San Remo or Garlenda (near Alassio). **Tennis** is less widespread

---

Eloquent Fingers

One spectator sport practised by 50 million Italians and watched by crowds of bemused foreigners, especially less expansive north Europeans and Americans, is the art of communication by gestures. Other peoples practice the art but none with quite the graceful flourish and eloquence of the Italians. The most Italian of all gestures is holding up pursed fingers, usually accompanied by a slightly anguished "Cosa vuoi?" ("What do you want?") or "Cosa fai?" ("What are you doing?"). Without a word, it often means: "You're crazy!" Beware of subtle nuances of interpretation. While a Spaniard pulling his earlobe is accusing you of sponging, an Italian is questioning a man's masculinity. A Frenchman stroking under his chin is calling you a bore, but an Italian may just be expressing an apologetic negative. The vertical horn-sign of the first and last fingers is universally recognized as "Cuckold!", but the same sign pointing horizontally is to protect you against the evil eye. Everybody knows the flourished forearm with clenched fist is a sexual insult, but don't be upset by the flattened hand raised sideways like a chopper to signify a departure.

than in other major western European countries, but growing in popularity. Your hotel can help you find a hard or clay court.

Skiing is first-class in the established resorts of Cortina d'Ampezzo and Courmayeur, with a perhaps more explosive thrill on Mount Etna.

ENTERTAINMENT

From time to time, the Italians move the melodrama of their lives indoors and call it **opera.** Most famous of the high temples of this art is, of course, Milan's La Scala (see p. 148), privileging the works of Verdi, Bellini, Rossini and Puccini. The taste for the grandiose musical spectacle has spread all across the western world, but the greatest stars and divas need a triumph at La Scala for true consecration. Its season is from December till mid-May. For good tickets, you should plan well in advance through your travel agency, but your hotel may be able to help with seats from last-minute cancellations.

The other great opera houses are La Fenice in Venice, Florence's Teatro Comunale and the great Teatro San Carlo of Naples. But Bologna, Parma, Perugia, Rome and Palermo also have fine regional houses, beginning around December or January and going on till late spring or early summer.

In the summer, **open-air opera** is the great attraction in Rome's ancient Baths of Caracalla and Verona's Roman Arena, when performances of *Aïda* and other extravagant productions may bring horses, camels or even elephants onstage.

Orchestral concerts of symphonic and chamber **music,** for which it is usually easier to get tickets, are held in the opera houses outside and sometimes concurrently with the opera season, but also in Milan's Conservatorio and Rome's Accademia Filarmonica Romana. Florence, Spoleto, Perugia, Ravenna, Rimini and Stresa all hold important music festivals. In Tuscany, San Gimignano and Lucca stage open-air concerts, while Amalfi's are given in the cathedral cloisters.

Lovers of **Neapolitan folk music** can enjoy a whole week of it in early September at the Piedigrotta festival.

A great open-air festival of **jazz, pop** and **rock** music is held in the parks and gardens of Rome for the *Estate Romana* (Roman Summer). Alassio's jazz festival is in September. Milan has the best discos and nightclubs, while others are attached to hotels at the seaside resorts. Most Italians go over the border to France to gamble, but Venice has a winter **casino** in the Palazzo Vendramin-Calergi.

Naturally enough, **theatre** requires a good knowledge of Italian. You'll find the best productions in Rome and Milan, the latter famous for Giorgio Strehler's Piccolo Teatro.

One of the most entertaining ways to polish your Italian is at the **cinema**, where all foreign films are dubbed into Italian (though a minor revolution is taking place in a couple of movie-houses playing original

Everybody joins this Sicilian singalong in a typical restaurant.

versions in Milan and Rome). In summer, Rome's great cinema event is the series of Italian and foreign films projected at the Massenzio Basilica near the Colosseum. International film festivals are held at Venice and Taormina.

Festivals

The attachment to regional customs and religious festivals has dwindled in the 20th century, but many keep going for the tourist trade.

We offer here a far from exhaustive list of processions and festivities around the country.

January:	*Piana degli Albanesi* (near *Palermo*) colourful Byzantine ritual for Epiphany.
February or early March:	*Venice* Carnival, masked balls and processions in magnificent costumes; *Viareggio* Carnival; *Agrigento* Almond Blossom Festival.
April:	*Rome* Pope's Easter Sunday blessing.
May:	*Assisi* Calendimaggio Christian and pagan festival; *Naples* Miracle of San Gennaro (liquefaction of the saint's blood); *Camogli* (Riviera) Fish Festival, communal fish-fry in giant pan; *Gubbio* candle race, crossbow competition; *Orvieto* Pentecost feast of the Palombella (Holy Ghost).
June:	*Pisa* San Ranieri, jousting and torchlit regatta on Arno river; *Florence* Costumed medieval football game.
July:	*Siena* first Palio (July 2, see p.104); *Palermo* Santa Rosalia; *Venice* Redentore regatta; *Rimini* Festival of the Sea; *Rome* Noiantri street-festival in Trastevere (see p. 66).
August:	*Siena* Second Palio (August 16).
September:	*Naples* Piedigrotta, Neapolitan music and cuisine; *Venice* Historical Regatta.
October:	*Assisi* Feast of St. Francis; *Perugia* Franciscan Mysteries.
December:	*Rome* Christmas food and toy market on Piazza Navona; *Assisi* and *Naples* cribs in streets; *Alberobello* celebrations in *trulli*.

Venice's Redentore Festival in July celebrates the city's salvation from a devastating plague in 1577.

SHOPPING

The inspired vanity of the Italians has turned their country into a delightful bazaar of style and elegance for the foreign visitor. Of stupefying junk, too. The luxury goods of Milan, Venice, Rome and Florence, jewellery, clothes, especially shoes, but also luggage and household goods of impeccable modern design, are second to none in the world. Not inexpensive, but then the bargain here is not in the price, it's in the meticulous workmanship.

But the souvenirs also merit a homage to endless invention in the realm of the cheap—and not-so-cheap—and nasty: Leaning Tower pencil-sharpeners, Trevi Fountain water-squirters, musical gondolas, fluorescent volcanos, priapic Pompeians, Colosseum with plaster Christians fed to plastic lions, glass balls of the pope blessing the faithful in a snow storm, do-it-yourself *Last Supper* colouring-book. Maybe the sublime looks even more sublime when it hangs around the ridiculous.

Some souvenirs are, of course, more tasteful: gourmet delicacies, but save these purchases for the end, to get them home as fresh as possible—cheeses, salami, Parma ham, Milanese sweet *panettone* brioche, Lucca's olive oil, Siena's cakes, biscuits and famous *panforte,* a spicy

fruit-and-nut concoction, and the better Chianti and Orvieto wines that you may not find back home.

And if you've fallen in love with Italian coffee, why not buy a compact version of the *espresso* machine or streamlined coffee pot that does practically the same job on the stove? Italian kitchenware is in general beautifully styled with a great sense of colour and line.

In a country where civilizations have come and gone like commuter-trains, there's a considerable traffic in archaeological antiquities. But when anybody at an ancient site in Rome, Pompeii or Sicily offers you a Roman coin, Greek pot or statue, you can be fairly sure it's a fake. Of course, it may be a *pretty* fake, in which case you offer the price of a pretty fake.

Italian shoes are a step above the rest of the world's footwear.

For quality goods, Italians prefer shopping in small boutiques with a long tradition, very often a family business guaranteeing generations of good craftsmanship. As a result, you won't find upmarket department stores, but popular, lower-price

203

chain-stores—such as Coin, Standa, Upim or Rinascente. But these are useful for your extra T-shirts, suntan lotion or throw-away beach sandals.

Even when sales people do not speak English, they'll bend over backwards to be helpful. If you want friendly treatment in the more expensive stores, you must dress decently. Even the warmest-hearted Italian can, perhaps understandably, be snooty towards people dressed like slobs. Credit cards work almost everywhere these days, apart from a few Sardinian basket-weavers and Apulian potters. Shops in the big cities are only too happy to take your foreign currency, at larcenous rates of exchange, so stock up at the bank on shopping days (see p. 235).

Haggling is a thing of the past. You can get an occasional small *sconto* (discount) for bulk purchases, but the spread of foreign travel has taught shopkeepers in the remotest province the going international price for everything. Except among antique, art and second-hand dealers, where negotiation is part of the business, you may get a very cool response if you question the marked price.

Many cities are renowned for products of their traditional crafts: Naples' costumed terracotta figures for its Christmas cribs, Sorrento's inlaid walnut furniture and music boxes, Ravenna's mosaics, Pisa's alabaster, Gubbio's ceramics. For the rest, the widest range of products will be found in the big cities. (Unless you're buying things you want to use during your vacation, such as clothes or sports equipment, save your shopping till the end, so as to avoid lugging the stuff all around the country.)

Rome

The capital's smartest and most expensive boutiques (even if you're not buying, they're worth window-shopping just for the superb displays) are conveniently concentrated in a four-by-four-block area around Via Condotti. Closed to cars, it's bounded by Piazza di Spagna to the east and Via del Corso to the west. Here you'll find the finest leather goods (Gucci, Fendi, Pier Caranti). Women's fashions include the major French designers as well as the natives (Valentino, Armani, Gianni Versace and Missoni). Almost as expensive are the two children's clothing shops of Tablò. Among the men's clothes meccas are Cucci (with a C) and Battistoni.

In **jewellery**, for sheer exclusivity, there's nothing like the imposing marble façade of Bulgari (Via Condotti), the ultimate monument to Roman luxury.

Two streets dominate the market in **art** and **antiques**, Via Margutta and Via del Babuino.

On the outskirts of this high-class shopping district, you'll find mass-produced sweaters, jeans and other casual wear, as well as more moderately priced leather goods, on the bustling Via Tritone and Via del Corso.

If you're looking for second-hand **bric-à-brac**, try shops around the Campo de' Fiori and Piazza Navona. The Sunday morning **flea market** at Porta Portese in Trastevere is as much fun for the street-musicians as for the chance of picking up bargains. Keep valuables safe—pickpockets love this place.

Florence

If it has ceded to Milan its place as Italy's fashion capital, the old Renaissance city is still a centre of exquisite, if somewhat conservative elegance. The principal thoroughfares for the smarter **fashion** boutiques, for men and women, are Via de' Tornabuoni and Via de' Calzaiuoli.

Florentine **leather goods** remain unequalled. You can smell out the country's, indeed Europe's finest craftsmen at work in leather factories around San Lorenzo and Santa Croce. Watch the making of handbags, wallets, gloves, belts and desk-equipment without any obligation to buy. Look out, too, for the leather school tucked away behind Santa Croce's sacristy in what were once Franciscan monk's cells.

Ponte Vecchio is the most picturesque place to shop for very reasonably priced **gold, silver** and **jewellery**, designed with centuries of tradition behind them.

Multicoloured glass mosaic jewellery—brooches, pendants, bracelets and rings—are all over town, handmade in local cottage-industry, amazingly cheap and very attractive.

Inlaid wood or *intarsia* is a venerated craft here, perfected in the 16th century with the inlay of semi-precious stones. Using the same techniques, **furniture** is likely to be expensive, but framed pictures of Tuscan landscapes or views of Florence are more moderately priced and, as souvenirs go, tastefully done. The town also specializes in **bookbinding** and stunningly beautiful **stationery.**

Antique shops are centred mainly around Borgo Ognissanti and San Jacopo, Via della Vigna Nuova and della Spada. Even if you cannot afford the mostly prohibitive prices, they're worth visiting as veritable little museums of Renaissance and Baroque sculpture and furniture. If the creative geniuses are long dead, master craftsmen continue the tradition of superb reproductions, at negotiable prices.

Venice

One of the many great adventures here is separating the treasure-house from the tourist-trap, distinguishing priceless gems from pricey junk. By and large, the better, but more expensive shops are around the Piazza San Marco. The busy shopping street of Mercerie has good quality boutiques growing progressively moderate in price as they approach the Rialto. For cheap purchases, head for the Strada Nuova leading behind the Ca' d'Oro to the railway station.

The bargains or at least more authentic and tasteful products are to be found, like the havens of tranquillity, far from these main tourist-centres, in artisans' workshops on the Giudecca, in the Dorsoduro behind the Zattere, over by the Ghetto, to be hunted down individually and guarded as precious secrets.

Two true institutions stand out among the **jewellery** shops: Missiaglia on Piazza San Marco and Sfriso on Campo San Tomà near the church of the Frari. For a cross-section of Venetian craftsmanship in more moderately priced jewellery, as well as **ceramics** and **glass mosaics,** take a look at Veneziartigiana, just off San Marco in Calle Larga.

The famous **glassware** poses a problem of quality and price. Much of the stuff is unspeakably ugly, but there is also an admirable renewal in both classical and modern design. Just hunt carefully. Necklaces of crystal or coloured beads are popular. Prices in the Murano island factories are marginally better than "downtown". When choosing gifts to be packed, remember: if real giraffes are fragile enough as it is, glass ones will never make it home; go for a rhinoceros.

Visit the island of Burano to see **laceware** being made in the time-honoured manner, on the doorstep. Modern reproductions of traditional patterns can be bought on and around Piazza San Marco, along with beautifully embroidered tablecloths and napkins.

The venerable Legatoria Piazzesi (by Santa Maria Zobenigo) is the last of the great Venetian printing presses, still producing exquisite handmade **paper goods,** stationery and bookbindings. And you can give your fancy dress balls a touch of Renaissance class with the finely crafted papier-mâché **masks** produced for the great Mardi Gras Carnival by workshops also turning out delightful toys, dolls and funny hats.

The range of **fashion** boutiques around San Marco is small but select, with a special emphasis on top-class **shoes** and other **leather goods.**

Milan

With the commercial leadership of the country, Milan has also taken over as **fashion** capital. For women's and men's clothes, you'll find all the great Italian designers—Valentino, Gianni Versace, Fendi, Krizia, Armani, Missoni and Ermenegildo Zegna—on and around Via Monte Napoleone. Here, too, are the leading **jewellery** shops.

The Galleria Vittorio Emanuele has plenty of smart, bright and more moderately priced boutiques for younger tastes. Bargain-hunters in jeans, shoes and cheaper fashions head for the popular stores along Via Torino and Via Manzoni.

Fashioned in the glassworks of Murano, here's one goldfish that won't die on you.

You'll find the **modern art** galleries and **antique** shops in the neighbourhood of the Brera Gallery and the side streets of the Via Monte Napoleone—Via Borgospesso, Via della Spiga and Via Sant'Andrea.

The town offers by far the best range of **household goods.** This is the place to find the very latest design in *espresso* machines and other kitchen gadgets.

EATING OUT

The spice of life so treasured by Italians is there in abundance every mealtime. From the unique punch of the early morning coffee via a steaming midday plate of basil-and-garlic flavoured *tagliatelle al pesto* to a last shot of after-dinner *grappa*, eating and drinking here is always a heart-warming experience.

Where to Eat

Only in a few hotels catering specifically for foreign tourists will you get English- or American-style **breakfast.** Otherwise head for a good *caffè* on the piazza and settle, happily, for the local *prima colazione* of superb coffee, *espresso* black or *cappuccino* with foaming hot milk (sprinkled in the best establishments with powdered chocolate), and toast or a sweet roll. Italian tea is as anemic as English coffee, but the hot chocolate is excellent.

Ideal for those adopting a healthy "sightseer's diet" of one main meal a day, preferably in the evening, with just a snack for **lunch,** stand-up bars in the city known as *tavola calda* serve sandwiches and hot or cold dishes at the counter. If you want to picnic in the park or out in the country and don't feel like preparing the food yourself, get your sandwiches made up for you at the *pizzicheria* delicatessen. Ask for *panino ripieno,* a bread roll which they fill with whatever sausage, cheese or salad you choose from the inviting display at the counter.

For **dinner,** even if you don't have to be overly budget-conscious, it's useful to know that the most elaborate restaurant *(ristorante),* with prices matching the real or apparent opulence of its décor, is almost invariably the worst value. Apart from an occasional "gastronomic temple" that you'll find in such specialist gourmet guides as the one published annually by the newsmagazine *L'Espresso,* the service is too often snooty and obsequious, the cuisine pretentious and mediocre. In a family-run *trattoria,* Venetian *locanda* or, especially in Naples and the south, a *pizzeria* which serves much more than just pizza, the ambience, half the value of an Italian meal, is infinitely more enjoyable and the food has more real character. Don't expect to find too much character in the average hotel dining room.

It's the custom to round off the bill with an extra tip in addition to the service charge.

This waiter will convince you pasta is a well-balanced diet.

What to Eat

The classical cuisine of Tuscany and Bologna and the pizza and pasta dishes of Naples are available everywhere, but you can try other regional specialities as you travel around the country. Despite the plethora of sauces for the pasta, the essence of Italian cooking is its simplicity: fish cooked with perhaps just a touch of fennel, other seafood served straight, cold, as an hors d'œuvre, Florentine steak charcoal-grilled, vegetables sautéed without elaborate disguise, at most marinated in lemon, olive oil and pepper.

Any *trattoria* worth its olive oil will set out on a long table near the entrance a truly painterly display of its **antipasti** (hors d'œuvre). The best way to get to know the delicacies is to make up

your own assortment *(antipasto misto)*. Both attractive and tasty are the cold *peperoni,* red, yellow and green peppers grilled, skinned and marinated in olive oil and a little lemon juice. Mushrooms *(funghi),* baby marrows *(zucchini),* aubergines *(melanzane),* artichokes *(carciofi)* and sliced fennel *(finocchio)* are also served cold, with a dressing *(pinzimonio)*. One of the most refreshing hors d'œuvre is the *mozzarella alla caprese,* slices of soft white buffalo cheese and tomato in a dressing of fresh basil and olive oil.

Try the tunny or tuna fish *(tonno)* with white beans and onions *(fagioli e cipolle)*. Mixed seafood hors d'œuvre *(antipasto di mare)* may include scampi, prawns *(gamberi),* mussels *(cozze),* fresh sardines *(sarde),* but also, chewily delicious, squid *(calamari)* and octopus *(polpi)*.

Ham from Parma or San Danieli (near Udine) is served paper thin with melon *(prosciutto con melone)* or, even better, fresh figs *(con fichi)*. Most salami is mass-produced industrial sausage from Milan, but try the local product of Florence, Genoa, Naples and Bologna and look out for Ferrara's piquant *salame da sugo*.

Popular **soups** are mixed vegetable *(minestrone),* clear soup *(brodo),* with an egg beaten into it *(stracciatella)*.

Remember that Italian restaurants traditionally serve **pasta** as an introductory course, not as the main dish. While they won't kill you, even the friendliest restaurant owners will raise a sad eyebrow if you make a whole meal out of a plate of spaghetti.

It is said that there are as many different forms of Italian pasta noodles as there are French cheeses—some 360 at last count, with new forms being created every year. Each sauce, tomato, cheese, cream, meat or fish, needs its own kind of noodle. In this land of painters and sculptors, the pasta's form and texture are an essential part of the taste.

Besides spaghetti and macaroni, the worldwide popularity of pasta has familiarized us with *tagliatelle* ribbon noodles (known in Rome as *fettuccine),* baked *lasagne* with layers of cheese, tomato and meat, rolled *cannelloni* crêpes, and stuffed *ravioli*. From there, you launch into the lusty poetry of *tortellini, cappelletti,* and *agnolotti* (all variations on ravioli), or curved *linguine,* flat *pappardelle,* quill-shaped *penne,* corrugated *rigatoni* and potato-flour *gnocchi*. Discover the other 346 for yourselves.

And there are almost as many sauces. The most famous, of course, is *bolognese,* known more succinctly in Bologna itself as *ragù*. The best includes not only minced beef, tomato puré and onions but chopped chicken livers, ham, carrot, celery, white wine and, vital ingredient in Bolognese cooking, nutmeg. Other popular sauces range from the simplest and spiciest *aglio e olio* (just garlic, olive oil and chilli peppers), *pomodoro* (tomato), *carbonara* (chopped bacon and eggs), *matriciana* (salt pork and tomato), Genoese *pesto* (basil and garlic ground up in olive oil with pine nuts and parmesan cheese) and *vongole* (clams and tomato), to the succulent *lepre* (hare in red wine) and startling *al nero*, yes, pasta blackened by the "ink" of the squid—wonderful. Don't be ashamed to ask whether Parmesan cheese should or should not be added to some of the more subtle pasta sauces.

For prince and peasant alike, the Po valley's ricefields have made **risotto** a worthy rival to pasta, particularly in and around Milan and Bergamo. The rice is cooked slowly in white wine, beef marrow, butter (not oil), saffron and Parmesan cheese. Delicious with mushrooms, chicken or seafood.

For the main dish, veal *(vitello)* has pride of place among the **meats**. Try the pan-fried cutlet *(costoletta)* Milanese-style in breadcrumbs, *scaloppine al limone* (veal fillets with lemon), *vitello tonnato* (veal in tunny fish

sauce), *alla fiorentina* (with a spinach sauce). The popular *saltimbocca* (literally "jump in the mouth") is an originally Roman veal-roll with ham, sage and Marsala, while *osso buco* is stewed veal shinbone. You'll find calf's liver *(fegato)* served in a Marsala sauce, *alla milanese* in breadcrumbs or *alla veneziana,* thinly sliced, fried with onions in olive oil.

Beef *(manzo),* pork *(maiale)* and lamb *(agnello)* are most often served straightforward, charcoal-grilled or roast *(al forno)* but, particularly in the south where the beef may be less tender, the meat is cooked in a tomato and garlic sauce *(alla pizzaiola).*

The most common **chicken** dishes are grilled *(pollo alla diavola),* fillets with ham and cheese *(petti di pollo alla bolognese)* or, like veal, in a tunny fish sauce *(tonnato).*

All the **fish** that you see displayed as *antipasti* are prepared very simply, grilled, steamed or fried. You should also look out for *spigola* (sea bass), *triglia* (red mullet), *pesce spada* (swordfish) and *coda di rospo* (angler fish). Be careful when ordering the *fritto misto.* Although this most often means a mixed fry of fish, it may be a mixture of breaded chicken breasts, calf's liver, veal and vegetables.

Aristocrats among the cooked

vegetables are the big boletus mushrooms *(funghi porcini),* which sometimes come stuffed *(ripieni)* with bacon, garlic, parsley and cheese. Try red peppers stewed with tomatoes *(peperonata)* or aubergine *(melanzane)* stuffed with anchovies, olives and capers. Baby onions *(cipolline)* and zucchini are both served sweet-and-sour *(agrodolce).*

Of the **cheeses,** the famous parmesan *(parmigiano),* far better than the exported product, is eaten separately, not just grated over soup or pasta. Try, too, the blue *gorgonzola, provolone* buffalo cheese, creamy Piedmontese *fontina,* the pungent cow's milk *taleggio* or ewe's milk *pecorino.* Roman *ricotta* can be sweetened with sugar and cinnamon.

Dessert means first and foremost *gelati,* the creamiest ice-cream in the world. But it's generally better in an ice-cream parlour *(gelateria)* than the average *trattoria.* Serious connoisseurs send you to Parma and Bologna for the best, but they lower their voices when Neapolitans are around. The deliciously refreshing coffee- or fruit-flavoured *granita* has very little to do with that miserably insipid concoction which English dictionaries helplessly evoke as "water ice" (think *sorbet* and you're getting close).

Nothing varies more in quality than the Italian version of trifle, *zuppa inglese* (literally "English soup"). It may indeed be an extremely thick but sumptuous soup of fruit and cream and cake and Marsala or just a very disap-

How could you resist stopping for lunch at a tempting trattoria like this?

pointing sickly slice of cake. You may prefer the chocolate trifle or *tirami sù* ("pull me up"). The *zabaglione* of whipped egg yolks, sugar and Marsala should be served warm or sent back.

Easier on the stomach is the fruit: grapes *(uva)*, peaches *(pesche)*, apricots *(albicocche)* and wonderful fresh figs *(fichi)*, both black and green. Fruit salad is *macedonia*.

Regional Specialities

Though most regional delicacies have spread nationwide, a few specialities are still to be found principally in their place of origin.

Rome goes in for hearty meat dishes. If its *saltimbocca* veal-rolls have gone around the world, gourmets insist you mustn't wander too far from the Piazza Navona to get a real

stufatino beef stew or *coda alla vaccinara* (oxtail braised with vegetables). Romans also claim the best roast kid *(capretto)* or spring lamb *(abbacchio)*. The capital's Jewish ghetto originated the *carciofi alla giudea,* whole artichokes, crisply deep-fried, stem, heart, leaves and all.

The coastal resorts of **Sardinia** cook up a pungent fish soup *(cassola è pisci)* and roast eel *(anguidda arrustia)*. Inland, kid *(capretto)* and suckling pig *(porceddù)* are roasted on the spit, as is the island's greatest delicacy, wild boar *(cinghiale)*. There's a great variety of country bread, the best being the charcoal-baked *civriaxiu*. Try it with the local *pecorino* ewe's cheese.

Tuscany produces Italy's best chicken. Try *pollo alla cacciatora,* "hunter's style", with mushrooms, tomatoes, shallots, herbs and strips of ham. The flavoursome charcoal-grilled T-bone or rib steak *(bistecca alla fiorentina)* is often big enough to cover a whole plate and will serve two people, very, very happily. Hearty stomachs enjoy the *trippe alla fiorentina,* tripe with tomato, marjoram and parmesan cheese. On the coast, look out for the *cacciucco,* a spicy fish stew of red mullet, squid and crab in tomatoes, onions, garlic, Chianti and croûtons. *Baccalà alla Livornese* is a simpler but similarly spicy cod stew.

The cuisine of **Umbria** has great finesse. The roast pork *(porchetta)* is especially fragrant with fennel and other herbs, and look out for a succulent spit-roasted wild pigeon *(palombacce allo spiedo)*. They are proud, too, of the *cacciotto* and *raviggiolo* ewe's cheese. In and around **Perugia**, the supreme pasta dish is spaghetti *ai tartufi neri* (with black truffles). Especially at Christmas time, the traditional *cappelletti in brodo* is served, a soup of ravioli stuffed with pork and veal.

Milan has contributed its risotto, breaded veal, *osso buco* and sweet *panettone* brioche to the nation. But it's kept for itself and its more robust visitors the *casoeula,* pork and sausages stewed in cabbage and other vegetables. Tough industrialists are weaned on *busecca alla milanese,* tripe with white beans. To fend off the autumn rains, the polenta maize-flour bread served with so many savoury **Lombardy** dishes becomes, as *polenta pasticciata,* a stout pie of mushrooms and white truffles in a béchamel sauce.

In **Venice,** when you see someone smacking a cod against a gondola's mooring-post, likely as not it's being "tenderized" for the great *baccalà mantecato* (cream of salt-cod), a smoother version of the French *brandade de morue*. The *grancevole,* beautiful red Adriatic spider-crabs, are treated more delicately as a centrepiece of Venetian seafood. Risotto is as popular here as in Lombardy, particularly with scampi or mussels, as well as the delightfully named *risi e bisi,* rice and green peas. An original creation of Harry's Bar, rendezvous of the international smart set down by the Grand Canal, beef *carpaccio* is sliced raw and thin as Parma ham and served with an olive oil and mustard sauce. During Carnival time, have the mussel soup *(zuppa di peoci)* to resist the February mists. But **Ravenna** can lay claim to the Adriatic's most bracing fish soup, *brodetto,* full of sea bass, squid, eel, red mullet and all kinds of shellfish.

Bologna has a position of leadership in Italian gastronomy similar to that of Lyon in France. Its old specialities are now the mainstays of the national cuisine, but some things are just not as good away from home: *tortellini* pasta coils stuffed with minced pork, veal, chicken and cheese; *costolette alla bolognese* (breaded veal cutlets with ham and cheese); and the monumental *lasagne verdi,* baked green pasta with beef *ragù,* béchamel sauce and the all-important nutmeg. The key to the classic Bologna *mortadella* sausage is the flavouring of white wine and coriander. One of the great rice dishes of **Parma** is the *bomba di riso,* pigeons cooked in a risotto with their livers and giblets, tomato purée and, of course, parmesan. Parma's *prosciutto* (raw ham) is world famous.

Turin is famous for its *bollita,* a most aristocratic boiled beef dish, with sausage, chicken, white beans, cabbage, potatoes and a tomato sauce. Not to be confused with the *fondu* from across the Swiss border, the *fonduta* of **Piedmont** is a hot dip of buttery *fontina* cheese, cream, pepper and white truffles.

In **Naples**, the tomato is king since the Spaniards brought it here from America in the 16th century. It's there, deliciously, in the simplest pasta, the thinner *vermicelli* for which *alla napolitana* just means with a tomato sauce. And it dominates the greatest not-so-fast food ever invented, the *pizza,* for which the classic version also includes anchovies *(acciughe),* mozzarella cheese and oregano. A handy, purely local version is the *calzone,* pocket-size pizzas filled with ham and mozzarella and folded over in a half-moon. The seafood is excellent, especially the sea bass *(spigola),* swordfish *(pesce spada),* squid *(calamari)* and octopus *(polpi).* Have your morning coffee with a crisp Neapolitan *sfogliatella* croissant filled with sweet ricotta cheese.

Wines

Italian wine is much more than just Chianti, but it wouldn't be a catastrophe if that's all it was. The best Chianti Classico produced between Florence and Siena (p.101) and distinguished by the proud *gallo nero* (black cockerel) label will please the most discerning palate. In a high-shouldered Bordeaux-style bottle, it's a strong, full-bodied red with a fine bouquet. Whereas most Italian wines can and should be drunk young, the Chianti Classico ages very well.

The best of the other Chianti reds, some in the more familiar fat basket-bottles, are *Ruffino* and *Montalbano.* (While straw is no guarantee of quality and authenticity, it's a fair rule-of-thumb that if the bottle's basket is *plastic,* the contents are similarly mass-produced and characterless.) Good Chianti whites are rare—try the *Trebbiano.*

Of the other Tuscany wines, the most appreciated reds are the earthy *Montepulciano* and rather dry *Brunello di Montalcino.* The best of the whites are the *Montecarlo* and San Gimignano's *Vernaccia,* both dry.

Orvieto in Umbria produces superb white wines, both dry and semi-dry. East of Rome in the

Alban Hills is the refreshingly light *Frascati.* The famous *Est! Est! Est!* (see p. 72) comes from Montefiascone on Lake Bolsena.

The very popular wines are centred around Verona and Lake Garda, notably the velvety *Valpolicella,* light and fruity, and the light *Bardolino. Soave* is a dry white with a faint almond flavour. The rosé *Chiaretto* comes from south of Lake Garda

Restaurant displays give a taste of pleasures to come.

and another rosé, *Pinot Grigio,* from Treviso.

Piedmont boasts some of Italy's finest reds, particularly the powerful, full-bodied *Barolo,* with a slight raspberry tang. *Barbera* has a lot of bouquet and tends to re-ferment in the bottle, producing a slight "fizz" that horrifies Frenchmen and delights Italians. The *Barbaresco* is the lightest of Piedmont reds. From south of Turin comes the sparkling *Asti spumante* a more than respectable alternative to champagne.

Among apéritifs, bitters like *Campari* and *Punt e Mes* are refreshing with soda and lemon. For after-dinner **drinks**, try the anis-flavoured *sambuca* with a *mosca* coffee-bean (literally a fly) swimming in it or *grappa* eau-de-vie distilled from grapes.

BERLITZ-INFO

CONTENTS

A ACCOMMODATION
(See also CAMPING)

Hotels *(albergo)*. There are five categories of hotels, graded by stars, from five down to one, with the rates fixed accordingly. The government issues a list of de-luxe, first- and second-class hotels for all major cities. Local tourist offices provide up-to-date hotel information but only in the smaller towns will they help you reserve rooms. At most airports and railway stations, hotel information desks provide free advice and booking facilities.

During high season and at Christmas and Easter, it is essential to book in advance in all the major tourist spots, and in Venice it is wise to reserve all year round.

Service charge, tourist tax and I.V.A. (sales tax) are often included in the room rate, but if prices are not listed as *tutto compreso* (all-inclusive), as much as 20 per cent can be added to your bill. Breakfast is usually not included in the rate. When leaving your hotel, remember to take the receipt of the payment with you.

Pensioni are family-style boarding houses, often with more character and a homelier atmosphere than hotels; but they will offer fewer facilities and may not have a restaurant; when there is one, you could well be treated to some excellent Italian family cooking.

Day hotels *(albergo diurno)*. This handy Italian institution, often situated close to major railway stations, does not provide overnight accommodation, but offers practical facilities for delightfully low prices. You can freshen up with a shower or bath, leave luggage or parcels, have a haircut, manicure or massage, have your laundry done or take a few hours rest.

Convents and monasteries. Some Roman Catholic orders take in guests at very reasonable rates. They offer comfortable rooms as well as meals. In other cases, monastries which have fallen into disuse have been converted into luxury hotels at luxury prices.

Inns *(locanda)*. There may not be a basin or hot water but prices are very low.

Villas and apartments. Families staying for a week or more will find it more economical, especially in the resorts, to rent a furnished villa or apartment. Most local tourist boards have information on companies arranging rental in these areas.

Youth hostels *(ostello della gioventù)*. There are over 50 youth hostels in Italy, open to holders of membership cards issued by the

International Youth Hostels Federation, or by the A.I.G. *(Associazione Italiana Alberghi per la Gioventù),* the Italian Youth Hostels Association, at:
Quadrato della Concordia, 9, 00144 Rome

a double/single room	**una camera matrimoniale/ singola**
with bath/shower	**con bagno/doccia**
What's the rate per night?	**Qual è il prezzo per notte?**

AIRPORTS *(aeroporto)*

Rome and Milan are Italy's principal gateway cities, while a limited number of international flights serve other airports.

Check-in time is 1½ hours before departure for international flights, 30 minutes before domestic flights.

Rome. *Leonardo da Vinci,* more commonly known as Fiumicino, lies 30 km. (19 mi.) south-west of the city centre and handles most scheduled air traffic. There are two terminals, one for domestic, one for international flights. *Ciampino,* 16 km. (10 mi.) south-east of the city, serves mainly charter flights. Fiumicino is linked to the city air terminal (at Termini railway station, Via Giolitti) by a frequent and inexpensive public bus service. By taxi allow at least an hour to Fiumicino and 45 minutes to Ciampino, depending on downtown rush-hour conditions.

Milan. *Linate,* 7 km. (4 mi.) east of the city centre, handles domestic and international flights. *Malpensa,* 50 km. (30 mi.) north-west of Milan, serves intercontinental traffic. From both airports there is a bus service every 20 minutes to the air terminal at Viale Sturzo 37. The two airports are also linked by a not-so-frequent bus service.

Where's the bus for...?	**Dov'è l'autobus per...?**
Porter!	**Facchino!**
Take these bags to the bus/taxi, please.	**Mi porti queste valige fino all'autobus/al taxi, per favore.**

B   BABY-SITTERS   B

Many hotels keep lists of baby-sitters (generally students) known to them personally, and the local papers will carry advertisements in English or under the heading *Bambinaia.* A number of agencies are also listed in English in the telephone directory under "Baby Sitters".

C CAMPING (campeggio)

There are about 1,700 official campsites in Italy, graded, like the hotels, by stars. Most of them are equipped with electricity, water and toilet facilities. They are listed in the yellow pages of the telephone directory under "Campeggi-Ostelli-Villaggi Turistici". You can also contact the local tourist office (see TOURIST INFORMATION OFFICES) for a comprehensive list of sites, rates and complete details. The Touring Club Italiano (TCI) and the Automobile Club d'Italia (ACI) publish lists of campsites and tourist villages, which can be bought at bookstores or referred to in the tourist office. You are strongly advised to keep to the official sites.

To camp in the peak summer season, you should reserve in advance through the Centro Internazionale Prenotazioni Campeggio (Federcampeggio): Casella Postale 23, 50041 Calenzano (Florence).

The *International Camping Carnet*, a pass that gives modest discounts and insurance coverage throughout Europe is required at many campsites in Italy. It can be obtained through the TCI or Federcampeggio.

If you enter Italy with a caravan, you should be able to show an inventory (with two copies) of the material and equipment in the caravan, e.g. dishes and linen.

May we camp here?	**Possiamo campeggiare qui?**
Is there a campsite nearby?	**C'è un campeggio qui vicino?**

CAR HIRE (autonoleggio)

The major international car rental firms have offices in the main cities and at the airports; they are listed in the yellow pages of the telephone directory. Your hotel receptionist may be able to recommend a less expensive local firm. You need a valid driving licence. Minimum age varies from 21 to 25 according to the company. A deposit is often required except for credit card holders; insurance is mandatory. It is possible to rent a car in one Italian city and turn it in in another; occasionally you can arrange to have the car delivered to your hotel.

Weekend rates and weekly unlimited mileage rates are usually available, and it's worth enquiring about any seasonal deals.

I'd like to rent a car	**Vorrei noleggiare una macchina**
(tomorrow).	**(per domani).**
for one day	**per un giorno**
for one week	**per una settimana**

CIGARETTES, CIGARS, TOBACCO *(sigarette, sigari, tabacco).*
Tobacco products and matches are price-controlled and can be
sold only at official tobacconists—easily recognizable by a large
white *T* on a dark background over the door—or at certain
authorized hotel newsstands and café counters. Many of the best-
known foreign brands are available, but they may cost as much
as 50% more than domestic makes.

Smoking is prohibited on public transport and in taxis, in most
cinemas and theatres, and in some shops.

I'd like a packet of...	**Vorrei un pacchetto di...**
with/without filter	**con/senza filtro**
I'd like a box of matches.	**Per favore, mi dia una scatola di fiammiferi.**

CITY TRANSPORT

Bus and tram. In addition to the usual bus network, some big cities
also have trams; Naples has four funicular routes. Each bus stop
indicates the numbers of the buses stopping there and the routes
they serve. Tickets for buses must be bought in advance from
newsstands or tobacco shops; you enter by the rear doors and
punch the ticket in the machine. Some trams have conductors
at the back who sell tickets.

Underground (subway). Rome, Milan and Naples have underground railway lines *(metropolitana,* or *metrò)*, by far the fastest
means of transport in these cities. Tickets are sold at newsstands
and tobacconists, or can be purchased from machines at the
stations.

Taxi. Taxis—easily recognizable in each city for their distinctive
colour—may be hailed in the street, picked up at a taxi rank or obtained by telephone. The yellow pages of the telephone directory
list all the ranks under "Taxi". Taxis remain cheap by North-
European and American standards, but you should always make
sure that the meter is running. Extra charges for luggage and for
night, holiday or airport trips are posted in four languages inside

all taxis. A tip of at least 10% is customary. Beware of the unlicensed non-metered *taxi pirati*, which charge much more than the normal taxi rates for trips in private cars.

Where's the nearest bus stop/ underground station?	**Dov'è la fermata d'autobus/ la stazione della metropolitana più vicina?**
When's the next bus/ train to...?	**Quando parte il prossimo autobus/treno per...?**
I'd like a ticket to...	**Vorrei un biglietto per...**
single (one-way)	**andata**
return (round-trip)	**andata e ritorno**

CLIMATE AND CLOTHING

With its northernmost point in the snowy Alps and its southernmost point washed by the Mediterranean sea, Italy's climate is naturally very varied. Inland in the north, temperatures tend to be continental, with hot summers and cold winters. The Ligurian coastal strip is famous for its mild winters. Towards the south, the weather gets warmer and more Mediterranean.

The busiest tourist season is July and August, but spring and autumn are the choicest times.

Bring light- to medium-weight clothing and rainwear if you're travelling in early spring and autumn. During winter you will need a light topcoat for the south, and a winter overcoat for the north. From May to September you should take along cotton summer clothes with a jacket or cardigan for the evening. Comfortable walking shoes are indispensable. Casual wear is the general rule in most places and few restaurants insist on a tie. Shorts and bare-backed dresses are frowned on in churches, and women may have to cover their bare arms.

Here are some average daily temperatures:

		J	F	M	A	M	J	J	A	S	O	N	D
Milan	max.	40	46	56	65	74	80	84	82	75	63	51	43
	min.	32	35	43	49	57	63	67	66	61	52	43	35
Rome	max.	52	55	59	66	74	82	87	86	79	71	61	55
	min.	40	42	45	50	56	63	67	67	62	55	49	44
Naples	max.	53	55	59	65	72	79	84	84	79	71	63	56
	min.	40	41	44	48	54	61	65	65	61	54	48	44

And in degrees Celsius:

Milan												
	max.	5	8	13	18	23	27	29	28	24	17	10	6
	min.	0	2	6	10	14	17	20	19	16	11	6	2
Rome	max.	11	13	15	19	23	28	30	30	26	22	16	13
	min.	5	5	7	10	13	17	20	20	17	13	9	6
Naples	max.	12	13	15	18	22	26	29	29	26	22	17	14
	min.	4	5	6	9	12	16	18	18	16	12	9	6

COMMUNICATIONS
(See also Hours)

Post offices *(posta* or *ufficio postale)* handle telegrams, mail and money transfers. Postage stamps are also sold at tobacconists and at some hotel desks. Post boxes are red. The slot marked *Per la città* is for local mail only; the one marked *Altre destinazioni* is for all other destinations.

Poste Restante/General Delivery *(fermo posta)*. For a short stay it is not worth arranging to receive mail, as the post is often slow. However, there is a poste restante service at the main post office in the cities. Don't forget your passport for identification when you go to pick up mail. You will have to pay a small fee.

Telegrams *(telegramma)*. Night letters, or night-rate telegrams *(lettera telegramma)*, which arrive the next morning, are far cheaper than ordinary cables, but can only be sent outside Italy.

Telephone *(telefono)*. There are public telephone booths at strategic locations in the cities, as well as in almost every bar and café, indicated by a sign showing a telephone dial and receiver. The telephone companies have offices in the major cities and at railway stations and airports, from where you can make long-distance or international calls.

Older types of public payphones require tokens *(gettoni)* with a value of 200 lire (available at bars, hotels, post offices and tobacconists); modern ones, with two separate slots, take both *gettoni* and 100- and 200-lira coins.

If the telephone is labelled *Teleselezione*, you can make direct international calls, but stock up with coins or tokens. Some telephones will take magnetic cards with a value of 6,000 or 9,000 lire, available at SIP (Italian Telephone Service) offices.

Insert the token or coin and lift the receiver. The normal dialling tone is a series of long dash sounds. A dot-dot-dot series means the central computer is overloaded; hang up and try again.

The English-speaking operators of the ACI's telephone assistance service provide tourists with information and advice. Dial 116.

Some useful numbers:

Local directory and other Italian enquiries	12
Operator for Europe	15
Intercontinental operator	170
Telegrams	186

Give me... gettoni, please.	**Per favore, mi dia... gettoni.**
Can you get me this number in...?	**Può passarmi questo numero a...?**
I'd like a stamp for this letter/postcard.	**Desidero un francobollo per questa lettera/cartolina.**
express (special delivery)	**espresso**
airmail	**via aerea**
registered	**raccomandata**

COMPLAINTS *(reclamo)*

To avoid unpleasant situations, observe the cardinal rule of commerce in Italy: come to an agreement in advance—the price, the supplements, the taxes and the services to be received, preferably in writing. The threat of formal declaration to the police should be effective in such cases as overcharging for car repairs, but this will consume hours, if not days of your visit. In hotels, shops and restaurants, complaints should be made to the manager *(direttore)* or the proprietor *(proprietario)*.

Any complaint about a taxi fare should be settled by referring to the notice, in four languages, affixed by law in each taxi, specifying charges in excess of the meter rate.

For all serious complaints, including outright theft, telephone the police *questura* (see POLICE).

CRIME AND THEFT

Cases of violence against tourists are still rare, but it's wise to leave your unneeded documents and excess money locked up in the hotel safe and keep what you take in an inside pocket. Handbags are particularly vulnerable; agile thieves, often operating in pairs on vespas or motorbikes, whisk past and snatch them from the shoulder, sometimes even cutting or breaking the straps to do so. Be particularly attentive on crowded public transport or in secluded streets and districts. It's a good idea to make photocopies of your tickets, passport and other vital documents, which will greatly facilitate reporting a theft, should it happen, and obtaining replacements.

If you leave your car parked somewhere, lock it and empty it of everything, not only of valuables, with the glove compartments empty and open to discourage prospective thieves.

I want to report a theft.	**Voglio denunciare un furto.**
My wallet/handbag/passport/ ticket has been stolen.	**Mi hanno rubato il portafoglio/ la borsa/il passaporto/il biglietto.**

CUSTOMS AND ENTRY REGULATIONS

For a stay of up to three months, a valid passport is sufficient for citizens of Australia, Canada, New Zealand and U.S.A. Visitors from Eire and and the United Kingdom need only an identity card to enter Italy. Tourists from South Africa must have a visa.

Here are some main items you can take into Italy duty-free and, when returning home, into your own country:

Into:	Cigarettes	Cigares	Tobacco	Spirits	Wine
1)	200	50 or	250 g.	¾ l. or	2 l.
2)	300	75 or	400 g.	1.5 l. and	4 l.
3)	400	100	500 g.	¾ l.	2 l.
Into:					
Australia	200	250 g. or	250 g.	1 l. or	1 l.
Canada	200	50 and	900 g.	1.1 l. or	1.1 l.
Eire	200	50 or	250 g.	1 l. and	2 l.
N. Zealand	200	50 or	250 g.	1.1 l. and	4.5 l.
S. Africa	400	50 and	250 g.	1 l. and	2 l.
U.K.	200	50 or	250 g.	1 l. and	2 l.
U.S.A.	200	100 and	4)	1 l. or	1 l.
1) within Europe from non-EEC countries 2) within Europe from EEC countries 3) countries outside Europe 4) a reasonable quantity					

Currency restrictions. Non-residents may import or export up to L. 500,000 in local currency. In foreign currencies, you may import unlimited amounts, but to take the equivalent of more than L. 5,000,000 in or out of the country, you must fill out a V2 declaration form at the border upon entry.

When leaving. If you're exporting archaeological relics, works of art or gems, you should obtain a bill of sale and a permit from the government (this is normally handled by the dealer).

| *I've nothing to declare.* | **Non ho nulla da dichiarare.** |
| *It's for my personal use.* | **È per mio uso personale.** |

D DRIVING IN ITALY

Entering Italy. To bring your car into Italy, you will need:

- an International Driving Permit or a valid national licence
- car registration papers
- Green Card (an extension to your regular insurance policy, making it valid specifically for Italy)
- a red warning triangle in case of breakdown
- national identity sticker for your car

Drivers of cars that are not their own must have the owner's written permission.

Note. Before leaving home, check with your automobile association about the latest regulations concerning *petrol coupons* (giving tourists access to cheaper fuel) in Italy, as they are constantly changing.

Speed limits. Speed limits in Italy are based on the car engine size. The following chart gives the engine size in cubic centimetres and the limits (in kilometres per hour) on the open road (limit in built-up areas is usually 50 kph).

Engine size	less than 600 cc.	600 to 900 cc.	900 to 1300 cc. (and motor-cycles more than 150 cc.)	more than 1300 cc.
Main roads Motorways (Express-ways)	80 kph 90 kph	90 kph 110 kph	100 kph 130 kph	110 kph 140 kph

Driving conditions. Drive on the right, pass on the left. Traffic on major roads has right of way over that entering from side roads; but this is frequently ignored, so be very careful. At intersections of roads of similar importance, the car on the right theoretically has the right of way. When passing other vehicles, or remaining in the left-hand (passing) lane, keep your directional indicator flashing.

The motorways *(autostrada)* are designed for fast and safe driving; a toll is collected for each section, according to the distance travelled.

Last but not least: Italian drivers make indiscriminate use of their horns. Follow their example whenever it could help to warn of your impending arrival.

Traffic police *(polizia stradale)*. All cities and many towns and villages have signs posted at the outskirts indicating at least the telephone number of the local traffic police or the *carabinieri*.

The traffic police patrol the highways and byways on motorcycles or in Alfa Romeos, usually light blue. Speeding fines can often be paid on the spot, but ask for a receipt *(ricevuta)*.

Breakdowns. Call boxes are located at regular intervals on the *autostrade* in case of breakdowns or other emergencies. You can dial 116 for breakdown service from the ACI.

Fuel and oil. Service stations abound in Italy, most with at least one mechanic on duty (who's likely to be a Fiat specialist). Most close on Sundays, and everyday from noon to 3 p.m. Fuel *(benzina)*, sold at government-set prices, comes in super (98–100 octane), unleaded (95 octane)—still rare—and normal (86–88 octane). Diesel fuel is usually also available.

Fluid measures

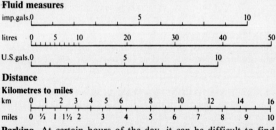

Distance

Kilometres to miles

Parking. At certain hours of the day, it can be difficult to find a parking place without risking a fine. Many cities have outdoor parking lots, supervised by attendants. Generally they are marked by large blue signs with a white "P". The main cities have towaway zones; if you park your car there, it may be towed to the municipal garages or parking lots. You will be able to retrieve it after paying a hefty fine at the post office. On Sundays and holidays the municipal garages are closed and cars cannot be recovered.

Road signs. Most road signs employed in Italy are international pictographs, but there are some written ones you may come across:

Accendere le luci	*Use headlights*
Deviazione	*Diversion (Detour)*
Divieto di sorpasso	*No overtaking (passing)*
Divieto di sosta	*No stopping*
Lavori in corso	*Road works (Men working)*
Passaggio a livello	*Level railway crossing*
Pericolo	*Danger*
Rallentare	*Slow down*
Senso vietato/unico	*No entry/One-way street*
Vietato l'ingresso	*No entry*
Zona pedonale	*Pedestrian zone*
driving licence	**patente**
car registration papers	**libretto di circolazione**
green card	**carta verde**
Fill the tank, please.	**Per favore, faccia il pieno.**
super/normal	**super/normale**
unleaded/diesel	**senza piombo/gasolio**
I've had a breakdown.	**Ho avuto un guasto.**
There's been an accident.	**C'è stato un incidente.**

E ELECTRIC CURRENT
Generally 220 volts, 50 Hz AC, but sometimes 125-volt outlets, with different plugs and sockets for each. The voltage might be indicated on the socket in hotels, but it's best to ask.

EMBASSIES AND CONSULATES *(ambasciata; consolato)*
Practically all countries of the world have embassies in Rome, and some maintain consulates in other Italian cities.

Australia	Via Alessandria, 215; tel. 84 12 41
Canada	Via G. Battista de Rossi, 27; tel. 85 53 41/4
Eire	Largo del Nazareno, 3; tel. 6 78 25 41
South Africa	Piazza Monte Grappa, 4; tel. 3 60 84 41
United Kingdom	Via XX Settembre, 80; tel. 4 75 54 41
U.S.A.	Via Vittorio Veneto, 119; tel. 46 74

EMERGENCIES

In an emergency you can phone the following numbers all over
Italy 24 hours a day:

Police, all purpose emergency number	113
Carabinieri (see POLICE) for urgent police problems	112
Road assistance (ACI) and advice for tourists	116

Careful!	**Attenzione!**
Fire!	**Incendio!**
Help!	**Aiuto!**
Stop thief!	**Al ladro!**

GETTING TO ITALY G

See a good travel agent before your departure for help with your
timetable, budget and personal requirements.

By Air

Scheduled flights

Rome's Fiumicino and Milan's Linate and Malpensa airports are
the principal gateways (see also under AIRPORTS), though certain
international flights operate into Bologna, Genoa, Naples, Pisa,
Turin and Venice.

Approximate flying times: New York–Rome 8 hours; Los Ange-
les–Rome 15 hours; London–Rome 2½ hours; Sydney–Rome
26 hours.

Charter flights and package tours

From the U.K. and Eire. There is a wide range of package tours
available. If you are planning on touring Italy, look into fly-drive
possibilities, with flight and rented car included.

From North America. Package tours including hotel, car or other
land arrangements can be very good value. In addition to APEX
and Excursion fares, there's the Advance Booking Charter (ABC),
which must be bought at least 30 days in advance.

By Car

Cross-channel car-ferries link the U.K. with France, Belgium or
Holland. From there you can put your car on a train to Milan
(starting points include Boulogne, Paris and Cologne). If you are
driving yourself, you will find that the excellent motorway network across the Continent is such that you can now drive from the
Channel coast to the toe of Italy without ever leaving a motorway.

By Bus

Express buses operate between London and the major Italian cities all year round.

By Rail

In Great Britain and Ireland, British Rail and its agents issue tickets to Italy's main cities with a validity of two months.

Both *Inter-Rail* and *Rail Europ Senior* cards are valid in Italy, as is the *Eurailpass* for non-European residents (sign up before you leave home). See under TRAVELLING AROUND ITALY for details of special tickets within the country.

GUIDES AND INTERPRETERS *(guida; interprete)*

Most hotels in the big cities can arrange for multilingual guides or interpreters. A selection is found in the yellow pages of the telephone directories under the entry "Traduzione", and local newspapers carry advertisements offering such services. There are also guides near most of the major tourist attractions, and portable recorders with commentaries in English can often be hired.

The Italian State Tourist Agency, CIT, and many private firms offer tours of all the major sights, plus excursions to other points of interest.

We'd like an English-speaking guide.	**Desideriamo una guida che parla inglese.**
I need an English interpreter.	**Ho bisogno di un interprete d'inglese.**

H HEALTH AND MEDICAL CARE

If your health-insurance policy does not cover hospital bills in foreign countries, you can take out a special short-term policy before leaving home. Visitors from Great Britain and Eire have the right to claim public health services available to Italians, since they are members of the EEC. Before departure obtain a copy of the proper form (E111) from the U.K. Department of Health and Social Security.

If you are in need of medical care, it is best to ask your hotel receptionist to help you find a doctor (or dentist) who speaks English. Local Health Units of the Italian National Health Service are listed in the telephone directory under "Unità Sanitaria Locale".

The first-aid *(pronto soccorso)* section of municipal hospitals handle medical emergencies.

Pharmacies. The Italian *farmacia* is open during shopping hours (see Hours), and there is usually one per district that operates at night and on weekends. The opening schedule for duty pharmacies is posted on every pharmacy door and in the local papers.

Bring along an adequate supply of any prescribed medication.

I need a doctor/dentist.	**Ho bisogno di un medico/ dentista.**
Where's the nearest (all-night) chemist?	**Dov'è la farmacia (di turno) più vicina?**

HOURS

Opening hours vary from region to region, and sometimes even from district to district in the large cities. In true Mediterranean fashion, much of Italy shuts down, or at least slows down, in the hours after lunch. However, in Rome and in the northern cities, the modern business day is gradually creeping in, with a non-stop day at least in the city centre. The following should therefore just be used as a guideline.

Banks. 8.30 a.m.–1.30 p.m. and sometimes again for an hour or so in the afternoon, Monday to Friday.

Churches generally close at lunchtime, approximately noon to 3 p.m. or even later.

Museums and galleries. Museums and sites are usually open Tuesday to Sunday 9 a.m.–2 p.m. and, in some cases, again 5–8 p.m. Closing day is usually Monday; if Monday is a holiday, the museums are closed the following Tuesday.

Pharmacies. Open 8.30 a.m.–1 p.m. and 4–8 p.m.

Post offices. Normally open 8.15 a.m.–2.30 p.m., Monday to Friday, until noon on Saturdays. Some main branches stay open till 8 p.m.

Principal businesses. 8 or 9 a.m.–1 or 1.30 p.m. and 4, 4.30 or 5–7, 7.30 or 8 p.m., Monday to Saturday. Sometimes closed Saturday afternoons.

Shops. Open 9 a.m.–12.30 or 1 p.m. and 4–7.30 p.m., Monday to Saturday (half-day closing is usually Monday mornings); food stores open 8.30 a.m.–12.30 or 1 p.m. and 5–7.30 p.m. (half-day closing is usually Thursday afternoons).

L LANGUAGE

Italians appreciate foreigners making an effort to speak their language, even if it is only a few words. In the major tourist hotels and shops of the big cities, the staff usually speak some English.

Remember that the letter "c" is pronounced like "ch" when it is followed by an "e" or an "i", while the letters "ch" together sound like the "c" in cat.

The Berlitz phrase book ITALIAN FOR TRAVELLERS covers all the situations you are likely to encounter in Italy; also useful is the Italian-English/English Italian pocket dictionary, containing a special menu-reader supplement.

Do you speak English?	**Parla inglese?**
I don't speak Italian.	**Non parlo italiano.**

LAUNDRY AND DRY-CLEANING

Most hotels will handle laundry and dry-cleaning. For lower rates you can either do your own washing at a *lavanderia* (or leave it with the attendant) or hand it in at a *tintoria,* which will usually offer a normal or express service.

When will it be ready?	**Quando sarà pronto?**
I must have this for to-morrow morning.	**Mi serve per domani mattina.**

M MAPS *(cartina)*

Newsstands and tourist offices have a large selection of maps at a wide range of prices. The maps in this guide were prepared by Falk-Verlag, Hamburg, which also publishes a complete map to Italy and to Rome.

MEETING PEOPLE

The real difficulty in Italy is *not* meeting people. They're everywhere, and for the most part, give or take a few soured by modern urban stress, as warm and outgoing as ever. Look out for the optimal hour of the late afternoon *passeggiata,* when people gather in the cafés and piazzas and the cares of the day are dissolved and the joys of the evening prepared. But remember to arm yourselves with a few introductory Italian phrases (see p. 243). It works wonders between tables at the trattoria. One last reassurance: in the big cities, the impressive emancipation of Italian women has largely put paid to that old habit of bottom-pinching.

MONEY MATTERS

Currency. The *lira* (plural: *lire*, abbreviated *L.* or *Lit.*) is Italy's monetary unit.

Coins: L. 5, 10, 20, 50, 100, 200 and 500.

Notes: L. 1,000, 2,000, 5,000, 10,000, 50,000 and 100,000.

For currency restrictions, see CUSTOMS AND ENTRY REGULATIONS.

Currency exchange offices *(cambio)* usually reopen after the siesta, until at least 6.30 p.m.; some are open on Saturday. Exchange rates are less advantageous than in banks. A flat rate of commission is common, so it is not worth changing small amounts many times. Passports are sometimes required when changing money.

Credit cards and traveller's cheques. Most hotels, many shops and some restaurants take credit cards. Traveller's cheques are accepted almost everywhere, but you will get much better value if you exchange your cheques for lire at a bank or *cambio*. Passports are required when cashing cheques. Eurocheques are easily cashed in Italy.

I want to change some pounds/ dollars.	**Desidero cambiare delle sterline/ dei dollari.**
Do you accept traveller's cheques?	**Accetta traveller's cheques?**
Can I pay with this credit card?	**Posso pagare con la carta di credito?**

NEWSPAPERS AND MAGAZINES

Some British and Continental newspapers and magazines are on sale, sometimes a day late, at the airport and stations and in the kiosks in the big cities. The *International Herald Tribune* is printed in Rome and is available early in the morning. Prices are high for all foreign publications.

Have you any English-language newspapers?	**Avete giornali in inglese?**

P POLICE

The municipal police *(Vigili Urbani)*, dressed in navy blue with
white helmets or all-white with shiny buttons, handle city traffic
and other city police tasks. They are courteous and helpful to
tourists, though they rarely speak a foreign language. Some do act
as interpreters, in which case they will carry a badge on their
uniforms.

The *Carabinieri*, who wear brown or black uniforms, deal with
serious crimes and demonstrations, and the *Polizia di Stato*
(national police), dressed in blue, deal with usual police matters.

Outside the towns, the *Polizia Stradale* patrol the roads (see
DRIVING IN ITALY).

The all-purpose emergency number, 113, will get you police
assistance.

Where's the nearest police station?	**Dov'è il più vicino posto di polizia?**

PRICES

To give you an idea of what to expect, here are some average prices
in Italian lire (L). However, inflation makes them unavoidably
approximate, and there are considerable regional and seasonal
differences. The following prices are based on those in Rome and
may be on the high side compared to less visited areas.

Airport transfer. *Rome*: bus between Fiumicino airport and
Termini railway station L. 5,000; taxi L. 45,000–50,000. *Milan:*
bus between Linate and city centre L. 2,500; taxi L. 25,000–30,000.

Camping. Adults L. 6,000 per person per night, caravan (trailer)
or camper L. 5,000–10,000, tent L. 2,500–3,000, car L. 2,500–3,000,
motorbike L. 1,200–2,500.

Car hire (international company). *Fiat Panda 45* L. 38,300 per
day, L. 599 per km., L. 592,000 per week with unlimited mileage.
Alfa 33 L. 67,800 per day, L. 816 per km., L. 939,000 per week
with unlimited mileage. Add 18% tax.

Cigarettes (packet of 20). Italian brands L. 1,600 and up, imported
brands L. 2,500–3,000.

Entertainment. Cinema L. 6,000–7,000, discotheque (entry and
one drink) L. 20,000–30,000, outdoor opera L. 15,000–35,000.

Guides. Half-day (3 hours) for individual or family L. 80,000.

Hairdressers. *Woman's* shampoo and set or blow-dry L. 18,000–27,000, permanent wave L. 45,000–70,000. *Man's* hair-cut L. 12,000–15,000, L. 20,000 with shampoo.

Hotels (double room with bath, including tax and service). ***** L. 400,000–600,000, **** L. 130,000–380,000, *** L. 70,000–240,000, ** L. 45,000–190,000, * L. 30,000–100,000.

Meals and drinks. Continental breakfast L. 7,000–15,000; lunch/dinner in fairly good establishment L. 35,000–80,000; coffee served at a table L. 2,500–4,500, served at the bar L. 600–800; bottle of wine L. 4,000 and up; soft drink L. 1,500–3,000; aperitif L. 2,500 and up.

Museums. L. 3,000–7,000. Free for children up to the age of 12 accompanied by an adult.

Taxi. L. 2,800 for first 250 metres or period of 1 minute, L. 200 for each successive 300 metres or 60 seconds. Night charge L. 2,500, suitcases L. 500 each, holiday surcharge L. 1,000.

Youth Hostels. 12,500 per night with breakfast.

PUBLIC HOLIDAYS *(festa)*

Italy has ten national holidays a year. When one falls on a Thursday or a Tuesday, Italians may make a *ponte* (bridge) to the weekend, meaning that Friday or Monday is taken off as well.

January 1	*Capodanno* or *Primo dell'Anno*	New Year's Day
January 6	*Epifania*	Epiphany
April 25	*Festa della Liberazione*	Liberation Day
May 1	*Festa del Lavoro*	Labour Day (May Day)
August 15	*Ferragosto*	Assumption Day
November 1	*Ognissanti*	All Saints' Day
December 8	*L'Immacolata Concezione*	Immaculate Conception
December 25	*Natale*	Christmas Day
December 26	*Santo Stefano*	St. Stephen's Day
Movable date	*Lunedì di Pasqua (Pasquetta)*	Easter Monday

Note: On all national holidays, banks, government offices, most shops and some museums and galleries are closed. Local feast days are held in honour of each town's patron saint.

R RADIO AND TV *(radio; televisione)*
During the tourist season, RAI, the Italian state radio and TV network, occasionally broadcasts news in English; from midnight to
6 a.m. there are brief newscasts in English and other languages.
Vatican Radio carries foreign-language religious news programmes
at various times during the day. British (BBC), American (VOA)
and Canadian (CBC) programmes are easily obtained on short-
wave transistor radios. RAI television broadcasts only in Italian,
as do the variety of private channels.

RELIGIOUS SERVICES
Roman Catholic mass is usually celebrated daily and several times
on Sunday in Italian, and you may find services in English in
Rome. Major non-Catholic denominations and Jews have congre-
gations in the big cities, often with services in English. Details are
published in the local papers.

RESTAURANTS
See also p. 208. You will find all types and classes of restaurant all
over Italy. In theory, a *ristorante* is supposed to be a larger and
fancier establishment than a family-style *trattoria*. But in many
cases the distinction is blurred beyond recognition: they're both
ways of saying restaurant, as is the less frequent *osteria*.

Restaurants usually serve from about 12.30 to 3 p.m. and from
7.30 p.m. to midnight, and each is closed one day a week. It's wise
to book a table by telephone, particularly if you want to dine
at peak hours (in cities around 1.30 and 9 p.m.; earlier in the
country).

The strictly Italian snack bar or *tavola calda* offers pasta,
slices of pizza and other snacks, sandwiches and salads, at a fraction of restaurant prices. They're crowded but quick; you may
have to eat standing up. *Pizzerie* are found all over. Snack bars
are open from early morning till late at night without interruption.

All restaurants, however modest, must now issue a formal
receipt indicating the tax (I.V.A.). In theory, you can be stopped
by the police as you leave the restaurant and fined if you are unable
to present the receipt.

To Help You Order...

What do you recommend?	**Cosa consiglia?**
Do you have a set menu?	**Avete un menù a prezzo fisso?**

I'd like a/an/some...		*Vorrei...*	
beer	una birra	meat	della carne
bread	del pane	milk	del latte
butter	del burro	potatoes	delle patate
coffee	un caffè	salad	dell'insalata
cream	della panna	soup	una minestra
dessert	un dolce	sugar	dello zucchero
fish	del pesce	tea	un tè
fruit	della frutta	water	dell'acqua
ice-cream	un gelato	wine	del vino

...and Read the Menu

aglio	*garlic*	gamberi	*prawns*
agnello	*lamb*	maiale	*pork*
antipasto	*hors d'œuvre*	manzo	*beef*
arrosto	*roast*	melanzana	*aubergine (eggplant)*
bistecca	*steak*		
braciola	*chop*	peperoni	*peppers*
calamari	*squid*	pesce	*fish*
carciofi	*artichokes*	pollo	*chicken*
cipolle	*onions*	prosciutto	*ham*
coniglio	*rabbit*	rognoni	*kidneys*
fagioli	*beans*	salsa	*sauce*
fegato	*liver*	sogliola	*sole*
formaggio	*cheese*	spinaci	*spinach*
fragole	*strawberries*	stufato	*stew*
frutti di mare	*seafood*	triglia	*red mullet*
		uova	*eggs*
funghi	*mushrooms*	vitello	*veal*

TIME DIFFERENCES

T

Italy follows Central European Time (GMT + 1), and from late March to September clocks are put one hour ahead (GMT + 2). Summer time chart:

New York	London	**Italy**	Sydney	Auckland
6 a.m.	11 a.m.	**noon**	8 p.m.	10 p.m.

What time is it?	**Che ore sono?**

239

TIPPING

Though a service charge is added to most restaurant bills, it is customary to leave an additional tip. It is also in order to hand the bellboys, doormen, hat check attendants, garage attendants, etc., a little something for their services. The chart below will give you some guidelines:

Hotel porter, per bag	L. 1,000
Hotel maid, per day	L. 1,000
Lavatory attendant	L. 300
Waiter	10%
Taxi driver	10%
Hairdresser/Barber	up to 15%
Tour guide	10%

TOILETS

Most museums and art galleries have public toilets. Restaurants, bars, cafés, large stores, the airports, railway stations and car parks all have facilities. On the whole they are clean and in good order.

Toilets may be labelled with a symbol of a man or a woman or the initials W.C. Sometimes the wording will be in Italian, but beware, as you might be misled: *Uomini* is for men, *Donne* is for women. Equally, *Signori*—with a final *i*—is for men, *Signore*—with a final *e*—is for women.

Where are the toilets? **Dove sono i gabinetti?**

TOURIST INFORMATION OFFICES

The Italian State Tourist Office *(Ente Nazionale Italiano per il Turismo,* abbreviated ENIT) is represented in Italy and abroad. They publish detailed brochures with up-to-date information on accommodation, means of transport and other general tips and useful addresses for the whole country.

Australia and   c/o Alitalia, 118 Alfred Street, Milson Point
New Zealand   2061, Sydney; tel. 2921 555.

Canada   1, Place Ville-Marie, Suite 2414, Montreal, Que.
     H3B 3M9; tel. (514) 866.76.67.

Eire	47, Merrion Square, Dublin 2; tel. (01) 766 397.
South Africa	London House, 21 Loveday Street, P.O. Box 6507, Johannesburg 2000, tel. 838-3247.
United Kingdom	1, Princes Street, London W1R 8AY; tel. (01) 408 1254.
U.S.A.	500 N. Michigan Avenue, Chicago, Il 60611; tel. (312) 644 0990/1.
	630 Fifth Avenue, New York, NY 10111; tel. (212) 795 5500.
	St. Francis Hotel, 360 Post Street, San Francisco, CA 94108; tel. (415) 392.62.06.

On the spot in Italy, the existing tourist administration is being progressively reorganized. Regional and local tourist offices, which were previously distinct under the names *Ente Provinciale per il Turismo* (EPT) and *Azienda Autonoma di Soggiorno, Cura e Turismo* (AAT), are merging into the *Azienda di Promozione Turistica* (APT). This means that for a while you could find that the tourist office in a given place has any one of those names. Best just to ask for the "ufficio turistico".

TRAVELLING AROUND ITALY

Car. An efficient network of *autostrade*, comfortable four-lane highways, and secondary roads makes for fast, smooth travelling from one end of the peninsula to the other (see also DRIVING).

Ferry *(traghetto)*. Ferries, most of which carry cars, and hydrofoils connect the mainland with Italy's many islands, both large and small, in particular Sicily and Sardinia.

Some crossing times: Civitavecchia–Golfo Aranci (Sardinia) 9 hours; Naples or Genoa–Cagliari (Sardinia) 12–15 hours; Genoa–Palermo (Sicily) 22 hours; Leghorn–Palermo 18 hours.

Plane. The Italian national airline, Alitalia, and its associate lines, ATI and Aermediterranea, offer connections between a great number of Italian cities. Ask about special reductions for domestic routes, usually early morning or late evening.

Train. The Italian State Railway (*Ferrovie dello Stato*) operates an extensive network all over the country. The fares are among the lowest in Europe. Choose your train carefully, as journey times vary a good deal. The following list describes the various types of train:

TEE	The Trans-Europ-Express, first class only with surcharge; seat reservations essential.
EuroCity (EC)	International express; first and second class.
Intercity (IC)	Intercity express with very few stops; a luxury service with first and second class.
Rapido (R)	Long-distance express train stopping at major cities only; first and second class.
Espresso (EXP)/ Direttissimo	Long-distance train, stopping at main stations.
Diretto (D)	Slower than the *Espresso,* it makes a number of local stops.
Locale (L)/ Accelerato (A)	Local train which stops at almost every station.
Littorina	Small diesel train used on short runs.

Tickets can be purchased and reservations made at a local travel agency or at the railway station. Better-class trains almost always have dining-cars or self-service cars which offer wine, beer, mineral water and food at reasonable prices. All trains have toilets and washing facilities of varying quality. If you don't have a reservation, you should arrive at the station at least 20 minutes before departure.

You can obtain a *Biglietto Turistico di Libera Circolazione* (BTLC) for unlimited first- or second-class rail travel on the entire national rail network for 8, 15, 21 or 30 days. Seat reservations are free of charge. There is also the *Biglietto Chilometrico*, which can be used by up to 5 people, even if not related, and is good for 20 trips or 3,000 kilometres, first or second class, over a period of two months. Both tickets can be purchased in Italy or in your home country.

Long distance buses. Inter-city buses abound. They are recommended as the best means of transport between the towns and outlying areas in Sicily, since trains can be slow.

W WATER
You can drink the water from the tap in hotel rooms, but with meals it is customary to drink bottled mineral water. If tap water is not drinkable—at public fountains, for instance—it will usually carry a sign reading *acqua non potabile.*

WEIGHTS AND MEASURES

Italy uses the metric system. For fluid, tyre pressure and distance measures, see DRIVING IN ITALY.

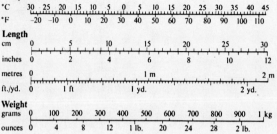

Temperature

| °C | 30 | 25 | 20 | 15 | 10 | 5 | 0 | 5 | 10 | 15 | 20 | 25 | 30 | 35 | 40 | 45 |
| °F | -20 | -10 | 0 | 10 | 20 | 30 | 40 | 50 | 60 | 70 | 80 | 90 | 100 | 110 | | |

Length

| cm | 0 | 5 | 10 | 15 | 20 | 25 | 30 |
| inches | 0 | 2 | 4 | 6 | 8 | 10 | 12 |

| metres | 0 | 1 m | 2 m |
| ft./yd. | 0 | 1 ft | 1 yd. | 2 yd. |

Weight

| grams | 0 | 100 | 200 | 300 | 400 | 500 | 600 | 700 | 800 | 900 | 1 kg |
| ounces | 0 | 4 | 8 | 12 | 1 lb. | 20 | 24 | 28 | 2 lb. | |

USEFUL EXPRESSIONS

good morning	**buon giorno**
good evening	**buona sera**
goodbye	**arrivederci**
yes/no	**sì/no**
please/thank you	**per favore/grazie**
excuse me/you're welcome	**mi scusi/prego**
where/when/how	**dove/quando/come**
how long/how far	**quanto tempo/quanto dista**
yesterday/today/tomorrow	**ieri/oggi/domani**
day/week/month/year	**giorno/settimana/mese/anno**
left/right	**sinistra/destra**
up/down	**su/giù**
good/bad	**buono/cattivo**
big/small	**grande/piccolo**
cheap/expensive	**buon mercato/caro**
hot/cold	**caldo/freddo**
old/new	**vecchio/nuovo**
open/closed	**aperto/chiuso**
free (vacant)/occupied	**libero/occupato**
here/there	**qui/là**
I don't understand.	**Non capisco.**

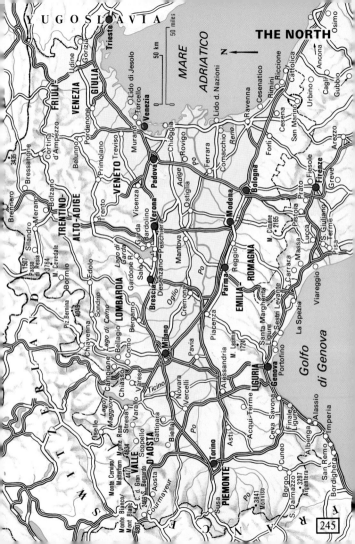

FLORENCE

247

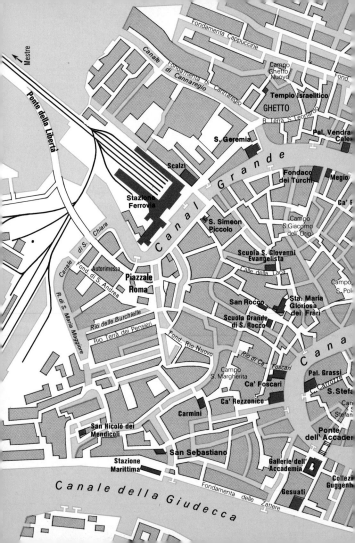

Cimitero S. Michele

Laguna Veneta

0   200m
0   1/4 mile

N

Madonna dell'Orto

Sacca della Misericordia

della Misericordia

Campo dei Gesuiti

Fondamente Nuove

d'Oro

Strada Nuova

Rio del SS.

Apostoli

Fond.a dei Mendicanti

Ospedale Civile

Scuola Grande di S. Marco

Pescheria

San Giacomo di Rialto

Santa Maria dei Miracoli

Monumento Colleoni

SS. Giovanni e Paolo

Ponte di Rialto

Fondaco dei Tedeschi

Salizz.

Campo S. Maria Formosa

R. di S. G. Laterano

Grande

San Salvatore

Mercerie

Pal. Querini Stampalia

Scuola di S. Giorgio degli Schiavoni

Pal. Loredan

Calle de la Mandola

Calle S. Marco

Torre dell' Arsenale

Procuratie Vecchie

Basilica di San Marco

Ponte dei Sospiri

S. Zaccaria

Sta. Maria della Pietà

Museo Storico Navale

Piazza S. Marco

Palazzo Ducale

RIVA   DEGLI   SCHIAVONI

La Fenice

Calle Larga 22 Marzo

Piazzetta

Molo

l. Contarini Fasan

orner ande)

Bacino di San Marco

Santa Maria della Salute

San Giorgio Maggiore

VENICE

251

Chiesa del Redentore

INDEX

An asterisk (*) next to a page number indicates a map reference. Where there is more than one set of page references, the one in bold type refers to the main entry. For index to Practical Information, see pp. 218–219.